Case
Workbook
in
Personality

Case
Workbook
in
Personality

Robert W. White
Harvard University

Margaret M. Riggs
New Hampshire Division of Mental Health

Doris C. Gilbert
California State University at San Francisco
Wright Graduate School, Berkeley

WAVELAND
PRESS, INC.
Prospect Heights, Illinois

For information about this book, write or call:

Waveland Press, Inc.
P.O. Box 400
Prospect Heights, Illinois 60070
(847) 634-0081

Preface

The purpose of this workbook is to supply students with useful material for studying individual lives. The workbook contains the life stories of four people coming from a variety of backgrounds. These subjects were first studied during their late teens or early twenties, and information is available about their subsequent lives. The material is given largely in the subjects' own words or in descriptions of behavior, with virtually no comments or interpretations by the examining psychologists. To keep it available for lower-level courses, we have not presupposed a knowledge of tests or other technical devices and have explained such scores as are mentioned. We have thus left it to the students' common sense and ingenuity to work out for themselves an understanding of these four people.

The study of individual lives is, in our opinion, a valuable, if not essential, adjunct to courses on personality, adjustment, and mental health. Such study counteracts tendencies to view personality only in the abstract, at a distance from everyday living. It challenges students to assemble evidence, find patterns and relations, and reach judgments about what was significant in each subject's life. It invites empathy and recognition of feelings, not only the subject's but also one's own in coming to understand the subject. It contributes to the wisdom that should be the result of courses on adjustment and personality. Most students, in our experience, respond to the challenge and find excitement in the work.

Each case should probably be given as a single assignment, allowing time not just for reading but for studying it carefully, making annotations according to the suggested outline and going back and forth over the material in search of organization. Subsequent discussion of the case in small groups is ideal, bringing out the different viewpoints of different students, but lively discussions are likely to arise even in fairly large classes. We have placed questions of the essay type at one or two points in each case history. That the students will see them is part of our plan, for they provide a certain guidance as to possibly significant themes in the subjects' lives. If a written examination on a case is desired, it may well be an open-workbook test with questions that call for assembling the relevant material.

Students and instructors alike should accept the fact that in material of this kind there are no strictly right answers. The task is to make good guesses about the experiences and influences that were significant in the growth of each personality. The material is not so complete as to provide final answers. Consensus can perhaps be attained on some of the evidence and interpretations, but there is a good deal of room for differences of opinion.

THE AUTHORS

CONTENTS

Introduction

SUGGESTIONS FOR USING THE MATERIAL IN THIS WORKBOOK

This workbook is intended to supply useful material for the intensive study of individual lives. It contains the life stories of four people who were first studied during their late teens or early twenties and who provided information about their subsequent lives. The material is given largely in the subjects' own words or in descriptions of behavior. No interpretations and few comments by the examining psychologists have been included. This leaves it to you to work out your own understanding of each of the four people. How does each person come to be as he or she is? How do they come to act, think, feel, and relate as they do?

Material of this kind can lead to understanding because personality is to an important extent a product of experience. It is a consequence of learning, and we therefore need to examine as many as possible of the situations over the course of life in which significant learning has taken place. When a subject in this workbook expresses an opinion, for example, you should consider what in his personal experience has con-tributed to his seeing things in this particular way. When a subject exhibits self-confidence, or on the other hand reveals strong feelings of inferiority, you should hunt out the past influences and present circumstances that have helped produce these outcomes. Each of us is the unique product of a partic-ular course of experience.

QUESTIONS

At the end of the original studies of each case, and again (except in Case 3) after the report of subsequent events, you will find lists of questions on the subject's personality and development. You may want to look ahead at these questions to obtain a better idea of what can be found out about a person from material of this kind. The questions can be located from the detailed tables of contents given at the beginning of each case.

The following outline embodies the general idea that each of us is the product of our experience. It shows the five chief areas in which personal growth takes place, and it

1

includes specific items to watch for. To obtain a general
view, begin by reading over the outline, together with the
comments made on each section. Then we can turn to proposals
for its systematic use.

OUTLINE FOR STUDYING PERSONALITY

1. SOCIAL AND CULTURAL BACKGROUND OF THE FAMILY
   Historical epoch
   Geographical and national origin
   Economic and social status
   Education and interests of parents
   Type of home and community
   Participation of parents in community
   Family traditions and values

Quite apart from the individual characteristics of the
parents and how they interacted with their children (see heading 2), the items listed here serve to establish important
characteristics of the environment in which the subject grew
up. Differences of social status, for example, mean differences in the environment of learning—differences in what can
be done, what is likely to be rewarded, what models are available for copy. The four cases included in this book differ
widely in background. It will be instructive to compare their
learning environments and consider how these contributed to the
differences in development.

2. THE FAMILY CIRCLE
   Personalities of parents as revealed in family life
   Parents' attitudes toward their children
   Standards and discipline: things encouraged and dis-
      couraged
   Fairness and favoritism
   Personalities of brothers and sisters; relationships with
      them
   Estimate of constructive, neglected, and harmful influ-
      ences in home life
   Effects on growth of confidence, interpersonal relations,
      and picture of self
   Changes in family interactions over time

The family circle has to be considered as a system of inter-
acting personalities. The situation of a rejecting mother and
an accepting father constitutes a different influence from
one in which both parents are united in rejection; rivalry with
one sibling may be offset by alliance with another. Assessing
the effects of the family circle on development implies working
out the whole pattern.
   The time dimension should not be neglected. Influences
change in the course of time: relations with parents or inter-

actions between two siblings are likely to evolve over the
years and produce different effects. Even parental favoritism,
if it exists, does not remain fixed as the children grow older.
Insofar as the material permits, the events a subject talks
about should be carefully placed in their chronological order.

3. SOCIAL DEVELOPMENT
    Early contacts with other children
    First years at school
    History of friendships and close companionships (through
       the school years and up to the present)
    History of memberships in groups (through the school years
       and up to the present)
    Relationships with members of opposite sex
    Preferred patterns of social behavior; needs satisfied by
       social interaction
    Estimate of social skills

    Social development outside the family circle has two decid-
edly different aspects: learning to get along with others in
groups, cliques, and gangs, where competition, cooperation, and
a general sociability are the main questions; and learning to
get along with single others as friends, chums, dates, and
lovers, where a relationship of depth and intimacy is possible.
Development along these two lines may occur at quite different
rates. Here again the time dimension must be kept in mind.
Moving to a new community may have important effects, and even
in the same environment subjects often report a succession of
changes in the patterns of their social interaction.

4. AVAILABLE CAPACITIES AND DIRECTIONS OF INTEREST
    Mental abilities; preferred ways of using the mind
    Physical abilities
    Practical abilities (making and repairing, cooking, busi-
       ness, organizing)
    Artistic abilities (craftsmanship, artistic skills, enter-
       taining ability)
    Affective traits (emotion and control, tension vs. relaxa-
       tion, depressive vs. excited moods, evidences of anxiety)
    Main lines of interest and special skills

    Natural endowments and constitutional differences make
their chief contribution under this heading. With material of
the kind presented here, however, these must remain largely a
matter of inference; it is difficult to isolate these ingredi-
ents from the effects of experience.
    In thinking about a person's immediate future, it is impor-
tant to consider what he has become able to do with comfort
and competence, what lines are less congenial, what actions
provoke anxiety and feelings of inferiority, and especially
what activities arouse deep interest so that the person wants
to do them and finds them inherently rewarding.

5. ORGANIZATION OF PERSONALITY
   Coping strategies and adaptive styles
   Ways of resolving conflicts
   Defenses and avoidances
   Initiative and persistence
   Identifications with models
   Self-images, self-esteem, and sense of competence
   Beliefs and values
   Plans, hopes, and aspirations

   Sense of competence, which is closely linked to self-esteem, is important for understanding both a person's past and future. How capable does the subject feel to control his own actions and influence his surroundings so as to attain his chief goals? The range is from serene self-confidence permitting easy initiations--very likely with a tendency to plunge in too rapidly-- to debilitating feelings of inferiority and helplessness that put the person at the mercy of surrounding influences. For most people the sense of competence is different in different spheres of experience, so that in each case the individual pattern as well as the overall level has to be discerned.
   Under this heading the time dimension is again important. Insofar as the material permits, you should try to picture the growth of organization over time, looking for significant moments of development in such items as coping strategies, initiative, and self-esteem.

SYSTEMATIC ANALYSIS

Studying the Material

   Unedited case material, especially when it consists mainly of interviews, does not yield its secrets in a single reading. On the surface the life stories may seem unremarkable, spiced only here and there by dramatic incident and excitement. Furthermore, the telling is likely to be repetitious and awkward. The life histories given here do not read like detective stories with well-constructed trails of clues. But they contain much more than first meets the eye. Previous users of these records often reported astonishment at the difference between what they gathered from a first reading and what they perceived after systematic study.

Applying the Outline

   The first step toward systematic study is to make effective use of the outline. When you start a case we suggest that you take several sheets of paper and copy the outline, allowing sufficient space under each heading and subheading to enter the relevant items as you meet them in the histories. For example, if a subject says something bearing on plans, hopes, and aspirations, you can enter your notation concisely under that heading, along with the page number on which the statement occurred. Working in this fashion necessitates slow progress through the material, but the payoff is high. At the end you have all the evidence on each topic where you can see it at a glance. The page numbers enable you to go back quickly to the original statements if clarification is needed.

This procedure is necessary because the material in its original form is never really well organized. Plans, hopes, and aspirations may be mentioned on five or ten different occasions, each time in a slightly different way. Attitudes of parents toward the subject may come out gradually in a dozen different incidents reported in a dozen places. Our memories are not large enough to hold all this scattered evidence in mind. The material has to be assembled and ordered before we can judge fairly what it signifies. Otherwise we recall selectively what happens to strike us, with the result that our personal preferences frequently hinder fair-minded appraisal.

INTERPRETATION

When the information has thus been put in order, the work of interpretation can begin. This work consists of pulling the material together in such a way as to account both for the subject's present qualities and for their origins and development.

Explaining Normal Development

Because clinical psychology has contributed heavily to the study of personality, it is easy to start by trying to explain what is wrong with a person. A patient coming for treatment is obviously concerned about what is wrong. Inquiry immediately comes to a focus on the complaint, whatever it may be, and treatment is directed at removing the cause of complaint. Students of personality as a whole, however, should not limit their attention to complaints. Ideally, the task is to understand everything about a person—the strengths as well as the weaknesses. If a subject shows highly desirable qualities, one should try to account for them. If it seems that a subject's personal life has been beautiful, one should try to explain this outcome. A career that has been a conspicuous success needs explanation just as much as one that ends in disaster. Successful development does not just happen. It is a legitimate and important topic for scientific inquiry.

This point is especially relevant because the subjects in this workbook were not studied with the purpose of detecting and correcting psychological ailments. They were all volunteer or invited participants in studies of personality; they were paid for their time and were not promised any other personal benefit. All were "normal," at least in the negative sense of not having sought psychological help from the interviewers. They were encouraged to talk about their strengths as well as their problems.

What Constitutes Explanation

The type of explanation that is made possible by materials of this kind can be illustrated by two examples of unusually good vocational adaptation.[1] The two subjects, called Chatwell and Merritt, were men in their early twenties who had completed college and military service. Seeking to establish themselves in civilian life, they found jobs that were wholly congenial yet utterly different.

Chatwell became a law clerk in a small firm, where he quickly began to shine because of his quick mind, excellent memory, and argumentative skill. He liked to show off and was at his best when arguing a case in court. These several qualities had first been encouraged at the family dining table, where his father liked to start intellectual arguments and where Chatwell, the eldest child, could both dazzle his parents and put down his siblings. Throughout school and college he continued to use his cleverness to impress superiors, developing strong powers of initiative and self-dramatization. With his contemporaries he relied on a strategy of verbal dominance. This did not make him lasting friends, but he valued independence and could always find new worlds to conquer. He was a perfect apprentice lawyer, impressing the senior partners with his brilliance and dramatically putting down opponents in the courtroom. Before many years had passed, Chatwell was a conspicuously successful trial lawyer whose services were in much demand.

Merritt entered a large bureaucratic business organization, where he quickly found a congenial position as a middle administrator. His mind, which throughout school and college had shown itself slower and more methodical than Chatwell's, was fully equal to the technical side of the work, and his interpersonal needs made for a perfect fit. His history showed childhood problems that he had solved by being a "good boy," showing deference toward parents and teachers and seeking approval and guidance from those in authority. His affiliative needs were also strong; in an unassertive way he sought the supporting friendship of his schoolmates and neighborhood acquaintances, with whom he

---

[1] R. W. White, The Enterprise of Living, 2d ed. (New York: Holt, Rinehart and Winston, 1976), Chap. 2.

tried to be a "good guy." In his position as a middle administrator he could be a "good boy" to his superiors and a
"good guy" to those below him. Toward those he supervised
he was considerate and friendly. Toward his bosses he was
deferent and cooperative, well satisfied to have them
responsible for all initiatives.

Notice that these explanations of vocational adaptation
point backward into the life histories. They call attention
to aspects of the subjects' experiences that tended to encourage certain qualities. These qualities, practiced and strengthened because they continued to serve well, form part of
present personality; they influence both the choice and the
subsequent enjoyment of vocation. Nothing in Chatwell's history developed qualities suitable for a middle administrator;
nothing in Merritt's encouraged his becoming a brilliant trial
lawyer. Had circumstances forced these men into the "wrong"
choices, they would probably have become cases of vocational
maladjustment.

Taking the Material at Face Value

In analyzing the material presented in this book it is important to begin by taking it at face value. The subjects
were cooperative: they tried to answer questions, follow instructions, and give candid accounts of their histories and
feelings. Their interviews contain a large amount of information that can be presumed to be both trustworthy and important.
The subjects were willing to tell a great deal in the confi-
dential and sympathetic situation provided by the interviews,
and they seemed to accept the challenge of making a contribution to psychological science. The best way to start trying
to understand another person is to give full and appreciative
attention to that person's own story.

Reading between the Lines: Self-Pictures

While fully respecting the subjects' conscious insight and
intentional self-disclosure, we cannot assume that they could
altogether see through their preferred self-pictures, lay aside
their habitual adaptive strategies, or alter their long-estab-
lished views of the world. Nor can we suppose them immune to
desires to make a good impression on the examiners and to stand
up well under psychological scrutiny.
The material must be viewed as conveying a self-picture to
the examiner. What impression does the subject apparently want
to make? Published studies show self-presentations of the most
diverse sorts. One subject, for example, presented himself
quite openly as an unusually sensitive, refined, talented indi-

vidual altogether superior to the common herd.[2] In sharp contrast, Merritt, whom we just encountered, recurrently spoke of himself and his family as normal, average, plain, reasonable, well-behaved people; this picture was important to him. A third subject, whose time and strength were being consumed by the daily exigencies of running a store, saw himself, and clearly wished the examiner to see him, as an alert citizen, well informed and well read, and a serious participant in cultural activities.[3] A fourth told his story in an amusing way that kept the examiners entertained even while they suspected a few picturesque exaggerations; yet in the atmosphere thus created he found it impossible to speak of very real abilities and accomplishments without sounding conceited and at the same time to disclose his real dissatisfaction with his failure to meet his own high standards.[4] Self-pictures can obviously occur in endless variety, being one of the most important manifestations of individuality.

Self-presentation is much influenced by the relationship that prevails between subject and examiner. Each subject, we can suppose, experiences a certain initial bewilderment about this relationship, wonders about the interviewer's expectations, and feels his way toward a comfortable interaction. It is hard to convey this interaction in print, especially when one cannot include the side remarks, murmurings, tones of voice, and gestures that form part of the communication. The first two subjects in this workbook were studied by teams consisting largely of graduate students in training; with a few exceptions the subject met a different person on each visit. This plan of study has certain advantages, but it is not conducive to developing a strong relationship between subjects and examiners, and it does not encourage much evolution in a subject's self-presentation. In the other two cases nearly all the meetings were held with a single experienced interviewer, whose continuing interest created an atmosphere increasingly favorable to self-disclosure.

Reading between the Lines: Unrecognized Tendencies

Certain aspects of normal human behavior are best understood as manifestations of unrecognized tendencies or motives.

---

[2] H. A. Murray and C. D. Morgan, A clinical study of sentiments, Genetic Psychology Monographs, 32 (1945), 3-311, the case of Commitless.

[3] M. B. Smith, J. S. Bruner, and R. W. White, Opinions and Personality (New York: John Wiley and Sons, Inc., 1956), the case of Benjamin Kleinfeld, pp. 210-218.

[4] R. W. White, Lives in Progress: A Study of the Natural Growth of Personality, 3d ed. (New York: Holt, Rinehart and Winston, 1975), the case of Hartley Hale, pp. 23-86.

These tendencies are effective--they influence behavior--but
the person is not fully aware of them. Often our private
thoughts and daydreams give us clues to urges that we tend to
exclude from our preferred self-picture. The urges most likely
to occupy unrecognized status are those that are hard to in-
corporate in a pleasing picture of oneself: dependence, hunger
for praise, timid avoidances, crude sexuality, envious rivalry,
resentful hostility, and wishes for power and glory.

Dependence, for example, is a residue of childhood, and
it takes the form of either a passive expectation or an active
demand that one's needs and desires be met by other people.
Such an urge may not be reported or even reportable by the
subject, but its existence can be inferred if there has been
repeated seeking of support from others. This might take the
form of looking for guidance, asking for help, preferring environments that remind of home, or becoming strongly attached
to a companion who supplies initiative. The evidence is especially strong if the behavior is inappropriate or obviously at
odds with the subject's professed independence, as when a person claims he needs no help but actually pumps his friends for
advice and aid.

In general terms, unrecognized tendencies are inferred
from repeated patterns of behavior that do not conform to the
subject's self-picture or stated intentions. The inference is
stronger when the repeated behavior is not appropriate to the
actual circumstances. Disclaiming or denying the urges represented by the behavior can also be taken as evidence for them,
but only under certain circumstances. For example, a person
might say that he is not interested in power and does not want
it thrust upon him. This could be a perfectly accurate self-
description. You could infer a contrary unrecognized urge
only if there was evidence that the person had behaved in ways
that tended to bring power.

THE SUBJECTS

In selecting four cases for this workbook the editors have
tried to include a variety of backgrounds. Their choice has
been limited, however, by the material available, as well as
by the willingness of subjects to have their life stories put
into print. Obviously, no series of four could be considered
a cross section of the population, and we make no claim that it
represents a balanced sample of the many varieties of personality. The subjects are simply four rather different people who
were willing to be objects of study and who cooperated well in
that undertaking.

All were originally studied when they were between the ages
of 18 and 22. In all but the third case, where the interval
was shorter, follow-up material was then obtained covering a
period of ten or more years. Readers may find it interesting
to pause at the end of the original study and try to imagine

what the subject will be like a decade or more later. It should not be supposed, however, that prediction can be successful beyond certain fairly general characteristics. Personality is much influenced by what happens: what events take place, what people are met, what changes of health or occupation or circumstances occur. These matters do not lie in the realm of the predictable.

The names given the subjects in this workbook are not their real ones, and alterations of detail have been adopted to protect anonymity. In fulfilling this obligation every effort has been made to confine the disguises to matters that are not significant for understanding, so that you can proceed with confidence in utilizing the material at hand.

1 Solomon Kompten

<u>Contents</u>

Preliminaries

    Solomon Kompten, a 22-year-old second-year law student, responded to a notice at his school's employment office about taking part in studies of personality. He was in need of money and gave this as his motive for entering the study. Although the procedure called for taking certain tests, most of the time was devoted to interviews. These were conducted by staff members at the research center and by graduate students; the subject usually met a new person on each visit.
    You will soon notice that Solomon tended to speak with clarity and confidence, as if his views of himself and his life were already well formed. He is placed first in this workbook because of this quality; there will be many opportunities in other cases to add stumbling speech, confused ideas, and inconsistent self-pictures to the other difficulties of interpretation. It should be remembered that the method of interviewing did not put much pressure on the subject to question his preferred ways of presenting himself. He gave the information for which he was asked, but there was usually not much inducement to examine it in depth. Only occasionally did he seem puzzled by his own behavior and curious about its explanation. The fact that a history is clearly given does not tell us, on the face of it, whether this is the whole story or whether important unrecognized tendencies lie behind what the subject presents. Trying to read between the lines is part of the work

of interpretation. This must be done, however, not as a guessing game but as a search for acceptable evidence.

The original study was made in the early 1950s. Solomon
had reached the age of 44 when he was asked to provide follow-
up information.

Following Section 8 you will find a set of ten questions
bearing on Solomon's personality at the age of 22. You might
want to look ahead at these questions in order to get an idea
of what is going to be involved in interpreting material of
this kind. You might also like to try not looking ahead to
the "Subsequent Events" (Section 9) until you have finished
working on the earlier part, thereby permitting yourself a few
guesses as to what Solomon Kompten will be like at age 44.

1. LIFE HISTORY

E: We want to start by getting the facts on the background of
your life, so why don't you begin by talking about your
parents, where they lived, what they did, and so on?

S: Well, both my parents were born in Europe, in what was then
called Russian Poland. My dad came to this country when
he was about 17 or 18, and my mother when she was a little
bit older. They met in New York and lived there for a
total of about twenty-five years, before and after they
were married. I was born in New York. We moved around
quite a bit; when I was 10 years old we had lived in most
parts of New York, and then around that age we moved out
to California, and moved around quite a bit there, but generally speaking we were living in San Francisco.

E: What does your father do?

S: My father is generally in the needle trade, a tailor. . . .
When he first came to this country he was in millinery, and
then always something connected with clothing. Men's
clothing, had his own tailor store, pressers, he was always
in the clothing line.

E: What about brothers and sisters?

S: I have a brother six years older than myself.

E: Are your father and mother still alive?

S: Yes.

E: And do you have any younger . . .

S: No.

E: Are there any other members of your family, aunts and
uncles, who were at all close to you in childhood?

S: Not especially so. When we were living in New York we
would go for extremely long periods of time without seeing
the family, and of course when we went to California, except for parts of the family which gradually followed us
out there, we had very little contact with the rest of the
family. There weren't any other relatives which were at
all close.

E: Which of your parents do you feel that you're closest to?

S: Well, I think I've learned a lot from both . . .   My
    parents seem to be of entirely different physical makeup.
    Mother's very nervous and quick and fast, and in some ways
    I'm like her, because I'm quite nervous and do things
    quickly; whereas my father is extremely calm, quiet, and
    the opposite of my mother in that he's not as active and
    emotional as she, and I seem to vary back and forth, show
    traits of both.

E: Do you have any preference for one or the other?

S: No . . .   I love my parents equally well. I think in
    childhood I was much closer to my mother, rarely seeing my
    father. It wasn't until I was older that I could feel as
    close toward both parents.

E: What about your brother, were you close to him?

S: Well, my brother was six years older, which meant that
    during most of the growing-up period we didn't pal around
    together; too much of an age difference.

E: What does he do now?

S: Well, he had a whack at being in business for a while, and
    then he gave that up, became a plasterer. Building trade.

E: How do you remember the atmosphere at home? Were your peo-
    ple interested in books or sports or . . . religion or . . .

S: Well, neither of my parents received very much formal
    education. My mother had not gone to any school at all, in
    either Europe or this country, when she first came over.
    She went immediately to work, and was busy most of the time.
    My father had a couple of years of education in Europe and
    attended American night school and got the equivalent
    possibly of a grammar school and partially a high school
    education. There were quite a few books around, but I
    never had any more or less guidance in studying them, since
    I was always going to school, and I was having opportuni-
    ties my parents never had. And I wasn't very far along the
    line when I could contribute more in family conversations
    than I could gain, I mean as far as formal education
    knowledge was concerned. The family was . . . neither of
    my parents are religious and . . . when they were brought
    up in Europe they had extremely orthodox families, extremely
    religious families, and they seemed to both go to the other
    extreme and object to religion entirely. My upbringing was
    entirely areligious, just was completely left out. It
    wasn't until I was much older that I began thinking about
    it seriously. Both my parents were always somewhat
    politically active or at least interested, would be
    interested, in various types of social organizations and
    political organizations, and I grew up in a sort of semi-
    political environment.

E: What sort of political interests were they?

S: Well, they were interested in world affairs, trade union
    movements in this country, working against all racial and
    religious discrimination, and . . . I was sort of introduced
    to this general atmosphere when I was quite young, and when

I was a fairly small kid I was interested in those things
myself.

E: What do you remember about school?

S: I liked school, I started when I was 4 1/2 years old, and
wanted to go to school very much, and I went to kindergarten for a year and a half.

E: You were probably pretty good in it, were you?

S: Yes, I was pretty good in grade school.

E: Which school were you in longest?

S: Probably the last one in New York. I must have been there
about a year or a year and a half, and that was the longest
at any single school.

E: That's pretty tough because you don't have much chance to
make friends.

S: I seemed to make friends pretty quickly, at least at that
age it was very easy to get into a group rather quickly,
but I always hated to leave it. But I seemed to have
very little trouble getting into another group when I came
to a new place.

E: How about your schooling in San Francisco?

S: Well . . . grammar school, let's see, I was in about the
fifth grade when I moved, and the New York schools were
quite a bit ahead, so I skipped a year, skipped two
semesters in a row, then . . . about the time I was ready
to go into junior high school I had some trouble with my
knee, put in a cast, was on crutches for about three months.
I couldn't go to a regular school so I went to a special
orthopedic school for about three months. . . . When I
came back I went to junior high school in my neighborhood
for three years, then high school for a year and an half--
the family had moved down to Wilmington and I finished high
school down there. After that I wanted to go back to San
Francisco, and we moved up again. I went to the University
of California at Berkeley.

E: Well, let's go back and see what you were mainly interested
in studying in school.

S: Well, before junior high school, I was always interested,
but I can't remember what it was, except it was pretty
interesting and I liked it to some extent. When I got to
junior high school it was the first time I began to take
different courses and I didn't care for math, languages,
and science. I liked anything else that had to do with
writing or history or geography, anything current. My
dislike for languages continued all the way through and
. . . I seemed to do poorly in those.

E: What about extracurricular activities?

S: I used to like sports very much.

E: Any one particularly?

S: Well, I used to play football and baseball, and I used to
run for the school, track. I did it in high school, until
my leg bothered me and I quit.

E: This was the same leg that you had your . . .

S: Same leg, it was all right for, it had been all right for a
   couple of years, and then all of a sudden, bang.

E: Well, what is the trouble with it?

S: It's a bone disease of some kind, origin they say is not
   known. They know very little about it, and the only cure
   they know is to stick it in a cast for a couple of months.
   They say it's a shattering of the bone that sort of mends
   itself . . . and the only trouble I've had since is that I
   just can't run. Or do any sort of strenuous exercise.

E: And you've had this ever since you were 10?

S: First had it when I was about 12. Was fixed up for a couple
   of years, and then bang. It was all right until I was
   about 15.

E: How about student government in the schools, things like
   that?

S: Well, I was in various school organizations in junior high
   school . . . held offices . . . president, secretary,
   treasurer of various clubs. I was in the boys' glee club
   when I was in junior high. High school paper . . . I think
   I ran for some sort of office and I was beaten, office of
   judge or something of the sort. I participated in debate
   and oratory at school and represented the school in various
   contests . . . and . . . well, during college, I was in a
   lot of organizations and held offices, which were not
   officially recognized by the school, they were off-campus
   youth organizations.

E: I was going to ask you about the sort of discipline at home.
   Do you feel you were very strictly brought up?

S: Generally speaking, not strictly. I think my parents tried
   bringing my brother up fairly strictly and decided that was
   kind of a bad deal, and eased up when they came to me. I
   remember a couple of incidents where my father was the
   disciplinarian and . . . once I was hiding from him and
   fell down a flight of stairs (laughs).

E: Why were you hiding from him?

S: I don't know, I've forgotten what I'd done, must have been
   something bad . . . and my mother would never mete out the
   punishments, that was my father's duty; and I went to a
   secret hiding place of mine, which was at the top of the
   cellar steps, and I just went too far and fell down.

E: What was the other incident you remembered?

S: Uh . . . something else when I was quite young. I remember
   my father giving me one good smack, and that was about the
   only time I ever remember that he hit me.

E: What sorts of things did he discipline you for?

S: I guess when I . . . I don't really remember, I suppose it
   was when I would talk back to my mother, or wouldn't eat,
   or wouldn't go to bed, and would be very insistent about
   doing what I wanted to do.

E: Did you ever feel that your parents had a different
   attitude toward your brother than toward yourself?

S: Not really, because we were so far apart, so it wasn't
    really a good basis for comparison. Especially when we
    were a lot younger, the six years made a big difference,
    and he'd always do things and I was always supposed to be
    too young to do them. And . . . he never gave my mother
    as hard a time as I remember giving my mother.

E: Why was that, a difference in . . .

S: Sort of a difference in makeup--he has always been and still
    is more tactful along--well, he won't be as stubborn as I
    am in certain situations, and will just as soon overlook
    something, and doesn't make an issue of it, where I'd be
    more apt to make an issue of it.

E: What sorts of things do you make an issue out of?

S: Well, I'll get in all sorts of . . . I'll usually say what
    I think and what I mean about a topic, and I'll take a
    lot of controversial stands, be ready to defend them and
    argue aloud, whereas many of these he wouldn't have any
    special interest in, so he wouldn't argue about them.

E: On the whole, you didn't quarrel much with him?

S: No. . . . Well, when I was very young I used to quarrel
    with him because I couldn't play with his crowd of boys.

E: But you feel the atmosphere was harmonious?

S: Pretty generally was; my mother and father got along very
    well and . . . to the best of their abilities they would
    always try to provide us with what we wanted, and . . . it
    was sort of an atmosphere where we were always trying to do
    things for each other.

E: How successful was your father economically?

S: Well, he had his up and downs, and he never reached great
    heights of any sort. My earliest recollection is that he
    had his own business and he was doing pretty badly then
    . . . and he pulled out of it before he went completely
    broke, then has worked for others since. Before we left
    New York, he was doing rather well . . . my brother and I
    have pretty bad cases of sinus, my brother much worse, and
    it was pretty important that we move out West, and ever
    since arriving in California, the economic situation was
    very bad. We came out there at the worst possible time
    . . . and I remember my father going to work for two
    dollars a day . . . and the first few years in California
    he began cashing in all his life insurance, and we were
    just about broke when the family moved to Wilmington; in
    fact, I think we had 27 dollars. Since then, why I think
    they're back on their feet pretty well.

E: Are you still financially dependent upon them?

S: Well, I don't--it's been a long time since I've really been
    financially dependent. I've been earning my own spending
    money since I was 11 or 12 . . . and by the time I started
    college, I had saved up about 900 dollars during high
    school, by selling papers. In fact, I did that when I was
    still going to college, and I'd work in the shipyards.
    After graduation from high school, and during, I worked at

at the post office . . . and . . . with the exception of
living at home and getting my room and board, really I've
done most of my own spending since I was just about in high
school. And now . . . I've taken some money since I've
been here, because I'd used up the money I'd saved, and
I've borrowed some money from the school.

E: But mainly, you worked your way through college?

S: Yeah.

E: Well, it sounds as if they were pretty considerate of their
children. They moved out West, then they moved back to San
Francisco.

S: Yes. The thing was that I wanted to go back to San Francisco and I was going back regardless of whether the family
would or not . . . and, luckily, they were able to find a
place. It was extremely difficult to find one, and . . .
I came up to San Francisco to get established, and Dad came
up with me to look around, and we found a house, and they
moved back with me.

E: What did you study at Berkeley?

S: Well, I was a political science major, took quite a bit of
economics, some history, and psychology. By that time I
had just about decided I was going into law, took pretty
much a general background, what I thought would be a good
background for it.

E: Well, I guess if you were working, you probably didn't have
much time for campus activities.

S: Well, the work didn't take much time and ... most of my
activities were in organizations--either in my community
or working at school, campus activities, but not student
government. I never could get worked up over the types
of things they were doing, such as the dances, and so forth,
was always more interested in . . .

E: The community things, what were they?

S: I was working in this local group of about a thousand
people--was the vice-president of it for a while and did
an awful lot of political work in it, and . . . we were
working for the Democratic Party and I was years too young
to vote (laughs).

E: So you've always had this political interest?

S: Yes, pretty much so.

E: Was your father a member of a union, was he active?

S: No, my dad . . . was not. And, in fact, he's always
worked on these small places which are never unionized,
but he's generally sympathetic toward union activity.

E: What about your campus activity, what sorts of things did
you do there?

S: Well, generally--at Berkeley there was no directly political
or religious activity on campus, that was state law--and
there were usually all sorts of subterfuges to attempt to
get around that. And that also meant no activity in the
fields of discrimination, legally. The organizations
would take some stands on these issues. I took a pretty

active role, helped them out legally, do a lot of writing,
school paper, and was pretty generally interested in the
field of jobs . . . especially discrimination there, and
we did activities directly on campus and in the community.

E: How did you do in your classes?

S: Well, the ones I liked I did extremely well in; the ones
I didn't like, I got about a C. Same general idea, I did
pretty well in economics, political science and psychology, and English . . . and I did poorly in the languages,
military science--I had no interest in learning that--and
in certain science courses like anthropology. I tried to
avoid as much of the natural science courses as I could; I
took only enough to meet the requirements.

E: What did you do during summers while you were in school?

S: I had all sorts of different jobs . . . about twenty
different jobs I held for short periods of time. I would
usually return to selling newspapers at that particular
spot because I would make more money at that. I worked at
a gas station for a short while, candy factory, and . . .
sold jewelry--one summer doing that. I did pretty well,
assortment of jobs, and toward the end of the summer a
bunch of fellows would take off a couple of weeks and go
on vacation.

E: What about social activities, did you go to a lot of
dances?

S: Yeah, pretty active all the way, there was . . . oh, from
about 14, 15. Especially the A.Z.A., which is the junior
part of B'nai B'rith, has supposedly a very full program
but centers mainly on sports and social activities.
Continual round of dances. My later years, in high school
and in college, I dropped out of that. Social activities
were either centered mainly on the various other organizations I was working with or . . . individual, through
friends.

E: What about girls, did you go steady when you were at school
or . . .

S: No. I'd go sort of steady for short periods of time
(laughs). I'd always stay with one girl for a short period,
and then get somebody else. Changes were rather frequent.

E: Well, when you were a kid, did you think you were falling
in love or was it just sort of flirtation?

S: Oh, I had lots of crushes, but they'd never last more than
a couple of weeks, if they lasted that long. About junior
year in high school I went steady with one girl.

E: Well, now, what do you plan to do when you finish law
school?

S: Well, it depends on what kinds of opportunities there are,
which, at this point, is a bit hard to tell. I roughly
plan to go back to San Francisco . . . and although when I
first decided to go into law I didn't think I'd practice
law, more and more I've decided I would practice.

E: What did you want to do?

S: I wanted to be in the political arm of the trade union
    movement, such as political action committees, and so
    forth. That's still a possibility, but it's not one of
    those things that you jump into, but rather get into after
    a long period of time. Then I decided I'd like to
    specialize in labor law, and I still pretty much want to do
    that.

E: Then you had this interest in political and trade union
    movements, and also wanted to go to law school ever since
    you were a kid?

S: Yeah. Pretty much so. At least in high school, it was
    sort of a debate between journalism and law. And journal-
    ism at that time had the upper hand. But at the beginning
    of college it swung the other way.

E: Why was that?

S: Well, where I wanted to go to college I thought courses
    preparing for law would be in the long run the better
    training.

E: You tell me that about your junior year you started going
    steady with a girl. Were you engaged to her?

S: No. I caused quite a bit of difficulty. She was divorced
    and had two children, quite a bit older than I. And . . .
    we had a good time and a rough time all wrapped into one.
    Caused difficulties with both families.

E: Was she temperamental?

S: Very much so, and her family didn't like the idea, and my
    family didn't like the idea.

E: Why were they against it, because of her age?

S: Well, there was a seven-year age differential. Her mother
    wanted her to marry somebody who was much older, and my
    parents wanted me to marry somebody who was much younger.
    At that time neither one of us was contemplating marriage,
    and we wanted no interference. We broke it off ourselves
    afterwards, putting up a big battle when anyone else had
    wanted us to.

E: When was this?

S: We had gone together about a year.

E: And do you still keep up with her?

S: No. I was home last summer and saw her for a while. My
    interest kept up for quite a while afterwards but . . . not
    anymore.

E: Well, what about since then?

S: There was one prospect, in which I almost made a bad mis-
    take. A little while after starting law school here I got
    engaged to a girl from San Francisco. She came out East
    and we met in New York with the intention of getting
    married. I was awfully scared about this . . . not being
    sure that this previous affair had really been ended as
    far as I was concerned . . . and I made the decision that
    it wasn't, at the very last moment. She was here and we
    had already gotten a license--and I felt like a heel for
    quite a long time after this.

E: What sort of girl was she?

S: Well, I liked her very much, but she seemed to be immature
    in a lot of ways. I didn't think a couple more years would
    change that . . . and we had some sort of an intellectual
    difficulty. She would get very emotional about things and
    rush headlong into them without thinking, and she always
    thought that I was a bit too slow. And I thought this
    might cause a lot of difficulty. Physically she became
    very ill after we had planned on getting married, and I
    thought that I was the cause of quite a bit of this.

E: After the break?

S: No, before the break. After the breakup she's gotten
    better (laughs).

E: Changing the subject, do you think that your life has been
    a happy one, or . . .

S: Yes, I do . . . I've been despondent many times, but never
    continually. I've been pretty happy most of the time.

E: What were you despondent about?

S: Well, various things would crop up. I was generally de-
    spondent for a long period of time when I broke off with
    this first girl. I just didn't like the idea of breaking
    up, and I didn't like the idea of getting married. I was
    also despondent when I felt I hadn't been very nice toward
    this other girl.

E: Well, what do you think were your most satisfactory
    experiences, what gives you the most pleasure?

S: Well, I'm most always satisfied when I'm doing things I
    like and doing them well. Had a lot of fun when I was
    working in organizations; to a great extent that usually
    overshadowed my school work. I felt something was being
    accomplished. I was very happy when I was going with this
    girl. I enjoy parts of college, which consist in sitting
    around having coffee after class (laughs). Bull sessions
    and beer parties and things of that sort . . . but not the
    work--the work always seems to be too far away from reality,
    merely provided a couple of the basic tools to talk about,
    but wasn't anything to get excited over.

E: What do you think were the most unsatisfactory experiences?

S: I'm going through a period of that right now . . . dull,
    boring classes. When they could be so alive and
    stimulating.   . . . And when I've loused up something I
    think I should do better.

E: You probably haven't got much time for those political
    activities.

S: Last year I had no time, I studied twelve, fourteen hours
    a day--surprised myself in being able to do it, and was
    disappointed in the results. It wasn't any better than in
    college, and I felt pretty unhappy not doing anything I
    wanted to do; this year I've gone pretty much over to the
    other extreme and . . . giving school my secondary atten-
    tion--and I think I'll be doing better at it.

E: What about in your childhood, what do you remember as being satisfactory or unsatisfactory?

S: I used to play a lot of games, used to make them up--when there was bad weather or when I was laid up in bed with a cold, which when I was a kid was quite often--stayed at home and played games.

E: By yourself?

S: Yeah. Or sometimes with another fellow. I did a lot of reading, and I still enjoy reading something I'm interested in . . . and . . .

E: What sorts of things?

S: Pretty generally things I'm ordinarily interested in politically . . . economics. Some fiction, very little-- used to read a lot of fiction when I was a kid, read all the kids' books . . . and I enjoyed those very much.

E: What about the other side, the unsatisfactory?

S: I don't remember anything that was especially unsatis- factory.

E: Not normal (laughter). There must have been something.

S: I'm sure there was, I can't remember what it was (laugh- ter). Well, I remember I used to like to play outside when it was real late, and I would be unhappy when I was called in.   . . . I hated going to bed.   . . . I hated eating the things I was supposed to eat.   . . . I can't remember the things I didn't like to do.

E: Well, if you go back in this early-memories business, you could probably remember something else that was disagree- able.

S: Well, I remember I didn't like very much getting beat up, and I received a lot of beatings when I was a kid.

E: Who from?

S: Oh, the older boys. I was always the youngest in the crowd. In New York when I was very young I would always be left out of the games. Fellows were four or five years older than I and I would have to sit and watch most of the time.

E: This was your brother and his . . .

S: Yeah, my brother and his gang; there weren't many kids my age. Or else I preferred hanging around with the older ones anyway. I always seemed to like the things they were doing better.

E: Going back to your activities in school and college, just what did you do, and what was it you especially liked?

S: Well, after having trouble with my leg, and not being able to enter into sports, I . . . entered and oratory contest. I was helped by one of my instructors up there, and I did pretty well in that, and went around to men's clubs meetings and represented the high school in various speeches. I picked my own subjects and they were usually current topics. I was about 16. And worked on the school paper . . . and I was interested in those school organi- zations that were cropping up, and then we conducted a poll at school, presidential choices of the high school

students. When I was in college I wanted these organizations to put on a mock congress and I ran that. Twenty
or thirty different organizations. Then my last year at
college, in 1951, there was a very large mass movement of
various student organizations about discrimination within
the community. We organized a strike against shopkeepers
who discriminated against Negroes. This caught on pretty
well, and we got quite a big student strike, which lasted
for several months and some shops went bankrupt. Of course
we were charged with the usual offenses, blocking traffic,
and one day, out of nowhere, spontaneously, approximately
300 high school students broke our lines up--we were sure
it was not so spontaneous; we have fairly good proof that
it was organized by the police and they received payment
for it--pretty generally there was a big mess about this
whole thing. With the injunction slapped upon us limiting
us to one picket, we were afraid to put out one picket by
himself. One picket couldn't defend himself very well, but
he also couldn't be accused of blocking. Ten couldn't be
accused of blocking either over a fairly large area, as
long as they kept a fairly good distance apart, which we
did.

E: You think the police were on the side of . . .
S: We had got wind that there might be some trouble, and three
    times we specifically asked that police be there, and they
    were not there, no one was there until after our line had
    been completely broken and several people were hurt, and
    then the police arrived to (laughs) take us in. And we
    were not arrested but given a stern tongue-lashing.
E: What does your family think of your political activity?
S: They feel pretty much the same way. They have no objection
    to it, they just think I shouldn't spend too much time
    which might detract from my school work.
E: So they feel very strongly about your doing well in school?
S: Yes. They didn't care particularly what I chose, but
    wanted me to do well in what I did choose.

2.   CHILDHOOD MEMORIES

S: Once, when I was about 4 years old, I lost my bicycle. I
    looked down the street and just returned home without it,
    not thinking to take it back. . . . Another time when I
    was about the same age, I had received a beating from some
    of the boys in the neighborhood. I remember once not
    wanting to drink some milk, some chocolate milk--I used to
    like that very much--and I was bribed with a piece of
    chewing gum to drink it. . . . When I was about 6 or 7 I
    remember playing some games in empty lots at night. We
    used to amuse ourselves by throwing things at people passing
    by while we hid behind trees. . . . I remember I got my
    mother angry at something and my father was supposed to
    mete out some punishment and I went to my usual hiding

place at the top of the cellar steps, and in the dark I
fell down the steps.

E: How did you feel about that?

S: I remember crying like a baby, which I was. I remember
my parents found me and took me upstairs, patched all my
bruises.

E: How old were you about then?

S: Well, under 7.   . . . When I was at home I used to mostly
tag around with my brother--<u>try</u> to tag around; he was older
than I.   I remember once it was raining very badly when I
was at school and . . . well, the streets were completely
flooded. And I took sort of a long way home, it took me a
couple of hours to get home and I was completely drenched
when I got there. And I found out that my mother had left
home and gone to the school to meet me to bring me some
rain clothes to wear. She came back after a while,
drenched, and gave me a bawling out for leaving school
without waiting for her.

E: How did you feel about that?

S: Well, I was very sorry that she had to go out and get
herself wet too. I didn't mind so much getting wet.

E: But you did mind her getting wet?

S: Yes. I felt very guilty about it. I should have thought
about it.

E: Do you remember more about your brother?

S: Well, I always wanted to play with all his friends. Most
of the boys in the neighborhood seemed to be about his age,
and I used to tag behind him all the time.

E: How did you feel about that?

S: Well, when they'd let me play with them I felt pretty good.
When they didn't, I'd sit around and watch.

E: How about your father?

S: Well, most of the time Dad was in the store. Sometimes old
customers would come in and I'd sit around and listen to
them talk. Most of the time he was working. Once in a
while my grandfather would come over. Every time he came
he used to bring us candy bars.

E: What is your earliest memory--the first thing you remember? Close your eyes and think back.

S: Somehow something sticks in my mind about my being in a
crib. I used to hate a crib. I used to put up a good
fuss about being taken there. I sort of remember . . .
I might have been a couple of years old . . . standing
up in the crib and trying to get out.

E: Can you remember a little bit more about that?

S: No, that's all. Just standing up in the crib holding
onto the bars, not liking where I was . . . wanting to be
out of it.

E: You've told me before about hiding . . . your usual hiding
place at the top of the cellar steps whenever your father
was supposed to punish you. Do you remember anything
about when he did punish you?

S: I only remember being struck once by him. I had more a
    fear of verbal punishment than anything else. I just
    didn't like to get bawled out.

E: Oh, I see. Can you tell me any more about this time when
    you were struck by him?

S: Well, I remember we were in the street, my mother and
    father and I, walking. I don't know what the incident
    was. But my Dad struck me. I sort of walked off and
    wouldn't walk with them. I don't know what the matter was.
    I must have been 5 or 6. I wandered off about fifteen
    blocks and a policeman picked me up and took me home
    (laughs). I was gone several hours.

E: And how did you feel about that?

S: Oh, by that time I was getting pretty tired (laughs). I
    guess I didn't mind so much.

E: Do you remember why you run away?

S: No. This is the first time I've thought about it in years.

E: How do you remember your childhood as a whole?

S: . . . I liked it pretty well. I liked going to school. I
    used to cry a lot before I was old enough to go. My mother
    had to talk to the school authorities about letting me in
    at 4 1/2.

E: Do you remember any particular troubles?

S: Noooo. The one time I remember getting beat up, I came
    home crying. It was because I was Jewish, and I asked my
    mother what a Jew was. I don't think it was because of my
    curls. Usually my brother was something of a protector.
    The only time I'd get a beating was when he wasn't around.
    If he was there, he'd either step in and prevent it or
    something.

E: And how did you feel toward your brother?

S: Well, he was always pretty good to me. I liked him. The
    only time I'd get angry was when he wouldn't let me play.

E: Well, now that we're on that, let's see what you can
    remember between the ages of 7 and 12.

S: Well, I moved around quite a bit. I think I lived in the
    Bronx about a year, until I was about 8. We lived in
    Brooklyn about a year, and we lived in Manhattan. I don't
    remember too much about the Bronx, except that my brother
    was working in Dad's store after school, and once in a
    while I was allowed to come in and help too. I felt pretty
    important when they let me do that--be a delivery boy.
    Usually at about that age I was allowed to play with the
    other boys a little bit more, became more of the crowd,
    wasn't always kept out because I was too young. Then (the
    next move) . . . it was a poor place; we were very crowded.
    I used to spend a lot of time at the beach in the summer
    time. It was so hot we used to sleep on the beach. And I
    remember I got interested in making model airplanes every
    once in a while. It was a big business, trading plans and
    trading models, things of that sort. . . . We used to
    live in a pretty rough neighborhood where there were always

gang fights, and wouldn't venture very far away from home
without going with the entire group. And sometimes our
neighborhood would be invaded, and there'd be more or less
of a pitched battle. I remember one day in the winter time
it snowed, and we set up a fort, and we fired snowballs
across at each other for three full days--usually they were
loaded with rocks. This was great sport, one of the
happiest memories (laughs). I was more or less the muni-
tions man. It was my job to make the snowballs. The other
ones threw them.   . . . I remember in the summer, my
brother would spend a lot of time playing basketball--all
day long he'd play basketball. I used to play that with
some boys who lived next door. I remember at this time we
were extremely poor. For a while there I didn't have any
shoes and didn't go to school, even though I lived just
across the street. When I was about 9 years old we moved
to a little better class slum, but still the slums (laughs).
I remember going to school there. I liked school pretty
well. I remember being very popular with the kids in
class. I had a lot of friends I used to play ball with
either in Central Park or in Riverside Drive. I remember
when I was about 10 years old we used to go around picking
up cigarette butts and hole up in the park some place and
smoke them. We really felt adventurous. Once I was caught
by my father . . . I think that was the second time I got
a beating--I forgot this time.   . . . One of my closest
friends was a Chinese boy, and he used to come down to my
place and I used to go to his place a lot, and I picked up
a couple of Chinese words.

E: How old were you then?

S: This was all when I was 9 or 10.

E: Do you remember anything about your mother about that time?

S: I was kind of thin, and my mother went to see one of my
teachers in school, and they decided I should be sent to
a convalescent home for a while, to get fattened up
(laughs). And I was sent to some place out on Long Island
and was there for about ten weeks. I hated it very much,
which everyone else did, too. We felt as if we were in
prison and always schemed about running away, but it was
kind of hard to do because we were pretty well watched.
Our mail was censored in and out, and we couldn't very well
plead to our parents to be picked up. I remember I was
supposed to be there twelve weeks, but my mother got the
idea things weren't going so well. They weren't allowed
to visit. So after ten weeks she came and got me out of
there, and I was never so happy in all my life. I remember
I made all sorts of promises that I would be a wonderful
eater, and I religiously kept up these promises for at
least a day (laughs). I remember that when I returned to
my school and neighborhood I was very well received by my
old buddies and was very, very popular after that.

E: Do you remember about coming to California?

S: Well, it was on the train, so I enjoyed the trip very much.
I remember when we first got there it was raining like hell
for three days, and I thought California was probably always rainy. I was very disappointed with the city and the
big buildings--I had thought it would be the wide-open
West. I remember when we first got established there we
got a great big house and rented out some rooms. Times
were very very bad, and my father couldn't get the line of
work he had been doing in New York. He finally landed a
job at something like 2 dollars a day, and this was his
income for quite a long time after. I remember I didn't
have any long pants to wear, nothing but shorts or knickers.
I had heard that in the West everybody wore long pants, and
I felt very embarrassed that I had to wear short pants for
a couple of weeks until finally a cousin of mine who lived
in California visited us and was horrified that I had no
long pants and went out and bought me some.   . . . I
didn't like California for about the first two years. I
missed the friends I had in New York, liked New York much
better.   . . . I liked school better. I liked most of
the people I knew, but I still missed a couple of friends
especially that I had in New York.

E: And how did you get along with the boys in general out in
California?

S: Pretty well. For the first time I came across a place
where we had room to play football and baseball. I got
along pretty well. I always felt very talented that I
was 10 years old and could play with boys about 12 and
wasn't excluded from the games because I was too young.
. . . I went to work on my stamp collection again and took
a big interest in it once more.   . . . When I was about 10
I began selling magazines after school. A magazine agent
came up to me in the street and asked me how I'd like to go
to work; I said, "Fine," and I began selling magazines
after school and made a fantastic sum of about 35 or 40
cents a week. I used to save it up during the week, and on
Saturdays I'd have a chow mein lunch, which I liked very
much, and buy three candy bars and go to a show. I felt
very independent because I was paying for all this myself.

E: Those were hard times for your parents?

S: Things were still pretty bad. I remember that in addition
to renting out rooms, my mother would sometimes . . . do
laundry . . . and things like that . . . for others. With
all that, I remember she used to go downtown to do a lot of
shopping and would always come back with a lot of candy and
cake for us. At that age I was nuts about candy, and there
was always candy in the closet. She would just about give
me as much as I wanted. I sort of got in the habit of never asking for big things, but there was always enough of
little things to go around . . .

E: What do you remember about your father those days?

S: Well, for quite a long time my father was trudging around
    looking for a job. Gradually he got to selling life insur-
    ance. Most of the time I saw my father, he was kind of
    depressed, having a pretty rough time of it. He usually
    was gone all day long, and when he had work, if he had a
    chance to take on any extra work, he'd do it. He'd always
    be quite busy.

3.   FAMILY RELATIONS

E: Well, this time we're interested in such questions as your
    attitude toward child-training, how you think you should
    bring up children, things like that.
S: Well, most of this is going to be original thoughts because
    I haven't thought about it. Pretty generally, I guess you
    ought to try to treat children as much as possible as
    adults.   . . . So that when they get a bit old enough,
    they'll have some sort of understanding as to what's going
    on, sort of taking on the family council, at least it will
    appear so, get a sense of responsibility, sense of having
    a hand in all the decisions . . . to . . . attempt to be
    pretty considerate of their needs, their special desires,
    and I guess they've got as much right to want to bang away
    on their drums as you have to want to sit quietly in your
    easy chair and read a book
E: So you think in general, they have rights . . .
S: Yeah, they have rights too.   . . . And unless they go to
    extremes, they ought to be somewhat left to do the things
    they like and want to do, ought to be channeled in the
    direction you want to bring them up.
E: You mean that instead of dictating, you ought to . . .
    direct with a light hand, but still give them their head
    as much as possible?
S: Yeah. I remember reading something years ago by George
    Bernard Shaw, was very impressed by it, something about
    children, telling them about Santa Claus. It said up to
    the age of about 5 or thereabouts they believe all these
    wonderful lies about Santa Claus, then you have a family
    pow-wow, call the child in, and say, "Well, Buster, you're
    old enough and you're intelligent enough to see how things
    are. There really isn't any Santa Claus, but when you
    were a young little boy, why you wanted to think that way."
    And sort of approach it the right way, instead of being
    disappointed in the fact that there's no Santa Claus, it
    will inflate his ego by playing on "now he's at the age
    where he knows the bigger things in life." And I like this
    way of approaching on a sort of responsible attitude.
E: You feel it's necessary to give the impression that he's
    sort of let in on something that he'd been kept out of?
S: Yeah. If you tell a kid not to play in the street or some-
    thing, he's not going to see any sense to that, but per-
    haps, and I've tried this, and it hasn't worked (laughs),

try to show the reason for not playing in the street, and
it might soak in a little bit more, it might not; instead
of your being some sort of a dictator with some divine
power, show that there was some sense to it.

E: How'd you try that?

S: Well, I was going with a girl who had a couple of kids.
One 2 and the other 4 or 5 years old. Generally speaking,
they had pretty much free rein, and I liked the way it
seemed to work out. I think they ought to be given a lot
of their own objects and be sort of trained to take care of
things. Think they should have some things of their own
which they have the responsibility of taking care of.
Shouldn't run around picking things up after them; you
ought to let them take care of them.

E: How about such things as punishment?

S: Well, I think punishment may be necessary, but certainly it
ought to be the last means of coercion you ought to use.
It's hard to tell when you . . . when they get to the age
when you can talk to them. I think you ought to try persuasion and some sort of reasoning--sort of a correlation of
reasoning and discipline; you reason with them when you
think hey can. understand, and use discipline in what you
think would be difficult for them to understand. If this
doesn't work, maybe a form of subtle bribery might; you
don't have to explain all the ramifications of if you do
one thing, you deserve something else . . . but you have to
make it a little more direct. And if this fails still,
then . . . some sort of punishment, in still a bribery
sense, by denial of something they desire, denying them
ice cream when the ice cream man comes around every day.

E: I can never hold out with my kids.

S: Well (laughing), it's easy to break down, but it's at least
denial at the usual time and usual place, even if only for
a short while. If you can keep it up for a half hour
(laughing). I don't know what kinds of incidents would
call for punishment, but if you had to give him a spanking,
might be necessary, I mean after the anger dies away I
think there would be a great effort to show him a great
deal of affection, perhaps, and to explain the reason for
the punishment, even though he might not listen very atten-
tively, or be able to understand, but show why the punishment was meted out.

E: Seems to me, then, that you don't favor any one approach,
but rather a wide variety of approaches according to the
circumstances.

S: Yes, what the individual circumtances call for.

E: I was interested in the fact that you mentioned that some
of your opinions had come from George Bernard Shaw. I was
wondering, in general, where they came from. Have you
learned anything from your brother?

S: Well, some, through observation. I think he has an overly
disciplined manner; his girl, about 3 years old, just

appeared to me to be correct in every manner. Very, very
pleasant to be with, perhaps, because she never seems to be
troublesome, but also has a very deadening effect on the
individuality. I've never even seen her cry. I've never
seen his kids make a lot of noise, and I think it's sort of
because they're always subdued generally, rebuked very
quietly if they make noise, and I think it might be a
little stifling. It might be nice to have a kid around the
house who doesn't make much noise, but still . . .

E: Do you have any idea why the two of you would take different attitudes toward it?

S: Uhh . . .   Well, there's a large difference in our approach
to a lot of things.   . . . I think he's more likely to
pick up more . . . conventional ways of doing things without giving too much thought to it; instead of deciding on
these points himself, he's more likely to accept the
accepted ways of doing things.

E: I was just wondering if there was anything in your own
background, because I find in my own experience in trying
to raise my youngster, and my wife finds, that frequently
we're either reacting in terms of the ways we were raised
or reacting against them.

S: Well, this might be so; he was much more strongly disciplined than I was. At least before he got married, we were
talking about it, and he seemed to think that was not the
way to raise children. He's not being a stern father by
any means, but just a little bit too coercive, I mean the
child is too angelic (laughs).

E: Do you think that you two suffered the lack of attention
acutely?

S: No. But I never remember being with my father very much
. . . I always associated my father with being at work,
early in the morning and late at night, which he was, and
certainly in his time off, it was time to relax, get sleep,
busy doing other things. There's also a great difference
in environment. I can never remember my father playing any
sort of games . . . and my brother and his wife are quite
often playing with the children. And, of course, now that
my father is much older and has more free time, he plays
with the grandchildren, he has more time to play with the
grandchildren than he had time to play with us.

E: You probably had more time with your mother.

S: Not too much of that either.   . . . Well, both my parents
were born in Europe, and that had some effect on their
attitudes of looking at children. At very early ages they
were working and . . . the types of games we would play as
children was something quite new to them.

E: Apparently your mother was the main person who raised you.
What sort of tactics did she use?

S: Seemed to be usually bribery to me. I was extremely fussy
with my food, and I'd always be bribed to eat. I never
came to accept bribery, but I never objected because I

wanted the bribe. She would give me chewing gum, I could
go to the movies . . . stay out a little bit later, this
would be to get me to eat and do other things, but it always seemed to be mainly to eat. If I didn't want to come
in at night, I'd be bribed that I could go to the movies
on Saturday.

E: How about schooling?

S: Yeah . . . that would be tried, but it was usually settled
with a bribe. Scold, I'd object, usually wouldn't make
much of an influence. But when my father scolded I jumped.
I guess it was just the idea that I never saw my father
too much, and this was somewhat of an outsider doing the
scolding. My mother I knew much better, seemed to know how
I could get around her.

E: Did you feel the difference between your father and your
mother in any other way?

S: No, just in lack of presence; my father was away at work
most of the time, and I saw him very little in the evenings.
My mother I was in constant touch with.

E: Did you feel an equal amount of affection for them?

S: Well, I felt a little closer to my mother because we seemed
to share more of the everyday things. But outside of that
I felt an equal amount of affection, placed my mother and
father equally. There were more incidents that my mother
and I had gone through together.

E: Did you feel that your dad was able to give you an adequate amount of affection, being out of the house so much?

S: Yeah . . . the only times I seemed not to feel it is when
I would see somebody else's father, for example, playing
ball, being out with the guys, and I would want my father
to be out there too. And once or twice he made a sincere
effort at it, but he was so terrible (laughing) that I
never egged him on again.

E: Now, getting back. Pretty early in the game you advocated
a minimum amount of interference in the way the kids grew
up. You felt they should be directed in general but not
specifically. Yet I suppose you have some ideas of what
the kid should grow up with. I wonder what the picture is
in terms of whether you figure the kids should be left to
go their way, or whether they should be directed, sort of
given ideals.

S: Well, my parents tried to make a musician of my brother.
The way they chose it was to buy a violin and get violin
lessons for him. He hated it, dropped it as soon as possible. I think the better way would have been to concentrate
on introducing him to good music at a very early age. If
we grew up and sort of became accustomed to it and sort of
have the desire ourselves to want to play . . .

E: Where did this value on music come from--in your parents?

S: Well, neither of them can play an instrument or had any
training . . . just think it's a general appreciation of
good, fine things. When they were young . . . when they

got married . . . they'd go to some sort of concert and
stand up through the entire thing. So I think they were
trying to do something, but not going about it in the right
way.

E: They valued music very highly?

S: Yes, they sincerely valued it, not just that they thought
it was the thing to do. Yet the way they approached this
made us—I guess my brother, anyway—object. I know we had
some records around the house, but I never remember actually hearing them. I was never really introduced to them
when I was a kid. I didn't take to the idea much of
learning to play the violin, and I objected very strongly,
and they didn't inflict it.

E: How about their religion?

S: My grandparents on both sides were extremely religious,
both my parents received very orthodox, very formal training—both had completely rejected it before they came to
America—and I got no formal training in religion whatso-
ever. It was more of a vacuum in my life than anything
else; there wasn't any antireligious training, but there
wasn't any indication, no coercion whatever, toward it.

E: Your grandparents didn't come over here?

S: Yes, they did. In fact, my folks brought them over, most
of the entire family's come over. And . . . when we went
visiting my grandparents, for example, it was a big—well
it was a game with me, I watched very intently when my
grandfather prayed. When I was in my grandfather's house,
act the way a nice little boy should act, had respect for
my grandfather, but outside the house, why . . .

E: Your parents felt that even though they had given up
religion themselves, because your grandparents had it, they
should respect it?

S: Yes. They were respectful toward the religion, but my
grandparents certainly were aware of the fact that they
were not religious. . . . I remember there was a church,
a Negro church, and I went into it out of curiosity when
I was a child, and if everybody else stood up, I stood up,
copied what people were doing around me because I didn't
want to stick out like a sore thumb. Out of curiosity.

E: What in general did your parents say to you about religion?

S: It wasn't anything against belief in the supernatural or
anything like that, it was sort of — I don't think my
parents felt that way especially—but it was certainly
against the form of their church or any church. Against
the organization of the thing more than against the ideas.

E: Did your parents urge you to go to college?

S: That seemed to be sort of my own choice. My brother decided not to go on past high school. It was a decision
that he made, and the only difference was to learn a trade.
And I really never discussed it with my parents when I was
in high school. I was always assuming that I was going to
college. It was more of an announcement to my parents when

I decided when and where I'd go, and the feeling there was,
why anything I decided was all right, and they would help
me out as best as they could.

E: And your mother has had a good deal of sickness?

S: Yes.

E: Does this affect your relation?

S: Well, it seemed to make her very irritable. Quite often I
think she might be unjustified in getting angry. She's
very easily excitable.

E: Did you feel that it had emotional impact?

S: Yeah, it did, it upset me, but it didn't last long.

E: Does it get you upset--is that carried over?

S: No, I don't get upset nearly as often, but I still have
difficulty in really having a smooth time for any length of
time with my mother. Very likely to snap at her when I
wouldn't snap at anybody else. Although it's much better
now than ever before.

E: How about your dad over the course of time?

S: Much closer. We both feel that my mother's jumpy, and we
can talk about it fairly objectively now. It's like one of
those things I heard years ago, kid says when he was 14 his
father didn't know a damn thing, but when he was 21, his
father was an awfully smart man, surprised at how much the
old man learned in 7 years. I think that's pretty appropriate as far as I'm concerned, too. Much closer as we're
getting older.

E: Now you mentioned that your folks said you should stay on
the ball, at least as far as learning a trade was concerned.
Was there much of an emphasis on succeeding in general,
doing a good job?

S: Not especially. In school I was doing pretty well anyway.
I seemed to be pushing myself more than . . . the push I
got from home. It was--I was always in the thick of
competition, I liked to do well in the things I was in,
anyway. If I didn't do as well as I should have in school,
it would bother me more than anybody.

E: What was your mother's attitude in general when you were a
kid? Did she feel that you had to be taken care of more or
less fairly closely or left to yourself?

S: I was looked after fairly closely. I was the kind of kid
who was always having colds, getting laid up. Seemed to go
to a lot of trouble to--lot of emphasis on the food I
should eat. I remember resenting very much being taken
care of, looked after. Always thought there was an overly
. . . amount of care.

4.   CURRENT LIFE

(At the outset the subject was asked to describe in as much
detail as possible the course of a typical day in his current
life.)

E: So you got to class after 9 o'clock. Now how closely can
    you remember things connected with that hour?

S: 9 o'clock class, I'm <u>always</u> bored stiff. It's a terribly
    boring class, taught on a high school level . . . and I
    take my notes very accurately because it's the only way I
    can suffer through an entire hour.

E: Keeps you awake?

S: Yeah, while I'm writing I can stay awake better . . . and I
    remember thinking how disgusting this was, that this nice
    young fellow was looking so sincere and earnest in every-
    thing he said, and he was making a lot of noise and re-
    peating exactly what he wrote in his own book, which I had
    read . . . and gave nothing original. That's an exception,
    thank god, but I was exceedingly bored the first hour .
    Second hour is a "Corporation" class, same room, so I just
    shove over, mosey around a few minutes, smoke a cigarette
    in between classes . . . talk to some of the boys around
    my seat . . . and . . . not quite so bored during the
    second hour. Same thing when that class is over at 11,
    smoke a cigarette, talk to some of the boys . . .

E: Your feelings about the second hour, how do they stack up
    against the first?

S: I had gone through the same process that I did in the first
    several months before, since I missed this particular class
    for over two months straight . . .

E: You missed it?

S: Yeah, again there was absolutely nothing original in the
    lectures that wasn't gleaned from the cases itself, and
    this used to be my first class in the morning, so I just
    used to sleep through it--then go to the next one, and
    glance at somebody's notes, and see I didn't miss a thing.
    I had copied the notes from the previous year, and they
    were exactly the same . . . and felt no pangs of conscience
    whatsoever at having missed "Corporations." But now that
    I have a 9 o'clock class, I have to get up anyway (laugh-
    ing). Then my next class is "Property" at 11. There's
    nothing original here either, but this course I don't mind
    so much because it's extremely difficult to grasp and we're
    all stenographers in this course and rather enjoy it--take
    a great amount of notes, try and take down everything
    that's said . . .

E: That's the point of it on . . .

S: That's the way the guy teaches , yeah. He just talks
    straight for an hour, very quickly, and lays the entire
    course out. However, it is quite a difficult course, and
    if we didn't do it this way, I don't know how we'd ever get
    it in the time that's given for it, so I don't feel badly
    about having this one . . . on the same order as the other
    two.

E: So what would you be doing from, say, noontime, when you
    finished classes? How do you usually go about spending
    your time?

S: Several alternatives. Go on and have lunch at the same
    place I had breakfast . . . go home and make some lunch
    . . . go and have some coffee . . . gradually wander back
    to my room sometime after 1 or so.   . . . If there wasn't
    anything I had to do in the afternoon, I would sometimes
    go to bed for about an hour . . . lie down . . . after
    reading the paper. I'll always read the paper, probably
    after lunch. Then I'll either do some kind of work that I
    have . . . type verious letters--I'm secretary to the
    Student Lawyers' Guild and I usually have a whole bunch of
    letters to take care of. I'll either do it then or some-
    times do . . . some work, usually working on reviewing on
    an outline.

E: You mean reviewing for courses?

S: Yeah. I'll spend perhaps a very small amount of time doing
    the actual daily work--most of my studying goes into
    reviewing.   . . . That would be in the afternoon . . . we
    go out--all the fellows in the house go out to eat very
    early, we usually go together, some time about 5 o'clock.

E: You have supper real early?

S: Yeah, about a quarter after 5 or so.   . . . That's the
    first supper (laughing).

E: You mean you have a snack or something later on?

S: Well, it becomes a very full meal, usually; we buy stuff
    and keep it lying around, and we'll all go out later.

E: Well, then, usually now, you'll go out about 5.

S: Yeah, about 5. Supper easily takes about an hour. After
    that, why, we always seem to make our stop at the corner
    drugstore for the papers and the magazines, and buy cigars
    and cigarettes . . . and usually mosey back together to
    the room.   . . . Then, depending on what night of the
    week, it is or . . . just exactly how much work there is,
    or what was being planned for the evening . . . we usually
    break up into bull sessions for a while, or whip out the
    cards and play a game of casino, which usually takes some
    time . . .

E: After you've been studying?

S: This is before we even start, right after we come back from
    dinner . . . nobody wants to go to work--we'll always look
    for excuses. And we'll do that for a while, and gradually
    somebody says he has to go study, and he'll go off to his
    room to sit and stare at the walls . . . and my routine is
    to open books up on my desk, get everything nice, and pick
    up a cigarette, and get up on my feet and start going
    visiting, making the rounds through the house.

E: After you set yourself up to study?

S: I get the things prepared right on my desk, I've taken a
    look at it and I feel disgusted (laughter)--we start the
    rounds, which is a very usual procedure. Took me four
    hours one night to get a piece of red lead from the next
    room. People, with the exception of one fellow in the
    house, ask no privacy, and don't expect to give any to

anybody else, bust in and out of each others' rooms.

E: It's really a good friendly . . .

S: Yeah, it's really open and free, and if you want something in the other guy's room, you walk in and take it, walk right out again.

E: And how about when you go visiting around--and everybody is perfectly willing to shoot the breeze?

S: Sometimes my roommate objects, because he's the most studious fellow in the house. He studies most . . . and always passes his insults around very freely, but everybody's gotten used to that now, and they completely ignore him. He doesn't really object . . . but at times he would like to spend more time on his studies. With that one exception, why nobody ever objects, very anxious to find a decent excuse to put the books away. Most of the other fellows are third-year guys and they're completely disgusted.

E: How long does this go on?

S: Well, the--something like this would keep up for a while. I will either get kind of jumpy about doing this, or if the other boys decide to get back to work, I will either sometimes have a meeting which I attend, or I'll take off and go to a show for a couple of hours. . . . Come back about 10 or 11 and try to do as little work as possible before I got myself sleepy. Read a book, or some magazines lying around . . . if I can't avoid it, I'll do about an hour's work, or a half-hour's work, finally get a game of cards, sit around and make something to eat, and have a bull session again.

E: What time will this be about?

S: This will be close to 12, or later. . . . This is liable to keep up anywhere from 12 to 4.

E: And you say you put twelve hours a day on the books last year?

S: I would say that was an average, seven days a week--probably including class work, but there wasn't more than fourteen hours a week of that.

E: Didn't it take its toll on you, didn't you feel it?

S: Yeah, I did. But when it got bad I'd take off then too; I'd never work when I didn't feel well. The only reason I could do that--I never could sit that long, but my roommate is solid, he can sit at the desk fourteen, fifteen hours a day, and he does it. So he was a good one to watch, if he was able to do it, I was able to sit down and keep up for a while. He could sit morning, noon, and night, but by the time night came around, I had to quit.

E: Now these discussions you have with the other fellows in the house, is there any particular thing they revolve around?

S: Politics, religion, sometimes law.

E: Sometimes have bull sessions on the law?

S: Once in a while. More or less arguments than bull sessions, though. Some guy will throw something out that he
happened to be working on . . . and everybody in there,
being a junior lawyer, would be eager to pounce upon the
subject . . . and bull about it--nothing especially vital,
just something to talk about. For example, one of the
fellows is writing a paper on labor law, he's the only
Republican in the house, and . . . still a pretty liberal
fellow from anybody else's point of view, and we love to
harangue him on his topic, and hit him from all sides,
objections to the central thesis of his paper, and this
might keep up for a couple of hours. Or . . . we'll always talk about the individual biases or prejudices of
somebody else, and this is usually a ganging-up process,
three or four will gang up on the other. And . . . he'll
be defending himself and his views, for several hours at
a time.

E: What do you plan to do when you get out?

S: Oh, I'd like to go in with a couple of guys fairly soon,
but it's . . . pretty much impossible, and I can't--I've
got to make some dough when I get out, enough to live on,
which means work for somebody else.

E: You'll be through this year pretty soon; do you have to
provide for yourself for next year?

S: Well, I don't have any income except for what I can earn in
summer, and odd jobs--like being paid for these interviews.
I'm quite a bit in the red now.

E: Where does that come from?

S: Mostly home. My savings expired the first year. I had
some extra expenses the first year, which . . . sort of
cleaned me out--some of it loans from school, some of it
loans from home.

E: Money that has to be paid back?

S: Oh yes, at least I feel an obligation to pay it back.

E: You can see your way clear to the end all right, financially?

S: By continual deficit financing, and by borrowing, I can.

E: But it's worth it to you, it's something you planned on
doing?

S: Yeah. Sort of faced this problem when I was in college.
I knew I would . . . well, I figured then what it would
cost me, which I would have to borrow over a three-year
period, and it's running out just about that way, and I
decided then it would be worth it, and I still think,
even now, that it's worth it, with all the gripes I have.

E: You mentioned the Student Lawyers' Guild, connected with
the school?

S: It's a national lawyers' organization with student chapters
in various law schools.

E: You're secretary?

S: I'm secretary of the local chapter.

E: Have meetings fairly often?

S: We have . . . a pretty active program. We bring in outside
    speakers, have . . . various sorts of affairs. Sort of an
    active lawyers' organization. In the law school we tend to
    be somewhat active, writing briefs on civil liberties
    cases, working on various types of investigations . . .
E: Do you like that?
S: That's a lot more practical, I like it. I like the subject
    matter it's concerned with--it's the civil liberties angle
    . . . the various types of work we do. Yeah, I find that
    much more interesting.

5. HEALTH AND PERSONAL HISTORY

E: I'd like to learn something about your health history.
S: I've never had anything serious. I suppose I had all the
    kids' diseases.
E: You probably did.
S: They tell me I have high blood pressure now, which is some-
    thing relatively new. Didn't have it when I went to col-
    lege.   . . . I had a little trouble with my knee when I
    was about 12 years old, and my knee was in a cast for about
    three months. And since then, I haven't been able to run
    or take part in very heavy sports.
E: Do you know what the character of the trouble was?
S: Well, they weren't quite sure themselves, they--the most I
    could find out then was that it was a shattering of the
    bone, cause unknown. It seemed to have healed all right
    after the cast, but I still felt it every time I'd run. I
    was running one day in a race and felt it--fell flat on my
    face, my knee just gave way.
E: Well, as you get older you won't care so much about
    running; you'll try to avoid it whenever you can.
S: I do that now, it's a convenient excuse (laughter).   . . .
    There's nothing else I can think of.
E: Then your health has been a problem to you only in respect
    to that one thing, which came when?
S: Somewhere about eight, ten years ago.
E: Did it bother you much at the time?
S: Just in climbing steps, I could walk around all right.
    And . . .
E: Did it bother you psychologically, take away one of your
    forms of excellence?
S: Well, it meant I couldn't play ball or be on the track
    team for a while.
E: I was thinking that at that age that kind of thing might be
    quite a wound to one's pride.
S: By that time I had a houseful of ribbons anyway, so it
    didn't make much difference.
E: Oh (laughing). You had laurels to rest on . . .   Did you
    have any experiences of sex play with other boys, mutual
    masturbation, and so forth?
S: No.

E: How would you have felt about that?

S: Never thought about it until I moved out to California.

E: You were lucky then not to strike it sooner.   . . . Did you have actual experiences in California, or were you just saying that you learned about it there?

S: Well, uh . . . it's rather a commonplace thing, I mean . . .

E: Sure.

S: Come across it almost every time you go hitchhiking, you're bound to be picked up by a . . . gentleman who makes over-tures, and it's common along the streets, and when you're older, it's found in bars. And it's a talked about thing. You become familiar with it through talk, and . . . it's not something that's between boys, really, it's something associated between older persons, really.

E: Yes.   . . . How do you feel about that kind of thing? Does it upset you?

S: No.

E: Have such events happened?

S: No. I can remember back to when I was old enough to really think about it, and . . . I've heard it's considered to be a medical or psychological factor, and sort of accepted that explanation to it.

E: You were pretty well informed, as things go, I think, on these points.

S: I had a smart bunch of fellows around.

E: They didn't need the Kinsey Report?

S: No, no, we were quite familiar with most of those things, except they didn't have the exact figures, I suppose (laughter).

E: When did you start getting interested in girls?

S: Oh . . . I suppose when I was about in junior high school. When I was about 11, 12 years old.

E: You started right in early then?

S: Yes (laughter). Before they always seemed to be sort of in a crowd.

E: Yes.

S: Well, you see, even before then, they weren't . . . not in the crowd, but outside the crowd, I mean they were shunned more or less before that.

E: There's a time in there when boys and girls separate as if they were poison to each other. Just before puberty.

S: Yes, just before . . . we moved to California, and I remember in New York it was all attachment with boys.

E: Well, you started then being aware of an interest in girls in junior high school; did you have a special object for your affection, or did you move around?

S: Uhh . . . there were special objects, but they didn't last very long (laughter). They came one at a time.

E: You were one who could be smitten then?

S: Yes. I suppose I was smote or smitten quite often.   . . . It was when I was 13 or 14 that I was really smitten, I guess.

E: Yes. . . . At that time they were all on a short-duration basis.

S: Yes.

E: I can imagine that your parents were happy that they were
on a short-duration basis.

S: Let's see. . . . I remember my parents objecting when I
was 13 or 14, to going out. With girls. Told me to wait a
little bit. But then they didn't seem to take it seriously. I confined most of my activity to the afternoon and
the early evening. And they didn't seem to be unduly
bothered about it.

E: Were you able to talk with your brother about these things,
or were you separated?

S: Well, he was six years older than I was. Which meant that
he was running around himself quite a bit, and I more or
less followed his example instead of taking his counsel
(laughter).

E: That's a nice way to put it. . . . You parents came
around in the course of time, I suppose?

S: Somewhat. It wasn't until I was about 19 that . . . we had
to have a big knockdown battle over something--but until
that time, things ran pretty smoothly, and there weren't--
I mean, I was given pretty much of a free rein.

E: Yes. At what point did some of these interests get over
into physical relations?

S: Oh . . . in high school, about 16.

E: Then your first sexual experience came about the same time.
Was it with one of the girls that you liked?

S: No, I wasn't smitten at the time.

E: You were not smitten. What led to it, then, curiosity?

S: Curiosity was the big element; then, being one of the boys,
wanting to be one of the big boys more than anything else.

E: You get a status.

S: Yes, very much so.

E: Again, did you feel any guilt about it, or any upset about
it?

S: No, no. More of an achievement than anything else.

E: Achievement, yeah. . . . Was a perfectly happy experience
in itself, as well as one can expect the first time?

S: Well, it wasn't what I thought it was.

E: That's almost always true. Played up too big, for the
first time in our minds.

S: That's one of the big disappointments in life when you find
out what that is (laughter). I think it makes you grow up
a little bit faster.

E: Has that feeling of disappointment remained with you, or is
it just in connection with your inexperience?

S: It's certainly not disappointing any more. That was just
something, I suppose, that had been built up so largely
that nothing could fulfill the expectations. It was disappointing that it wasn't fulfilled to the utmost.

E: You said at 19 some difficulties began with your parents.

S: Yes. That's when I think I was really in love.   . . . I
begin going . . . well, with an older woman who had been
divorced and had had two children. That's what caused the
objection of my family. And that caused quite a hard time
for almost the duration of the relationship, about a year.
And . . . the difficulty was mainly with my mother. I felt
about interference in the family--by that time I felt I was
old enough to handle myself more than anything else, and
. . . tried to quiet my mother's fears as to the possible
consequences. I was going to college then. And it didn't
seem to be the actual relationship which was causing my
mother anxiety . . . but the fear for the future, and . . .
I tried to convince her that even there it was sort of my
problem, and I thought I could handle it, girl and I would
handle it together. And that's the way it worked itself
out.

E: You were 19; that must have made you resent quite a bit the
interference.

S: Well, I think I resented it even before, pretty much so in
high school, about 15, 16.   . . . I had not received very
strong parental pushing one way or the other, and . . . as
long as I acted within a certain extreme, why everything
was all right. And it wasn't until I reached an extreme
point that the family would step in.

E: What your mother didn't like about this relationship was
that you might marry the divorced woman with the children?

S: Yes. She couldn't see why I was putting myself in such a
position with five or six years of school ahead. The woman
was about seven years older than I was.

E: It was more that you were going to get tied up in an
impossible financial burden, taking over a family of three
all at once.

S: I had no ideas of doing it at the time.

E: I was going to ask you that. You sounded as if you thought
that your mother's fears were quite ungrounded.

S: The reason I say that is that . . . we discussed it, the
girl and I discussed it many times, and we both knew, at
least at that time, that nothing permanent would come,
that . . . I thought she was a pretty smart girl, and we
were able to discuss the thing pretty well, and it was
just more or less a relationship until something would
break it off. And it was later that I regretted that
attitude. But I don't see how at that time it could have
worked out any other way.

E: Certainly would have been a terrific undertaking for you at
that stage of your life.

S: Yeah, I think I realized that, and I think she realized
that too.

E: Still, the feeling sense, it evidently meant a great deal
to you, perhaps you only let yourself know that . . . later.

S: Well, that might have been it--because the first several
   months, anyway, I just wouldn't think about the problem
   entirely, just tried to put it aside, and . . . well, as
   time went on, I just couldn't push it aside anymore; it was
   something I really had to think about and solve it. And in
   the midst of happiness there was quite a good deal of un-
   happiness that went with it. And after breaking up--I
   mean, it lasted for quite a long time--this big grouchy
   feeling.

E: Mm, yes. Was the breaking up itself difficult? Reaching
   the decision?

S: Yes, it was one of these things where it probably took
   several months, breaking, then reuniting, then breaking,
   uniting. It was quite protracted.

E: Oh, yes. That takes an awful lot out of your emotions,
   too.

S: Yes, I think so.

E: Had you been in love before with a girl that was older?

S: Well, I'd never felt that way before, and . . . most of the
   girls I had gone with were older. They--first of all, I
   was a year or two ahead of myself in school, and met mostly
   older girls. Seemed to be interested in older girls, but
   this was the first time I had gone with somebody that much
   older.

E: Well, this . . . older woman, that relationship was different in quality or in depth from anything you'd experienced
   before?

S: Yes.

E: Is it possible for you to analyze the nature of the attraction you felt for her? This is a mean question to ask anyone.

S: No, I've often thought about it, so I guess it's pretty
   fair (laughter). She was probably the most intelligent
   woman I've come across. We were very much interested in
   the same things.   . . . She was very emotional in that
   she would really . . . deeply participate in the things she
   was interested in--I admired her in many ways . . .

E: When you say she was very emotional, you mean that . . .
   being with her gave things a quality of excitement?

S: Well, she was very absorbed in what she did, very intense
   in what she did--was a very rich feeling, and very enjoyable experience. Emotional in other ways, too. I mean
   she . . . after we broke up, spent quite a lot of time
   visiting a psychiatrist. Settled a lot of personal problems she had. Just boundless energy. And we were engaged
   in a lot of similar activities, and very closely together
   by working together.

E: Did she feel very strongly toward you, too? Was it mutual,
   the feeling?

S: Yes.   . . . In fact, she told me first that she was in
   love with me, after . . . a month or two, and at this time,
   I was sort of wrestling with the problem myself, realizing

the signs to it, and it was several months before I would
face it squarely and discuss it with her.   . . .

E: Have you had any other girls that you were interested in
since in this way?

S: Probably not to the same degree.   . . . About a year after
we broke up, before I started law school, I was pretty
interested in a girl, a young girl, for about the first
time; she was about 20, 21. After I came here, well, we
got engaged, more by phone calls and letters than anything
else, and . . . I'm still trying to analyze this one
(laughter)--she came out here, we were supposed to be
married last . . . last Christmas. We spent three days
together, and she went back home. We just had a couple of
nights of good long talks.

E: Did the fact that she was younger make any difference? Did
she seem therefore less interesting to you, perhaps less
rich as a person?

S: No, I don't think her age had anything to do with it . . .
but certainly that was one of the conclusions I came to.
. . . I tried my best not to make any comparisons, and we
discussed that out, too, and she had the feeling that I was
comparing, that . . . I didn't want to admit it, but I had
the feeling I was, too . . . and we thought it was best not
to go through with it.

E: Were you the active agent in breaking it off, do you think?

S: Yes. I was changing my mind six times a day for the period
of two or three days, but I was active in breaking it off.
I felt very badly about the way it worked out--and I tried
to meet again, really, to talk the whole thing over once
more, had no intention to start it up again, but I felt I'd
played a very dirty trick on her, and I wanted to talk the
whole thing through . . . and she left very angry . . .

E: Was she the active agent in bringing the engagement about,
then?

S: Well . . . probably more so than I was. I think she had
planted the idea and kept on harping on it. I know when
I had left home, which was about three months before she
had come out here, end of the summer, I had no idea of
getting engaged, married to her. And . . . then we decided
that she would come out here Christmas time, nothing definite then, but then after--through the mails is a bad way
--then we'd gotten more and more definite till we decided
we'd get married at Christmas.

E: Mm.   . . . You met her not any long time after you'd
broken off with the other one, is that the right inference?

S: Uh . . . less than a year.

E: I imagine that wasn't long enough.

S: I don't think so. I don't think I was being honest with
myself saying it was, it wasn't.   . . . In fact, it probably wasn't till last summer, that I think it was about
long enough. It . . .

E: Takes time to work your way through those things.

S: I think so.

E: Usually more than you think or hope that it's going to.

S: I thought that time had taken care of things, but it hadn't.

E: Would you now pretty much like to get married if you found the right person, now that your education is well along?

S: Yes.

E: You're all ready when you can make the right choice.

S: Making the right choice is going to take a long time (laughing).

E: Oh yes, yes.   . . . Well, you know that, and that's an asset.

S: Well, I mean, I think I've . . . slipped in the wrong direction often enough to try not to slip again.

E: Yes.   . . . Well, that's pretty generally everyone's history, isn't it? You're making a vital choice, and you fumble a few times, and if you're lucky enough to see your way out of those first fumblings, not commit yourself to a difficult situation or a lifelong mistake, why then you're able to approach it with some maturity.

S: I had thought that most people with that manner of trouble didn't fumble quite as badly, but recently I've changed my mind after speaking to quite a few of the fellows I'm living with. They've fumbled just as badly, so I don't feel so badly.

E: Well, it's very good of you to tell us all about yourself in this way, and . . . it helps us in studying personality, to have a person willing to go right into his history as you've done.

S: Oh, this is just as interesting for me as it is for you, I imagine (laughter).

6. ABILITIES

The only standard test of ability given to Solomon Kompten was the Wechsler-Bellevue Adult Intelligence Test. The items of this test are divided into verbal (e.g., comprehension, arithmetic, similarities) and performance (e.g., picture completion, block design, object assembly). It is customary to state a verbal I.Q. and a performance I.Q. separately, together with a full I.Q., which is not simply an average but is calculated independently from all the scores. In Solomon's case the verbal I.Q. was 142, the performance I.Q. 111, and the full I.Q. 130. According to Wechsler's classification, the performance I.Q. would be called "bright normal," while both the verbal and full I.Q.'s belong in the "very superior" category.

It is coming to be the general view that so-called intelligence tests predict scholastic performance—measured often by grades in school—relatively well, but they do not predict much else with acceptable accuracy. In studying the individual case it is advisable to learn about abilities by securing information about what a person has actually done.

His or her own summary opinions such as "I am bright," "I am
not bright," or "I am clumsy" need to be amplified as much as
possible by finding out instances of, for example, the alleged
clumsiness, and other instances in which the subject was
perhaps not clumsy at all. The material presented thus far and
to follow provides a large opportunity to infer Solomon's intelligence, including the capacity to act upon ideas as well as
think about them and expound them. The test scores constitute
information, but they should be seen in relation to life performance when this has been included in the study.

     To increase the latter kind of information, there was an
interview on abilities, defined not technically but in common-
sense language like business ability, memory ability, and
persistence. Solomon spoke disparagingly of his mechanical
ability, which he rated only as "fair" in comparison with other
men of his age.

S: My brother is pretty good at it, and I've never been able
     to do the things he's been able to do.   . . . I remember
     when I had shop in school, I got along all right, but I was
     kind of slow at it. It took me a while to catch on to
     working with things with my hands, carpentry or metal work,
     and radio shop. I could do it all right, but . . . I never
     really got it well. If there was something to be fixed
     around the house, I would let my dad do it.
E: That's what I was going to ask--did you ever put it to
     practical use?
S: Very little. I mean, I've done some . . . fix the roof,
     things of that sort, but no playing around with plumbing
     or anything like that. I always watch.
E: Did you ever work on a car?
S: Well, I helped my brother when he took one apart . . . I
     was kind of young then. Since then I haven't had my own
     car to tinker around with, so . . . I know very little
     about a car . . . except I did work one summer in a gas
     station, intending to learn about cars, spent most of my
     time filling up cars with gas (laughing).

     He gave himself "excellent" ratings in three of the eleven
abilities that made up the list: leadership ability, thinking
ability, and intuitive ability. Of the latter he said:

S: Well, I don't like the connotations that intuition has, but
     . . . much of it is not based on guess, but is more of a
     prediction, which I don't think is merely guesswork, but
     which is a relation back to what I know about a particular
     subject. For example, if I'm talking to a person, and I
     know him fairly well, I can usually--I'll usually try and
     think through his particular background, his particular
     type of education, before I approach him in a certain way
     and . . . will approach different people differently,
     according to more or less the category I place them in. I
     can try to push them one way or try to predict their actions

according to that type of . . . thinking.

E: Well, how about if we had used the word "insight" rather
than "intuition"?

S: I'd prefer it. For example, I used to like to play the
horses very much . . . and I certainly wouldn't rely on
intuition on anything of that sort. I'd have a feeling,
but I used to very thoroughly cover the racing form . . .
and . . . try to place things pretty much in context; but
. . . I seem to succeed fairly well, and that's more the
way I would try to approach any other problem, not just
guess about something, say I feel this way. I might try
to relate it to why I feel this way; sometimes, though, I
can't, I can't relate the feeling I might have to why I do
that.

E: Do you ever find yourself anticipating wishes of others?

S: Yes.   . . . For example, I will many times answer questions which weren't asked, or I'll answer certain doubts.
When I'm fairly familiar with the person and I've heard
about an event which occurred to him, I can try to predict
his action.

Answering a question concerning his <u>social ability</u>, on
which he rated himself "good," he said:

S: I can usually get along with people pretty well, even ones
I don't like, although I'm quite apt to say what I think,
what I believe, even when it's not too opportune to do so.
I will alienate some people that way. But generally
speaking, unless I have an intense dislike, I can usually
be very friedly with . . . a lot of people I basically
disagree with and . . . am able to make friends fairly
easily, although I don't especially go out of my way to do
so. If I'm at a party or something, and the thing is going
along rather slowly, I'll try to some extent to get the
thing livened up; sometimes it falls even flatter.

E: How do you generally apportion the time you spend on social
activities? Do you set aside certain nights?

S: (Laughing.) Oh . . . about eight nights a week. No, there
were never any special nights or special times, just whenever I felt like it, which was quite often . . . and . . .
I'm rather basically lazy, and it's always an excuse to get
away from work that I have to do or should be doing . . .
and I'm generally pretty active socially, and my phone is
usually jangling. Now, it's very much an escapist thing
and . . . although when I'm not overburdened with work,
there's still the desire for it to a certain extent, but
not to the extent that I go out and partake in it.

The subject thought poorly of his <u>memory ability</u>, but had
this to say about <u>thinking ability</u>.

S: Well, I would more or less place this at the opposite pole
    from memory--and one I dislike very much, and one I like.
    And . . . I've had discussions with people, and arguments,
    and I think they might memorize all the details, but
    usually they seem to be making a very illogical argument to
    me . . . and I think I approach it usually in a much better
    way by . . . having more insight into the basic problem and
    perhaps not knowing the details as well as they, but being
    able to give a perspective, a logical survey, and then the
    details just seem to fit in, once the groundwork is laid.

    When the interviewer turned to <u>artistic ability</u>, on which
the subject rated himself only "fair," the following dialogue
ensued.

S: Well, I like music very much, I know very little about it.
    For some reason I have a strong bias against poetry, and
    have never or just about never been able to appreciate
    anything in really poetic form. I'm not too familiar with
    great art, painting . . . there are certain things that hit
    me, that I like extremely well . . . generally, though,
    many things which appear beautiful to other people almost
    escape my view, so after it's called to my attention, and I
    concentrate on it, I can decide whether I like it very much
    or dislike it. My views are usually not in accord with
    most people I know. Except in music, there I like most of
    it.
E: Now, in regard to music, do you generally attend symphonies
    or do you just get it over the radio or . . .
S: I attend symphonies when I can afford them, which isn't too
    often--but . . . but . . . I . . . like listening to
    records . . . then again I don't have too much--I don't do
    it too often, I always feel rushed about the more pressing
    things, even though I always like to relax. Listen to
    opera, operettas. I'll do this sometimes, but not as often
    as I would like to.
E: Do you have special preference in music?
S: Well, I like . . . generally, symphonies over opera. And
    . . . within the symphonies, I like most all of
    Tschaikovsky's work; anything somewhat stirring I usually
    prefer. Lot of Bach and Beethoven that I like, too.

    Solomon did not rate any of the eleven abilities "poor,"
but he was somewhat disparaging of his own only "fair" <u>per-
sistence</u>.

S: Well, this really depends. Only when I'm interested, very
    interested, will I persist to the point . . . that I do
    something very well or very strongly--if I have no interest
    in a topic or in some type of school work, for example, and
    it has to be done, I will do it to get it over with, and
    will put it off as long as possible, and then be caught for

lack of time and have to rush to do it. If I do like it
. . . persistence rating would be higher, but it's only
when I've got the interest involved with it.

E: When you are interested, do you generally put everything
else aside until you've satisfied yourself?

S: Well, I put everything else aside, but it might take
proportionately more time than it should in relation to
other things, might concentrate to a great extent on this
--not quite to the point of excluding everything else, but
sometimes, pretty much so.

7. PERSONAL VALUES AND SENTIMENTS

E: Well, the interview today, the general idea to start off
with, is whether you yourself have formulated any general
philosophy of life, your general orientation toward the
world. You could just take off on that.

S: Pretty good topic. I probably spend between twenty and
thirty hours a week discussing it.

E: In classes?

S: No, bull sessions.   . . . This is a little too broad,
though; we usually pinpoint it a little more (laughter).
Well, generally, I . . . I think the Golden Rule is a good
standard which--I don't consider myself religious, but more
or less which I adopted, desirable standard to attain.
Also the . . . ideas embodied in the Ten Commandments. I
believe more of it transcends religion. I attempt to
pattern my life, with varying degrees of success, I suppose,
generally in that direction. I don't believe in placing
myself above others to the extent of excluding others,
thinking myself as being better than someone else. I like
the word "democrat" with a small "d."   . . . Well, to
begin with, that's a very general summation.

E: Yes, that's putting the statement in the most broad terms
of how you feel toward human beings. Do you have any
general personal aims in relation to this broad framework?
Your own personal philosophy of how you fit into it?

S: Well, I don't believe in this more or less maxim that everything comes to him who waits; I prefer working to achieve
things you want. When I--well, years ago, when I was
thinking about what I wanted to do . . . I would consider
the various things, the various methods by which I could
best fit into this overall philosophical scheme.

E: You've had this same philosophical scheme that far back?

S: As far back as I can remember. I considered either journal-
ism . . . but even when I decided upon law, I wanted to do
the type of legal work that would go in the direction I
wanted things to move. For example, I believe very strongly
that in a democracy, political action is a very necessary
. . . means of attaining what people wish . . . and I wanted
to aid political, economic, and social movements which were
moving generally in the direction I wanted. I thought I
best could do this with a legal background, and either work
directly or indirectly from within the law.

E: Well, how did you feel that you yourself could--did you have the feeling that the newspapers weren't presenting things right and that you could do a better job?

S: No, not at that time. I just wanted to be there and see these things and write about them myself; it wasn't a straight reporting role, I wanted to be more of a columnist. Just writing opinion.

E: Just so that you could be heard by more people.

S: Yeah, I think so.

E: Well, did you have sort of a buddy that did all the same things that you did?

S: Well, my closest friend--two or three of my close friends, didn't. One was mainly interested in sports, but we were pretty close even though we didn't pal around together in my various activities. Also palled around very closely with a couple of people who generally agreed with my viewpoints, but disagreed with the actual tactics we used, handing out leaflets, and so forth, and they remained my closest friends even though we didn't belong together to the same organizations.

E: What was the main basis for your friendship?

S: Probably intellectual discussions; we always spent hours every day talking over our school work and arguing about things.

E: Even though they didn't agree, they still were interested?

S: Oh, yes. Then we were friends socially; as far as social affairs were concerned, there was a combination of all sorts of interests.

E: To get a little away from this sort of thing, within the same framework, do you have any particular people that you feel . . . best exemplify what you would say are your ideals in all of this activity, or any other activity, or any other ideals that you have?

S: . . . No. No particular individual, or no particular group. . . . Just any individual or group which seems to be in more or less basic things for the things I want.

E: You don't have any picture even in an abstract sense of an ideal person? what the best qualities of an ideal man should be?

S: Not exactly in those terms, except . . . that I think one of the things that any ideal person should have is a very deep sense of a social awareness, and if this is lacking, I think a person is not a well-rounded person, not a very--well, meaningful person.

E: Has it always been this way? Have you ever had any strong ideals, things that kids usually go through?

S: Yeah, I remember that I did a lot of reading in Upton Sinclair, and I know he impressed me quite a bit, but I don't think he ever approached an ideal.

E: You mean Sinclair as a man or just the things he wrote?

S: No, just the things he wrote impressed me. I think I read all of his novels. Oh, it was propaganda for socialism.

It interested me, I was very sympathetic toward the under-
dog . . . believed this kind of solution was correct. He
wrote about the jungle, king coal, work in the steel mills
--these are things I was reading about, thought he was
pretty much right. This--I don't know if I mentioned this
before, but, this period of Sinclair followed the Horatio
Alger period, and--(laugher) . . .

E: How early was that?

S: Maybe around 10.

E: You think he had any lasting . . .

S: No, they were just stories to read. . . . And I went
through the Tom Swift stage, too, quite far back. But up
to recently, I think that Sinclair is the only one that
stands out in my mind.

E: Well, do you recall religion being an important issue in
your earliest days in any way before you left New York?

S: Well, important in only one respect, that I got my first
beating when I was about 4 years old for being Jewish. I
remember coming home and asking my mother what a Jew was.

E: How did that happen?

S: I was playing ball with a whole group of boys from the
neighborhood, and I was the youngest of the group, and I
guess the most convenient target.

E: What sort of an effect did this have on you? What did your
mother say, and how did you feel?

S: Well, I don't quite remember what went on, but I do remember asking the question and . . . being quite at a loss to
understand why the devil I got a beating.

E: Mmm . . . and did you play ball with those same boys anymore?

S: Oh, I suppose I did.

E: This was just a routine thing.

S: Yeah.

E: Was this ever--I suppose in the general political activities too this was a central point, discriminatory practices
against all people, had a rather personal meaning to you?

S: Probably did. And yet, though, at this age, I don't
clearly remember associating the two things together; it
was more on an international scale than a national scale
that the political things were connected with.

E: Have you ever thought of reinteresting yourself in religious
affairs?

S: Yeah--there's one argument I can never think of an answer
for . . . that the very fact that I individually feel as
strongly as I do about certain things, which there is no
direct personal benefit to myself for . . . proves that
basically man has some sort of supernatural guidance . . .
this making him different from other forms of animals,
which, as far as we know, at least I'm told, do not do
things of this type.

E: Well, you haven't brought out very well where the basic re-
examination comes in; is it because of this one question

you can't answer?

S: Yeah . . . up till now, when someone says there's always
    been a beginning which is not from man, I've countered that
    with . . . that might sound logical at first hearing, but
    must there always be a beginning? After all, the scien-
    tific axiom is that nothing is ever lost, but merely
    transformed, and that could apply also to the earth. How-
    ever, the introduction to the argument that there must be
    something spiritual in humans, or something above material
    feelings, I find a bit more difficult to answer . . . the
    fact that . . . if the premises this person advances are
    correct, that man is the only type of animal that exists
    this--this way . . . is a problem I haven't answered yet.
    Perhaps there is something else besides material existence.

E: Well, you have given me a pretty good account of your ideas
    and your general life aims, and so on. I think we're
    getting toward the end of the hour. I'd just like to ask
    you one further question, and then we can knock off. How
    do you feel that you as a person measure up to what you
    generally have devoted your life to in terms of your
    activities and ideas?

S: Well, again, that's a pretty hard question to answer. Gen-
    erally, I think I've measured up fairly well.   . . . In
    comparison with others who don't feel the way I do, I just
    think I'm head and shoulders above them, but with others
    who do--that's not a good basis of comparison--but with
    others who do feel strongly about either what I believe or
    have any strong beliefs about anything else, I think . . .
    I've done pretty well, could do much better, and intend to
    do better. At times I've done very well, and I've done very
    poorly. But it's pretty tough to have any strong belief in
    anything . . . and to possibly advance a strong belief in
    something is a continual effort, and, of course, there's a
    lot of . . . ups and downs in that.

8. EXCERPTS FROM OTHER INTERVIEWS

   Following is a series of disconnected excerpts from other
interviews, selected because they amplify previous materials or
contribute to the picture as a whole. Some of these dialogues
occurred spontaneously, others as a result of questioning on
points that had seemed obscure.

E: You mentioned something about a little game you used to
    play when you were a child and ill in bed. Do you remember
    what that was?

S: I played all sorts of games. Yeah, I remember I used to
    play all sorts of games--baseball, football, hockey, horse-
    racing game, track--just about any major sport.

E: I was referring to one that you sort of made up while you
    were at home.

S: Well, these I made up.

E: Oh, these you did make up?

S: Yeah.

E: Well (laughter), what sort of things were they?

S: Well, the company that puts out those Monopoly games swiped
    my idea (laughter). They were the kinds of things you'd
    play on a board and have various chances, either with a
    deck of cards or slips of paper or a little dial that you'd
    spin or something of that sort. There'd be two opposing
    teams, and depending on the game you were playing, slips of
    paper or marked decks of cards, there were all sorts of
    possibilities for various plays as at a football game. And
    you would captain both teams, of course, always choosing
    one yourself to win (laughter). I noticed a very fine
    football game was put out a few years ago by one of these
    companies which was very close, except they had the board
    all set out and figures to play with, lavish, but the same
    idea.

E: You'd play these by yourself?

S: Yes, others too, when other fellows came over, worked out
    pretty well.

E: This sort of brings up the subject of your parents. We've
    talked about them already, and I wonder if you can tell us
    something more. What are the ways they differed?

S: Well, she's the more active one in the family, very quick,
    and . . . more emotional, more nervous and tense. As
    regards my Dad, he's very slow, quiet.

E: Well, do you know if there are any points of view, ideas,
    or what have you, in which they . . .

S: Well, I think the contrast we just spoke about.   . . . My
    father would always be the cautious one, as to changing
    locations, and so forth. Mother would always be the agita-
    tor for a change. For example, our move out to California
    we debated for many years. My mother wanted to go ten
    years before we did.

E: She finally got her way (laughs).

S: Yeah (laughs).

E: Well, on this move to California, how did your father feel
    about it?

S: Well, they both wanted to go. They moved mainly because of
    my brother's and my health. It meant giving up an estab-
    lished position in New York, security of some sort . . .

E: Well, what about . . . are there any other points of differ-
    ence you can think of between them?

S: I've never heard them have an argument, so I'd have to
    guess.

E: That sounds like quite a remarkable relationship.   . . .
    Well, do you think that their relationship through the
    years has changed any?

S: No, I wouldn't say so. From what I can tell, it's a very
    satisfactory deal. There haven't been any special points
    of conflict.   . . . All in all, it's just about the

happiest marriage I've ever seen.

S: When I got to the ninth grade I finally had a course I really enjoyed, a year of it; I still correspond with the teacher I had then. It was a course with history and current events all thrown together. Four or five other fellows and myself formed, I think in the ninth grade, a Philosophers' Club--and we appointed this teacher our advisor. We used to meet with her once a week and discuss all sorts of topics which none of us knew anything about, and we used to feel important and she used to enjoy it very much. We did, too. Kept this up all the way through high school. We kept our association up after we all went to high school. This teacher often told me that she had wished that I had taken languages with her; she chided me many times at getting C's in Spanish and said I should have taken a course in Latin with her, and she would have made me learn (laughing).

E: What kinds of ideas do you recall about this club, that made it so important?

S: Well, the teacher was probably the most popular in the school, outside of the one I had in glee club. They were the two most popular teachers, very well liked, very friendly, very warm human persons . . . of course, the courses they were teaching had much to do with it. . . . For the first time we seemed to be--something in the school which was alive and interesting, the fact that we would discuss current events and things which seemed to really matter instead of . . . instead of talking about amoebas, which nobody knew what they were, and trying to learn the difference between Spanish pronouns when we didn't know very well what English pronouns were, and the type of course was much more interesting.

E: How did you get along with the kids in the civics class?

S: The kids? Pretty well. I got along pretty well with all the kids at the school. I went out for track team there, too, but about this time my leg got really bad, and it was impossible for me to run. . . . Then I had an English teacher who wanted me to try out for an oratory contest . . . so when I was supposed to be at gym, I couldn't participate in any more sports, so I would take that hour and spend it with him, and he would coach me for this oratory. We spent most of the time just talking, and sometimes I'd get up and he'd help me prepare a speech.

E: Did you have this English teacher for class too?

S: Yes. In the end I did a lot of oratory work. I won the school contest and placed about third, I think, in the regional contest. And after that another student and myself toured all the clubs in Wilmington who wanted us, Rotary and so forth, and we'd give speeches.

E: What were those speeches about?

S: We'd pick our own topics.

E: Do you remember some of the topics you spoke on?

S: Oh . . . student looks at the world or something, generally
    current things. We tried to give the general student
    impression of what we wanted, of what students wanted when
    they went to college, and so forth; and I did quite a bit
    of that.

E: You also mentioned that you still write to some of your
    old teachers, your English teacher for one, and for an-
    other . . .

S: Well, just once a year or so.

E: And the philosophy club teacher?

S: Also about once a year.

E: That is sort of remarkable, the interest on your part, and
    their interest in you.

S: Well, when I was in school I spent a great deal of time
    with them . . . some oratory contests. And then we spent a
    great deal of time together outside of that. I guess I was
    interested in their points of view; they helped me along
    quite a bit. The same thing is true of the other teacher.
    . . . We used to--every once in a while talk politics--good
    people in that respect. And one of them lived in San
    Francisco, and one of them lived near Wilmington, so when
    I'm around there, I think I'll drop in and see them.

E: Well, how do you account for the fact that this has lasted
    for so many years?

S: Well, I know lots of people who have sent (laughs)--just
    doesn't seem like so many years, and . . . well, I felt
    that I was seeing these two more than anyone else in the
    school, and they helped me out, and I had very good times
    in their classes, and learned quite a bit from them and
    this made a lasting friendship even though it was school-
    days . . .

E: Was it their personality, ideals?

S: Well, more of an interest in the same types of problems.
    And we'd get different answers on things, but always
    enjoyed exchanging opinions on them.

E: Then they don't necessarily think the way you do?

S: No, no. But we're interested in the same things, more or
    less in the same general approach, but we differ quite a
    bit.

E: What papers do you read?

S: I'll read . . . the extreme ones. Usually I'll read either
    the New York Times or the Tribune, the Daily Worker, some-
    times a Hearst paper, then I'll usually read several of the
    news magazines, Times, Newsweek . . . read the publications
    of the Communist party, and I'll read . . . sometimes the
    Catholic organizations.

E: Do you find any kids who go through this amount of infor-
    mation when you talk to them?

S: Some, not many.

E: Well, how did you start this, did you start in college?

S: Started way before.

E: Well, what was there about your life that got you so inter-
    ested?

S: Well, the economic situation at the time undoubtedly had a
    very strong effect. I knew things just weren't right. I
    knew my dad was working too long, my mother was always busy
    . . . although I had all the small things that I wanted,
    there was always money, I didn't know quite what it meant,
    what it could get, but that we didn't have enough of it.
    We lived in a very poor neighborhood for over a year, a lot
    of anti-Semitism and a lot of anti-Negro feeling. There
    was a dramatic incident of judicial unfairness to Negroes.
    It was brought home to me as a kid. I heard everybody
    talking about it.

E: Well, you seem much more strongly motivated along these
    lines than most people.

S: Well, I spend an awful lot of time on it. I enjoy it.
    Gives me the feeling that I'm doing something. I tried for
    a period of time not doing any of these activities, and I
    usually fall down on my academic work as well. So it sort
    of aids all my other work. I get better grades, for one
    thing, when I'm most active.

E: How does it work, do you think?

S: Well, I just seem to get awfully unhappy when I force myself
    to sit at a desk for twelve hours a day for just school
    work. I feel completely out of touch with what's going on
    around, and I can't see the value of what I have to do; I
    can't correlate my everyday activities, I'm out of touch,
    in a vacuum. And I feel very--oh, I used to have a tremen-
    dous guilty conscience that I was separating myself from
    life and putting myself in an ivory tower, that the law
    school is.

QUESTIONS ON SECTIONS 1-8

1. When a young man falls in love with a somewhat older
woman, the interpretation is often given that he is looking for
a mother substitute. To support this interpretation, there
should be evidence that he wants to be mothered by his partner,
and the interpretation is strengthened if he has been highly
dependent on his mother and on other older women, such as
teachers, during his earlier life. There are, of course, other
reasons for being attracted to someone older. Do you judge
that Solomon Kompten in his first important love affair was
looking for a mother substitute, or do you interpret this in
some other way?

2. It is sometimes predicted that ambitious parents who
have not had educational advantages will push their children
hard to do well in school as a means to economic success.
Taking all the evidence into account, how would you characterize the attitudes of Solomon's parents in this respect?

3. In the third interview Solomon was asked for his ideas
on bringing up children. What values are most prominent in his
discussion of this topic? In what respects do his suggestions
correspond to the way he himself was brought up, and in what
respects do they represent attempts to improve upon his own
upbringing?

4. Solomon's relationship with his brother changed in the
course of time. How would you characterize the different
phases of this relationship? What effects do you think this
relationship had on Solomon's personal growth?

5. Identification with models plays a part in the growth
of personality. What models seem to have been most influential
in Solomon's development, in the early years as well as more
recently?

6. On his relations with peers Solomon generally reports,
though without much detail, that he got along well and was
popular. Do you think he may have misjudged his popularity?
What qualities did he have that might be expected to make him
unpopular? What evidence is there, on the other hand, that he
was in fact popular?

7. Solomon rated himself high on both thinking ability
and intuitive ability. Some readers have thought that he was
not at all an "intuitive person" and had misjudged himself in
this respect. What evidence do you find relevant in reaching a
decision on this point?

8. Although we often speak of intelligence as if it were
a single variable, we recognize that in actual life people use
their minds differently and are, so to speak, intelligent in
different ways. How would you characterize Solomon's intelligence: in what ways does he use his mind best and show the most
unusual gifts?

9. Solomon is unusual in having developed as early as
junior high school a set of social-economic-political beliefs--
a sense of "the direction in which I want things to move"--
strong enough to prompt a good deal of action. What do you
find in his earlier experience that might have given these
beliefs their special force?

10. Compared to other men of his age, Solomon rates high
on self-confidence. What is there in his history that seems to
have contributed to his present strong sense of competence?

11. In what ways do you think Solomon's social and economic environment during childhood and adolescence left a
distinctive impression on the growth of his personality?

9. SUBSEQUENT EVENTS

Solomon Kompten opened his law practice in San Francisco
in the mid-1950s. At that time the House of Representatives
Committee on Unamerican Activities, of which Senator Joseph
McCarthy was chairman, was at the height of its power. Using
highly arbitrary methods, this Committee conducted what have

since come to be regarded as witch-hunts. The idea of a "dangerous radical" was extended to include people whose opinions were hardly more than mildly liberal. For a lawyer deeply committed to constitutional rights and freedom of opinion, the defense of people called to testify before the Committee could easily become a mission, one that involved real dangers. After a few years Senator McCarthy and his Committee were discredited and their activities curtailed. It is to this change of climate that Solomon refers when he says that the times, rather than his own commitment, were changing.

Following a short list of suggested questions, Solomon dictated his subsequent history.

After I graduated from law school I returned to San Francisco, studied, took the bar examination, and had one of the biggest surprises of my life when I found out I had flunked. It really was of no solace to me to discover later that that particular bar examination in California resulted in numerous failures and a change in the system of grading, because I lost six months of my professional life in restudying for the exam, and perhaps learned a pretty good lesson regarding ego. Defeats and losses have never had as great an impact upon me since.

While I was studying for the bar for the second round, I obtained employment with an attorney who was representing some of the lawyers who were subpoenaed by the House Committee on Un-American Activities, and I spent perhaps one of the most fascinating years of my life doing really what amounted to political work, rather than legal work, in helping to prepare their defense and testimony for the Committee. I received all of 50 dollars a week, but have never since that time felt that I was doing more productive work.

After that period of time passed, I went into the general practice of law in San Francisco, where I struggled for five years building a practice completely on my own. I suspect I did economically as well or even better than my classmates, but I really received no satisfaction from the practice or from the struggle to establish one. I knew few lawyers in the San Francisco area who would undertake a civil rights case, and I felt that this was what I wanted to do as well as establish myself economically. So I formed a partnership with an attorney whom I had met when we were both law students and who was practicing in San Francisco and who felt exactly the same as I. For the next few years we did build a successful general practice with heavy emphasis on free work and civil liberties.

For the first few years each of us, I suppose, received a great deal of satisfaction in what we felt we were accomplishing, not only for ourselves but for our community. The chores of practice and the burdens soon got to me, however, and gradually, as I came to do less and less work in the criminal area, I also began to do less and less in civil rights and civil liberties. I slowly began to develop more of a practice in

representing injured persons in personal injury cases, and as
my income increased I suppose so did my guilt. To some extent
initially I felt that this was an abandonment of earlier-held
principles, a sort of copping out, but I felt that times,
rather than myself, were probably changing. I no longer have
any feelings of guilt about the type of legal practice in which
I am engaged, but neither do I receive any satisfaction from my
work as I did in the earlier years, even though then I had economic problems which I no longer face.

I suppose, therefore, that my brief sketch on occupational
history sort of blends into your second general question concerning beliefs and values. I have changed in this area as I
have grown older. I no longer feel I am the idealist I was
some twenty or twenty-one years ago. I'm really no longer an
activist, and even though I can now contribute in economic
terms to those causes which I feel deserve such contributions,
that really is the extent of my participation. Whereas in the
past I would have been the writer of a petition, or the petition circulator, at least, I now might be the petition signer.

Also I have increasingly turned my time and attention to
those interests which give me direct satisfaction, such as my
participation in horse racing. This no longer can be put in
the hobby category, but probably is more of a business, even
though a relatively non-paying one. With the increase of income that did come along with a successful law practice, I was
able to begin taking some time from practice and began to do
some traveling about ten years ago, which I wasn't able to
afford before that. It is now not unusual to take three or
four weeks in Europe or a week or two in Mexico whenever my
wife and I feel like it. Yet traveling no longer provokes my
curiosity and I am just as content to remain at home, where I
can participate on a daily basis in activities such as racing,
which almost completely dominates my field of interest at this
point.

As to your question on health, my impulse would be to
answer that it has been fine and that I have had no serious
illnesses. This really means that I give little consideration
to the fact that about eight years ago I was hospitalized for
cancer, and did have a cancerous growth removed from the area
of my shoulder blade. Just prior to surgery I heard the doctor
say, "We might have to do a disarticulation of the shoulder
joint," but I was almost completely unimpressed that what he
was saying was that I might lose my left arm and shoulder, and
possibly my life, if the surgery were not successful. Fortunately, it was completely successful and I have had no problems
since. But I certainly did a lot of reflecting immediately
after surgery concerning what it was in life that I should be
doing, and I suppose it helped force me to concentrate on the
fact that I should be doing those things that I really wanted
to do and deriving whatever pleasure I could, since we are all
here for such a short time anyway. Other than that I have felt
reasonably well and don't feel that my health restricts activ-

ity in any way, although I certainly feel much older than my
chronological years. I feel that I have led life at a pretty
good tempo, and perhaps it is beginning to take its toll.

Presently, I am under medication for hypertension, with
which I have apparently flirted ever since I was in law school,
when I was first informed that my blood pressure was high; but
I have apparently never needed to be placed on medication until
very recently. I don't suppose that my life-style will change
to any appreciable extent, and I presume I will have to remain
on medication. For example, I am still a heavy smoker, still
consume great amounts of coffee, feel that I never get enough
sleep and that I must pack into each twenty-four-hour day as
much as I possibly can, and I do a pretty good job in the
packing process.

My personal life has not been such as I would have anticipated when I was a student. I married shortly after graduation from law school, and can't for the life of me even now
explain why I did. I did not feel physical love for the woman
I married, although I suppose I felt that we would make good
lifetime companions. The hardest decision of my life was to
leave, in view of the fact that we had three children, and I
did not want to leave whatever home life we had together. It
was the realization that we didn't have a home life as a family
and that a divorce would not be harmful to the children, at
least any more than a bad home life, that finally made me leave
for the last time. That was after eight or nine years of
marriage of which the last four or five were extremely unhappy.

I remarried shortly after my divorce and am very happily
married now, except for the fact that my wife and I have
problems due to her inability to accept my attitude toward my
three children. We have no children together, and she feels,
to some extent at least, that I have not felt love for her
because of this. I understand her feeling of frustration, but
it does cause difficulties in our relationship, especially
since she seeks the outlet of excessive drinking.

Interestingly enough, my present wife was born in Nazi
Germany. We are the same age, and although I do believe her
pronouncements that as a child she was totally apolitical and
unaware of what was happening in Germany, it was a great step
for me not to bear prejudice against her because of her birth
and upbringing. We have since visited Germany together on
several occasions, and I cannot help but feel even now resentment against Germans in my own age bracket or older.

Fortunately, I believe the relationship with my children
has been strengthened since my divorce from their mother, and
I am pleased to say that I have, by today's standards, three
very normal and healthy children, who are out of serious
trouble and all of whom seem to be doing very well. I have a
son who is now going to art school in his first year, who is
very bright and determined, and may or may not stay with art as
a career. My older daughter is in her second year at college
and is extremely sensitive and sweet, and, I think, very level-

headed. My younger daughter is in high school and seems very
average in her ways and emotions, but also very independent,
and I am sure she will be able to stand on her own two feet as
she matures.

My parents are still alive and are now living in San Fran-
cisco--that was my wife's idea, since they were extremely unhappy and lonely where they were after having sold their home
and moving to an apartment where they could not adjust. We
helped them to secure a condominium very close to where my wife
and I live, and we see them frequently. They are, of course,
very old, both in their eighties, and at times extremely un-
reasonable, in my opinion, to get along with, and I admire my
wife's ability to really go out of her way to be kind to them
and a good daughter to them. My brother has also moved to San
Francisco, and we do see each other a couple of times a week,
although there is no similarity of interest outside the family.

I have several times mentioned horse racing and might
explain that earlier in my first marriage, when I was getting
extremely frustrated at having to scratch the lawn on weekends
or stay home and do housework in order that the house my wife
and children and I shared not look like a garbage dump, I
discovered the possibility of attending the races. I gradually
began to attend on a weekend basis, taking all of 10 dollars
or so with me, as that was all I could afford to gamble, and
this became my weekend recreation. After a few years of small
wagering, I did win a few thousand dollars one day, and purchased a small interest in a race horse, which my partners and
I ran at the track. We got lucky and had a few wins, and I
purchased another race horse, and gradually I became a small
owner as well as a bettor. Since that time I have increased
my interest in racing, and as of this year I got into breeding
of race horses. I now spent two or three hours seven days a
week on business connected with breeding and racing, and I
continue to go to the races on every occasion I can where I
have a horse running. I certainly am not in the big leagues,
as this would require many millions, but I do have several
racing animals and several for breeding purposes, and expect I
will participate in racing for the rest of my life, to one
extent or another. Fortunately, my wife shares this interest
with me and has always encouraged me to be in racing and to
spend more time and money on it.

So you see I don't feel at all like the person I anticipated being when I was a law student. At that time I would
have felt that holding some office such as in the state legis-
lature or in Congress would have been fulfillment of a life's
dream. Now I wouldn't take it if it were offered to me.
That's probably more of a cynical attitude than anything else.
I feel that my gradual abstinence from political activity has
been proportionate to my growth of cynicism about the entire
political and human process.

This really leads to one of your last questions, as to
what I might advise a young man of 22, as I was when you first

met me. I suppose the modern generation has a phrase for it--
"do your own thing"--and I would advise any young man today to
do what he feels he wants to do and to make his own decision
in that regard. About the only time I recall seeking advice
was when I really didn't know what to do regarding my desire
to terminate my first marriage. I expressed my query to the
closest friend I then had, my physician, who has since died.
He astounded me with his response of "Do what you want to do,"
and I pounced on him very argumentatively and bawled him out
for such selfish answer. It took me quite a while to see the
wisdom in it. I now would give the same response to any such
question.

     All in all, I have been very optimistic in my approach to
life. I think I have had more ups than downs, and I do consider myself very fortunate to have a reasonable amount of
health, reasonable happiness from family life, and sufficient
money to enjoy material living, which I do enjoy, and yet to
continue having interest in some activity, even though to a
much lesser extent than previously, in matters outside my own
personal and family circle.

     I apologize for taking this amount of time to respond to
your request for up-to-date information. Perhaps it tells you
more about me now than anything else, since I am sure that as
a young man I would have dropped everything else that would
have prevented me from answering your request and would have
responded very quickly. But now I kept putting it off until it
was relatively convenient for me and would cause little interference with my normal activities.

FURTHER QUESTIONS

     1. One of the outstanding facts to be explained in Solo-
mon Kompten's subsequent life is the dying down of the once-
zestful interest in social reform and civil rights. He gives
certain reasons for this. Do you think they are sufficient?
Does the answer you worked out to Question 9 (following
Section 8) have room for the possibility that this central
cluster of commitments would be transient? How do you explain
the change in him?
     2. Unless you are yourself an enthusiast, you may have
difficulty in understanding the magnetic attraction that horse
racing has for Solomon. Try, nevertheless, to make some good
guesses about this vital element in his present life. Why is
it so absorbing? To what aspects of his personality, as
revealed in his life history to date, do you think it appeals?
What function does it serve in his current life pattern?
     3. What values are revealed in Solomon's description of
his three children? In what respects do these values represent
a change from those he held for himself as a young man?
     4. Do you think that Solomon feels unhappy about the way
his life has turned out? Does he feel that more has gone out

of it than has come into it since the earlier study, when he was 22, and shortly thereafter? Does the last paragraph of his communication have a bearing on this question?

    5. (A confidential question; do not let anyone grade you on it.) Were you pleased to learn that Solomon got his come-uppance on the first California bar examination? (Your answer may help you to detect personal feelings you developed during the first 8 sections of the material.)

2 Carol O'Brien

Contents

Preliminaries

Carol O'Brien was studied during the late 1940's when she was a sophomore in college. She had her nineteenth birthday during the course of the study. Her background and experience contrast sharply with those of Solomon Kompten. Of Irish descent and Roman Catholic faith, she grew up in a small, relatively self-sufficient, and stable industrial town in Rhode Island, living in the same house until she went away to college. She was invited to take part in the research, being paid for her time, because subjects with her background were poorly represented among those previously studied.

In comparing her with Solomon it is necessary to keep in mind that when studied she was four years younger, at a time in life when a great deal of development goes on during four years. She was much less communicative and coherent; in interviews she often fell silent, sat passively, and gave few evidences of lively interest. As the interviews were not recorded, Carol's silences had at least the advantage of giving examiners time to write down verbatim much of what she said.

At the end of Section 7 you will find a group of questions on Carol's personality at age 19. You may want to look at these beforehand. Her report on "Subsequent Events" (Section 8) came in more promptly than Solomon's and is much longer. This section is followed by "Further Questions."

As a first step in the study Carol was asked to write an

autobiography and was given a list of topics which she might
like to cover. She followed this list faithfully. The sequence of paragraphs is thus to be attributed more to the outline than to her own selection. Phrases taken directly from
the outline are underlined.

1. AUTOBIOGRAPHY

I was born in Wakefield, Rhode Island. My parents are
citizens of the United States and are of Irish descent. My
father graduated from Holy Cross College and Georgetown Law
School. My mother is a graduate of Rhode Island Teachers
College. My parents are of average social and economic status.
We live comfortably without pressing financial worry, yet we
aren't considered wealthy. My father belongs to Rotary Club
and mother to the Women's Club; both are members of the country club in town. My father is a lawyer, while my mother is
at home. Both my parents enjoy reading, contract bridge, golf,
and music. In addition, my father likes baseball, football,
and almost all sports from a purely objective point of view.
Just now he is interested in Red Cross work, since he is chairman of the Home Service Committee. My mother has a mild interest in raising plants. Both my parents are Roman Catholics
and Republicans.
   The general home atmosphere is one of harmony with occasional discord. In spite of these occasional quarrels, there
are no deep-seated rifts between any members of the family.
The family group has always maintained an affectionate attitude toward me. Because I am the younger of two children, the
rest of the family considered me helpless and young; therefore,
they always did things for me. My mother, in particular,
figured that she could do things much faster and quicker than
I. I always let my parents do things for me, because it was
much easier to shift the responsibility to someone else's
shoulders. When I reached the age of 12, I became very self-
conscious and afraid to do simple little things--for instance
--to give talks in English class, to play the piano before
strangers or at the Music Club, and to talk with strangers (I
was secretary of the Music Club, and had to call the newspapers,
and so forth). I was afraid to even speak to my father about
matters of any importance--going to college, and so forth.
When I was younger I used to be afraid to ask my father to
take me to the movies. I have always loved my father, but
held him in awe because his word was final in our house.
   My sister, who is very independent, always interceded for
me with my parents. She was always wonderful to me and tried
to help me overcome my shyness. I have never resented her in   *sister*
any way even though I had reason to be jealous of her, for she
is very beautiful and intelligent and has quite a bit of poise.
I never resented her because of her kindness and the fact that

there was never any chance for real competition or comparisons between us since she is seven years older than I. My father used to get disgusted with me for being so helpless and afraid. He finally refused to listen to my sister when she would ask things for me; therefore, I was forced to ask for myself, and I gradually overcame this uneasy feeling in relation to my father. My family considered me somewhat of a scatterbrain. I was much more energetic and boisterous than my sister; and unlike her, I was young for my age.

My parents always punished me when I did wrong. Usually, they deprived me of some pleasure, for example, going to the movies or playing near my house after dinner. My first reaction to punishment was resentment, sometimes expressed, other times repressed, which quickly turned me to shame when I thought it over. I never committed any serious, outstanding offense to my parents.

I received most of my religious training at school. My parents have always abided by what I learned, as they lived up to what they taught me with regard to morals. As far as drinking and smoking are concerned, my parents approve as long as these habits aren't carried to extremes. My parents taught me to have respect for law and order, to be honest and unselfish. Also my mother taught me to keep our community clean. She never let me throw papers on the street, and so forth.

Our family used to go on picnics together when I was quite young. We used to take a trip almost every year. On birthdays and holidays the family usually went somewhere together.

I have always lived in the small town of Wakefield. There are only a few industries in town; hence, my surroundings are more like the country than the city. Our house has two stories and ten rooms. My economic and religious position in the community is the same as that of my parents. As for social position, I belonged to various clubs connected with high school and church. A small percent of the population in Wakefield is Jewish (there are but two families of Negroes), the remaining are Italian, Polish, Irish, English, and Scotch.

When I was 4, I had chicken pox, at 5 I had gland trouble, from which I developed a twisted and stiff neck; however, this condition disappeared before I had to wear a collar of any sort. A few years later I had tonsilitis. In the third grade I had the regular measles. That was in February, and every year afterwards, for four years, I had German measles every February.

I can vaguely remember a few fleeting scenes of my early childhood. I recall one time when my grandfather, who occasionally took care of me when my parents went away, carried me to the end of the street to meet the rest of the family who were coming along in the car. I remember another time when my mother was dressing me in my pink coat to go out for a walk with my sister. Althoug these scenes may have preceded the following incident, I don't remember them as vividly. When I

was 2 1/2, photographers came and took our pictures (family).
I remember that we had to pose in different ways, and the
strong lights and the pretty dress that I wore which I always
liked. As the photographers were leaving, I remember that a
friend of my sister (girl) telephoned to ask her to go for a
walk. I don't recall whether she went or not.

All my life I have daydreamed, mostly of dangerous situations in which I was placed. Of course, I always allowed myself to come through with "flying colors," or else other people
would be in trouble and I would step in and "save the day."

I enjoyed reading Arabian Nights, the Oz books (in particular), fairy stories in general, books on travel, and the various girl-detective mystery stories. I don't recall having
any particular hero.

My first playmates were all boys; therefore, I never
played with dolls until I was 6 when two girls moved into the
neighborhood. My family always considered me a tomboy even
when I played with girls, mainly because I was very energetic
and at times mischievous (in comparison to my sister, who was
a quiet and obedient child). I have always loved animals and
had one dog of my own from the time I was 7 to the age of 13.
My dog and I went everywhere together, and the dog would growl
when my mother would get real angry with me. Generally, my
emotive behavior was cooperative and obedient; as I grew older
I became more sensitive and fearful.

I entered a parochial school at the age of 5 1/2. I was
13 1/2 when I graduated. I entered public high school the
same year and graduated at the age of 17 1/2. Until I entered
college, I was always close to the head of the class scholas-
tically.

I have made a few deep and many casual friendships. I
rarely quarreled with my friends, except when I was younger
and chummed with people who lived near me rather than people
with whom I was compatible. All through high school I went
with the same two girls (not exclusively), and we have never
quarreled. One of these girls was as self-conscious as I;
therefore, I am afraid we were a bad influence on each other.
We made quite a pair at Music Club; she played the violin and
I accompanied her on the piano. We were both so scared whenever we played that her bow would shake as did my hands. The
result was a sort of tremolo effect. The only basis for selection of my friends is the fact that we are compatible and have
a good time together. I was never a leader but one of the gang,
I wasn't ignored, but certain people bullied me, especially one
girl, with whom few people seemed to get along. I used to give
in to her rather than have an argument. Half the time I didn't
realize that I was being bullied (I thought I was merely being
agreeable) until some of my other friends called it to my attention. My behavior with groups is genial, submissive more
than aggressive, and slightly boisterous (if I know the people
real well; otherwise I let the other people do the talking and

joking).

In high school I always wanted to be popular (particularly with boys) and attractive. However, I realized that I
would never be pretty or popular, since I was too shy to do
much talking whenever boys were around; I was resigned rather
than frustrated. Realizing that I would never "set the world
on fire" socially, I attempted to make up for this deficiency
by getting high marks. This wasn't very hard to do because
not many of my classmates were particularly concerned with
getting high grades. Also, my parents were always pleased
when I received good grades. Although I attended all the
social functions at school and had some great times, I was
never as popular as some of my friends.

When I came to college, there was a reverse in affairs.
My life was more social than intellectual. I didn't get the
marks that I had in high school; however, I didn't really expect them, because I knew that college would be much harder
than the country club I had graduated from. Because of this
realization I am afraid that I didn't try as hard as I should
have. I lost much of my ambition along intellectual lines.
I was particularly poor in English and Spanish; therefore, I
assumed the attitude that everyone was much smarter than I and
that I couldn't do any better, so I didn't try very hard. In
my other subjects, geology and history, I did much better;
therefore, I tried to get good marks in these courses. College
was quite a change from high school, where I said before, I was
near the head of my class. However, I wasn't bothered by this
too much, since I had more social life in college than I did
in high school.

I don't recall any hero worship of any particular people.
The only person I ever attempted to imitate was my sister.
When I was young, I always had to do everything that she did.
She liked to draw, and whenever she did I likewise attempted
to draw. As I grew older, I relied on her advice to a great
extent. I accepted her views on many subjects, such as clothes,
people, affairs of the world, and so forth. Anything she considered all right, I thought was all right too.

I have always been interested in sports, especially skiing, skating, tennis, and basketball. I was never any good at
any of these sports, but I enjoy them anyway. I am very fond
of music and never get tired of listening to it. I love to
play the piano and do so for a long period of time if I am in
the mood. I also like to read and dance and have an interest
or perhaps more of a curiosity about medicine. When I was in
high school, I belonged to Music Club, Glee Club, Orchestra,
and Writers' Club (we used to write compositions, poems, and
so forth, which were criticized by other members of the club).
I also was on the staff which produced the class yearbook, and
I enjoyed this work very much. We spent most of our time trying to think of new ways to present the same old material.
Throughout high school, I was a member of the Girls' Club,

[handwritten margin notes: "never popular"; "College"; "thought everyone was smarter, didn't try"]

which had no particular purpose except to have a good time.
There were about twelve girls in the club, and for the most
part we chummed together throughout high school. In college
I belong to the Dramatic Club (behind-the-scenes work), and I
go to a singing group occasionally; I would like to join, but
I have felt that it requires too much time. I would like to
devote more time to clubs, but I don't feel that I have it to
give.

In high school I never felt at ease when boys were around,
unless I knew them well. I have now limited this uneasy feeling down to boys that I like or am trying to impress. However,
when I forget about making an impression, or when I get to
know a boy better, I don't feel a bit uneasy. I have never
been in love, but I had terrific "crushes" on various boys.
Either they were quiet and shy or witty and loads of fun.

I think that marriage is something permanent; therefore,
both parties should know each other very well before getting
married. I disapprove of hasty marriages. I think that a
couple getting married should, if possible, come from the same
general background, economically, socially, and religiously;
mainly I think the couple will agree on more things if they do.
If, however, they are truly in love with one another, I believe
that this love can certainly overcome any differences which
might arise from different backgrounds. I believe in marriage
for love and never for money, convenience, or any other reason.
I would like my husband to be intelligent, considerate, and
poised and to have the same general interests as I.

When I was young, I experienced great joy whenever I went
anywhere, special trip, party, and so forth, or when I was
praised. When I was in high school, and also now, I still experience joy from these things, but I also feel happy if a boy
that I like particularly shows any attention to me or if I
receive good marks.

The events that caused me the greatest sadnesses during
my life were death of my dog when I was 13 and the death of my
brother-in-law last June. I still cry over these events,
whereas other disappointments in my life fail to bother me any
more (disappointments in "love," for example). As I said before, I experienced great discomfort whenever I had to carry
on business with strangers, play the piano, read anything that
I wrote (Writers' Club), or give talks in English class.

I have no definite aims for the future, as far as a career
is concerned, I am sorry to say. I don't want a career unless
my position is very interesting. I couldn't stand a monotonous
routine position like office work. I don't like to consider
marriage as an aim, but I guess as far as aims are concerned
that is mine. If I am forced to have a career, I would like
to do something with psychology or interior decorating, design-
ing, and so forth. (I have no talent along this line, but the
work appeals to me.) I would love to travel, but I doubt if
I will ever have a chance to make extensive journeys. I have

always wanted to go to Switzerland and Hawaii.

   If I could remodel the world, I would first of all end
war and try to have a peace organization which will be lasting
and successful. I think the main trouble with the world is
the fact that it has become too materialistic. If people
would return to the teachings of Christ and have more religion
in their souls, I believe there would be fewer wars. However,
I believe that there will be war always because people aren't
perfect and never will be. As long as they are not perfect,
they will have certain imperfections of character, greed, self-
ishness, and so forth, which will lead them to be inconsider-
ate of others in order to attain their own ends. However, we
can reduce the number and frequency of these inconsiderations
by having people realize that there is a God, that He wishes
them to observe the Golden Rule and live in peace with one
another. When people disbelieve in God and become materialistic, they concentrate attention on themselves and overvalue
their own importance. Hitler was an example of a person who
put God out of his life and thus began to think that he himself
and his race were superior to all others. I would like a world
free from religious and racial prejudices; however, a long process of re-education will be necessary to achieve this. Unfortunately, people aren't willing to forget their prejudices
long enough to give them a chance to be forgotten forever.

   I would be content to play a very small part in this re-
modeled world. I would like to have a family, to live comfortably but not luxuriously. I would like to raise my children
to do what was right and to give them as many advantages as
possible, particularly education.

   I divide the social world into two parts, people I don't
like and people I do like. I can't stand people who are hypo-
crites, who assume false airs and pretend to be more than they
really are. I don't mind people who are conceited, if they
have reason to be; however, usually the only people who have
conceit have no reason for it. I detest people who cheat and
try to get ahead in a dishonest way. I think people who really
deserve to progress don't have to resort to cheating to do it;
therefore, people who cheat really don't deserve to get ahead
and shouldn't. Also, I dislike tattletales or stool pigeons.
In my opinion, people of this sort are sneaky and have no sense
of honor, particularly when one tattles on a friend. Usually
when people tattle, they do so for their own selfish ends and
for no other reason. I have had little experience with people
of this sort; nevertheless, it infuriates me to hear of cases
of tattling. I like and admire people who defend what they
believe to be right and who say what they mean (although, at
times, I believe it is better to spare a person's feelings)
and mean what they say. If people have a right to complain,
I don't mind; however, I dislike to hear people fussing over
petty troubles. I like people who are natural and unpreten-
tious, considerate of others, and who try to make others happy

[margin note: overvalue own importance]

by acting happy themselves.

I really don't know what the world actually thinks of me.
I seem to get along with most people and have always had
friends. People who don't know me very well usually think I
am quiet and shy. Some very kind people think I am witty;
however, others of franker nature consider my jokes just plain
corny, but they grin and bear it.

I think I am a rather passive personality. I don't have
much push or ambition, and I am seriously lacking in will
power. It is much more pleasing to me to do something easy
than hard. I realize that there are many things I should do--
study or work in general--but I don't usually have the will to
force myself to do the things I should, particularly when something more pleasant offers itself. If I were to become genu-
inely interested in other people instead of thinking always in
terms of myself, as, unfortunately, I find myself doing many
times, I think I would be much better off. I certainly hope
that I will be able to acquire this genuine interest in others,
because I am getting terribly tired of me, especially after
writing this autobiography.

[handwritten margin note: No will power]

2. CHILDHOOD MEMORIES AND FANTASIES

Subjects differ in the ease and comfort with which they
produce specific memories from early in life. Carol appeared
perfectly friendly, but she slumped somewhat in her chair and
waited for the examiner to take the initiative.

E: What is the most outstanding memory of your early childhood?

S: When I was about 2 1/2 the family had pictures taken. I
liked it; I was excited with the lights. I wore a dress
I liked very much. I also remember, I don't know why,
that my sister received a phone call at that time to go
for a walk. . . . I vaguely remember grandfather carrying
me to meet the family coming up the street in the car. . . .
I remember once Mother was making bread and I sat on the
dough; she didn't like that (long pause). . . . Once Father
asked me for a bite of my candy and I said no. He said,
"I'll fix you," and he came home that night with a box of
candy. Everyone had some but me. I felt terrible. I
finally did get some because my sister sneaked me a piece.

E: Do you remember any dreams or nightmares you had as a
child?

S: I used to wake up at night, frightened, and call for Mother.
I don't know what it was that frightened me. (There was
another pause. S rested her head against the back of the
chair. E did not interrupt this dreamy state. Finally S
spoke.)

S: I dreamt once that my father died. . . . I dreamt of fall-

ing from a cliff when I was 8. Once I dreamt I was late
for supper, I couldn't get home, something always kept me
from getting home; either I met girl friends, or I stopped
to play, or some other thing.

E: Did you have any favorite fantasies?

S: I always daydreamed that I saved the day, I was the hero-
ine.

E: Did you have an imaginary playmate?

S: No, I had a dog, I treated him like a human--told him my
sad tales. Once my sister told me not to go into the
woods. I went to a neighbor's house, then I went home and
told my sister that I had gone into the woods. She scolded me. I don't know why I did that.

E: Do you recall any toys that you liked especially?

S: I had a cupie doll and a teddy bear, I played mostly with
them, but not with dolls until I was 6. I played mostly
with boys until I was 6. . . . I had a swing and gym set,
I played on that until I hurt my arm, which was when I was
7.

E: Did you have any favorite games or play situations?

S: I used to go sliding with a boy a year younger than the
rest, who sucked his thumb. Whenever he came to the house
we'd run and jump on the couch. Mother didn't like that,
it wore out the springs . . . . I remember a birthday
party I had when I was 5. I was very selfish, I wanted to
keep all the prizes. My birthday is near Christmas, and
I have twice as many presents as I would otherwise. . . .
My first recollection of having anyone to play with (I was
4) was meeting this boy who sucked his thumb. I remember
I had on a pink linen dress. . . . I liked the Oz books.
I remember once that I had been told by a girl friend that
if you close your eyes when you are in bed and say, "I
wish I was in Oz" that you would be in Oz. I packed my
clothes one night in a suitcase, and I put in the pink
linen dress and did as the girl had told me. Mother said
it wasn't so. I said yes, my friend had told me. . . .
I went for walks with my sister. I used to want to sleep
with her. We talked about clothes and we used to fanta-
size--I would say I had a silver crown, and my sister
would say she had a gold one. Then I would try to go my
sister one better, but I couldn't think of anything better
than gold. . . . I remember once when I was in the first
grade I lied about something, and it involved an innocent
girl. She got punished. I felt terrible. The teacher
played favorites and I was one of her favorites.

There were many pauses. Conversations made by E were
welcomed and made S feel at lease, but at no time did she take
up the lead; she would lapse again into silence waiting for
the next question. Long silences were permitted to elapse because it seemed as if S could produce nothing that required

effort; only that which seemed to float in upon her as she
submitted passively to her reveries would she be able to contribute. E remarked on the natural difficulty of recalling
and asked whether S would be willing to meet her again, as
more things might occur to her in the meantime. This was arranged, and on the second visit there was more liveliness in
S's face as she slid into her favorite position in the chair.

E: Were you able to think of more memories?
S: Yes. I used to get car sick, I remember, almost whenever
    we would go to Providence, but not when we went to other
    places. My sister used to call me "baby," and my parents
    were annoyed because it invariably happened in the middle
    of traffic, or whenever we went through cities and smoky
    places. I guess it was the stopping and starting in traf-
    fic. A good deal of it is built up in your mind, my sis-
    ter said, and I guess it was true. My aunt would tell me
    funny stories so that I wouldn't be sick. . . . Christmas
    time I used to be very selfish. Even if I had played with
    the toys years and years, I would hide the toys so that my
    mother couldn't give them away to poor children. . . .
    Another time a woman gave me a doll. It had funny hair,
    and it began to shed all over the furniture. My mother
    threw that away and I was furious with her. . . . I used
    to hate to take a nap in the afternoon.
E: Do you still?
S: I don't now, I can do it very easily. . . . I was afraid
    of the ocean and the dark. I didn't learn to swim until
    I was 12. I remember when I was 3 or 4 I was taken to the
    beach. My mother was afraid of the water because her
    mother was almost drowned, but that wasn't what made me
    afraid--she told me this after my fear was established. .
    . . I remember when we went to the restaurant called Duck
    Inn, and we had just been to the beach and I had a shell
    with me. When I got home I discovered I had lost the shell
    and left it there. The next day my father came home with
    the shell; he said a duck had flown over his office and
    dropped it there. . . . One November skating was very good.
    I was wishing Santa Claus would give me a pair of skates.
    My father bought me some and said Santa Claus had made a
    special trip down. . . . I remember how horrible I would
    act when my mother would take me to see anyone. Once I
    had a perfectly wonderful time at this woman's house, and
    when she asked me if I had had a good time I said no--my
    mother looked at me. . . . Once I threw a stone at a friend
    of my mother's, for no good reason at all. She was being
    nice to me and I just picked up a stone and hurled it at
    her. . . . At 3 I was in a style show. Everybody else
    acted quiet and ladylike; I don't know what I did, but I
    saw in my sister's diary a few years ago mention of that
    style show and how horrible I had acted. I remember walk-

bad girl

ing along the rampart, in back of a girl with her hands
out, and I remember getting dressed for it but I don't remember acting badly. . . . There were two little girls I
met when I was 6. I began to play with dolls at that time.
One of the girls was very selfish, and her mother always
took her part in quarrels. Sometimes a little boy would
play with us. He and I would gang up against the two
girls. We used to go over to the park; we built houses
made of pine needles on the ground. . . . Once I was in the
bulkhead. The two girls were sliding down on the slope of
the bulkhead. One had on a pretty red skirt. She accused
the boy of pushing her and told her mother. I said the
boy didn't push her although I hadn't seen it. I just
felt he wouldn't do it. She said he made her slide down
and she fell. . . . I used to play with three or four boys
in the neighborhood. One of them was terribly mischievous
and used to break windows all the time.

3. EXCERPTS ON PERSONAL DEVELOPMENT

In an interview on health Carol added little to the few
remarks made in the autobiography. As far as she knows her
birth was normal; she was not breast fed. Her mother kept a
baby book for about a year, but Carol knows only that one part
of her development was slower than her sister's--she cannot
remember which part. She was considered an active child,
though underweight, and she did not grow quickly, being always
shorter than most of her friends. There was a period from 8
to 12 when she became quite plump, but her present weight is
112 pounds. Upon questioning she says that she has no desire
to be tall; she used to, but now she is satisfied with her
height and weight. Her fingernails are soft and nick easily,
and she still bites them to some extent, a habit for which she
was never punished.

Carol reports that she first learned about sex when she
was 11 or 12. She was going to camp, and her sister, thinking
that she might be going to menstruate, told her about "the
birds and the bees." She learned a little more at camp; the
girls talked. What she learned didn't seem natural to her;
she didn't see how it could happen. Her attitude now is different. She has done some reading, talked to her sister a lot,
and taken a hygiene course in school. In fact, she did not
menstruate until she was 15, at which point she was not at all
surprised, as she had been wondering why it didn't come earlier.
Asked about masturbation, she said that she had read about it
but had never done it. "It's not considered good for you," she
remarked. The source of her knowledge was some books which
appeared in the top of her closet. She has talked about it
with a few girls at college. At first she was surprised to
find out that they knew about it.

Fairly early, during high school, Carol had a crush on a boy who played the violin. He was very thin, small like herself, very shy, and rather attractive. This relation lasted for about two years. She began to take her music more seriously. They went skiing, played tennis, and attended school dances. They held hands at times but there was no necking. They did not kiss each other except for one time when they played post office.

After this there was a "purely platonic" relation with another boy whom she had known all her life. They had a good time together, laughing and joking and being crazy. Then there was a third boy with whom she went out about once a week. He was a little different. It wasn't so platonic; they kissed on occasion, though they never "really" went further than that. She never felt guilty about the kissing, but she wouldn't go further and he did not want to either.

There is no particular boy now in whom she is interested, but she has frequent dates. "I have as many as I want."

Her health at present seems to be very good, but "for the life of me I don't see why," because she always gets to bed late, usually because of talking with somebody, and never gets more than six or seven hours of sleep. She is an occasional cigarette smoker and a "sociable drinker" who has never been drunk.

In an interview on extracurricular activities during her school years, Carol chose to begin with her piano lessons. She started when she was 9 and took lessons for the next eight years. At first, as she reported, "I didn't like piano lessons, but took them under pressure. I practiced when my mother sat there with me." After four years her attitude changed because of her crush on the young violinist, whom she accompanied once or twice, although his sister usually performed this service. Some people say that Carol plays well, but she herself estimates her playing as "nothing remarkable" considering the number of years she took lessons. She sometimes played at the Music Club and sometimes gave solos or accompanied schoolmates at parents' nights. She named Beethoven and Chopin as her favorite composers.

Her experience with school dramatics was less successful. She was on the ticket committee and the stage crew but never had a part. She once tried out for a part but didn't get it. She stated that casts were not chosen on the basis of ability. But she was much involved with the high school yearbook on which she worked "real hard." "I was literary editor, but that's just a title, didn't mean a thing." She wrote "write-ups" for some classmates, made page layouts, and had to figure out "whether it was going to come out right." She also helped compose the song for graduation. Out of loyalty to the school she went to all home football games.

Carol has participated actively in several sports and outdoor activities. She does not claim to be especially good in

any of them. The other members of her family are similarly
inclined, and her summers at camp contributed to an emphasis
on physical activity.

Asked about hobbies, she denied having any. Both her
father and her sister are stamp collectors, and her father
tried to stimulate her interest by once giving her an album
for her birthday. "He was more interested in it than I was.
It _never_ appealed to me."

Answering a question about jobs, Carol said that she
never worked very much. She has, however, helped her sister
to take care of the children. Her only paid job was an easy
one as high school reporter for the local paper.

When queried about playmates and friends, she gave a year-
by-year enumeration of the other children who were most important to her. She did not enlarge much upon their mutual activities, but there were always one or more people she rated as
friends or chums. In college "five or six of us chum around
together," though not to the exclusion of numerous other acquaintances. "We like each other, we like to have a lot of
fun. We are just average." The last statement is intended as
a form of praise, for during her freshman years Carol was much
put off by social cliques in the dormitory. She distinguished
two: "pseudointellectuals who looked down on everyone else"
and "girls with false accents."

This criticism came out in an interview in which the examiner purposely encouraged her to talk about things that annoyed her at college. She expressed annoyance about several
petty college rules, rigidly administered, that had caused her
trouble.

E: Can you think of anything else?
S: Quiet hours. We are supposed to be quiet from 7:30 until
    8 the following morning. You can't help letting loose
    occasionally. A few seniors complain.
E: How are the rules enforced?
S: Proctors appoint people on each floor to keep the place
    quiet. I don't like the system. I like noise to study.
    I can study better. Some people can't stand the noise and
    others can.
E: What especially gripes you?
S: I don't like the attitude of some of the girls. They just
    rush in and say "Shut up." Of course, we make more noise
    than ever.
E: This is what makes you angry?
S: What makes me angry is that they make a lot of noise in
    the morning going down the hall.
E: Do these girls do other things that annoy you?
S: They are always dashing into my room when I want to sleep.
E: Why?
S: To see what time it is, as though I had the only clock in
    the whole dorm.

E: Maybe they want to come and chat with you.
S: No.
E: Would it be better if all seniors were living together?
S: I like mingling with the upperclassmen. They would have
    arguments and discussions. Sort of broadens you.
E: The seniors annoy you only because they want the place
    quiet?
S: Yes. If they would just come out and say "Be quiet," we
    would be, but they want to boss. They come out and say
    they will report you. This is is kind of high schoolish.
E: Anything else?
S: At times I wish I had more time to enjoy more things.
    Like clubs. Last year I painted. I liked it.
E: You don't have time this year?
S: I really waste a lot of time.
E: How?
S: Talking . . . playing bridge. Then I talk and it goes on
    and on and on.
E: What do you talk about?
S: Anything.
E: What in particular?
S: Nothing. I'll talk for two or three days and just play
    around, and then study for a few days.

4. EXCERPTS ON FAMILY LIFE

E: Can you tell me something more about your father?
S: Quite intelligent, I think. Gets along with people very
    well--knows how to handle them. At times he's very witty.
    He makes a good master of ceremonies. I know he does that
    once in a while at the Rotary Club, and so forth. Very
    much interested in and conscientious about his work.
E: In your autobiography you mentioned that you sort of held
    him in awe. What was it about him that made you feel that
    way?
S: I was a little afraid of him. Sometimes he loses his tem-
    per, and the fact that he is intelligent, and what he said
    went.
E: Do you remember any special incidents?
S: A couple of times I came home late, and he punished me for
    that.
E: Was he pretty strict?
S: No, he wasn't, but then he didn't let me run wild . . .
    the thing is, I never knew how things would strike him
    exactly. Things I thought he would be angry about he
    wasn't, and things I didn't think he would be angry about
    he was. With favors, he'd let me do things I didn't think
    he'd let me do.
E: Did he do most of the punishing that had to be done?
S: If I did anything really naughty he did, but just everyday

occasions, my mother would handle.

E: What kinds of punishments?

S: He deprived me of things I wanted to do, like going to
the movies. He'd make me stay in after supper.

E: Can you remember much about what your mother used to be
like when you were little?

S: She used to sing around the house quite a bit, and I used
to like to hear her . . . she used to consider me sort of
a bother at times because I was very active and used to
get into trouble. . . . I used to get in the way. . . .
She was always very thoughtful.

E: You said to one of the interviewers that your mother was
rather anxious about some things, that she sort of checked
up on you.

S: Lately she has been. She hasn't been well the past few
years.

E: What kinds of things was she anxious about?

S: Things that I should do myself--for instance, she always
sends me explicit instructions about getting clothes big
enough and not spending more money than they are worth. .
. . She used to remind me of things, and that would make
me very angry if I had remembered them. It was quite nice
if I had forgotten, though.

E: And there was that business of pestering the neighbors.
She didn't like that? What reasons did she give?

S: She didn't like pestering the neighbors because probably
they would be busy and wouldn't want me hanging around all
the time.

E: Did you mind being checked up on?

S: Yes, particularly if I had already done the thing, and if
I were in a great hurry to leave, it was annoying to have
to answer questions.

E: Tell me a bit more about your sister.

S: She's very intelligent, beautiful, quiet, and sweet and
everybody likes her, and she has quite a bit of common
sense . . . always knows what to do and when to do it.
. . She sizes people up very well, and she's always been
very nice to me and encouraged me.

E: In what ways?

S: When I was in high school I used to be very self-conscious,
and she'd try to help me get over it.

E: How did you feel toward her when you were younger?

S: We very rarely quarreled. I always looked up to her. We
used to tease each other occasionally. I remember I used
to annoy her very much when she had company. I'd tag
along and entertain her dates. I used to try to imitate
her. When we had company and Mother said to her, "Now,
Alice, go and play the piano," I'd start turning somer-
saults in the middle of the floor. Mother wanted her to
take me for walks. She was like a mother to me. Took care

of me when the folks were away. I like her <u>very</u> much (emphatically). She's 26 now, married, and lives with us. I
always used to try to imitate her.

E: Did you succeed?
S: No, I don't think I succeeded.
E: What were the characteristics that you admired?
S: She was very attractive. She could do lots of things. She
had a lot of common sense and independence.

S: She was happily married. The children are young, and she
hasn't done much since her husband died. She doesn't look
healthy but she is. She took her husband's death very
well. She was not overemotional. I was fond of him, too.
(In another interview S explained that her sister's husband
was killed while in military service.)

There was a large circle of relatives living nearby. The
paternal grandparents and the maternal great-grandparents were
born in Ireland. Carol's impressions of the relatives are
rather slight, with the exception of her mother's younger sister, who was more easygoing than her mother.

S: Aunt Katie was very funny. She used to tell me very amusing stories. Sometimes she would do satires on people.
She used to kid Mother once in a while. She's not married,
works in an office. Got along well with my father, although
at times she was inclined to vote against the man my father
voted for.

At the beginning of an interview on family relations and
discipline, Carol was asked to fill out a checklist of forms
of punishment used respectively by her mother and father. Her
entries were as follows:

F   1. Being scolded or reasoned with.
M   2. Being spanked.
F   3. Being denied some pleasure, for example, going to a
         picnic, party, circus.
F   4. Being sent away from the group, for example, to
         one's room.
M & F 5. Being made to feel you were not as good as your
         brother or sister or other children.
M   6. Being made to feel you hurt your mother or father.
F   7. Being made to feel you had fallen short of what was
         expected of you.
-    8. Being denied any demonstration of affection by your
         mother or father.
-    9. Being told by your mother or father that they could
         not love you when you were bad.

E: Were any other forms of punishment used?
S: No, I wouldn't say so.

E: How did you react to punishment?
S: I didn't like it too well. I was sort of docile about it.
    I would cry.
E: How often were you spanked?
S: About average frequency.
E: Which parent did you prefer to be punished by?
S: Father was more severe. I preferred Mother's.
E: Were you sometimes threatened by disciplinary action that
    was then not carried out?
S: It may have happened with Mother but not with Father, I
    don't remember it.
E: Did one parent indulge you more than the other?
S: Sometimes Father, sometimes Mother. Mother more in little
    things. Father sometimes indulged me in things I wouldn't
    think he'd let me do.
E: Which parent do you prefer?
S: I like them both.
E: Do you think your parents showed favoritism toward your
    sister or to you?
S: No doubt they loved us equally well. But my sister is more
    like Father than I am. I'm more like my mother than my
    father. That seems to be the general opinion. I look like
    my father. I think I'm sort of a mixed breed of the two.
E: Do you spend a good deal of your time at home?
S: Not too much. There's school, and I've gone to camp the
    last four summers.
E: What do you think was good, bad, or missing in your up-
    bringing?
S: I think the fact that I was a younger child tended to make
    me stay younger than I should have.

5.   SENTIMENTS AND BELIEFS

The nature of Carol's religious beliefs was investigated by
giving her a long questionnaire, which at various points had
spaces in which to amplify her replies. Afterwards an examiner
went through her questionnaire with her, seeking certain clari-
fications.

Carol checked statements that indicated a positive convic-
tion of God's existence. She conceives of God as a power,
force, or energy of a spiritual nature, but she checked many
attributes of a more personal kind, seeing God as an affectionate father who is interested in us, watches over us, hears and
answers our prayers, and possesses the ideal virtues of wisdom,
holiness, goodness, and so forth. She believes in an afterlife
in heaven, and here she wrote: "Heaven is the state of eternal
happiness in which one sees and adores God." Asked by the
examiner about the origin of this definition, she said that
she got it from the Church. She gave her assent to a long list
of Christian theological beliefs, that God created the universe
and all living things, that all men inherit a state of sin from

Adam's and Eve's transgression, and that Christ was divine.
She indicated belief in the healing miracles, the crucifixion,
and the resurrection of Christ.

In space provided to describe her childhood forms of belief,
Carol wrote as follows: "I always thought of God as a kind of
father who was everywhere and who watched over us. I always
thought of the devil, the way he is pictured by everyone, as
an evil working agent. I always considered the soul as a white
sheet that could be stained by sin, as ink would stain a piece
of cloth. I thought the soul was inside the body. I considered immortality as going to heaven and living in a continual
round of parties, and so forth, or as going to hell and living
forever in fire and burning." These views were modified during
adolescence, when she became less sure about the devil and
began to think of the soul as connected with mind and conscience.

Carol goes to mass every Sunday, as do her parents and sister. She prays at least twice a day. She has experienced
God's nearness or presence, which has made her feel "secure,
happy, and comfortable." Answering questions about what she
thinks prayer, taking communion, and confession have done for
her, she lists first in each case that "it has helped me spiritually," and further that "it has a psychological effect." Of
receiving communion she adds, "it helped me to remain good or
relatively good for a while after." She attributes to religion
"a sense of security and benevolence." It also serves to
"bring morality into consciousness." One of the questions
read: "What effects on your character or conduct do you think
it would have if you lost all your major religious beliefs?"
The answer: "I would most likely become too materialistic,
cynical, insecure, and would no doubt lead a worse life." She
is aware at times of an overpowering sense of sin. Asked what
she feels sinful about, she replied, "lying, and moral things,
anything that's not right."

On the questionnaire Carol checked an item expressing dis-
belief in the theory of evolution. She also indicated that her
courses at college had not challenged her beliefs.

E: Don't you feel that your courses in biology, psychology,
     or geology contradict any of your religious beliefs?
S: No, I don't think so.
E: How about the principles of evolution?
S: They didn't announce the topic of evolution in class.

Carol says that challenges came mostly from discussions
with other girls. She finds these fruitless. "I came to the
conclusion that one very seldom convinces the other person
because the discussion usually turns into an argument. The
other person usually insists on proof for everything one says
and one can't always give proof for faith. Either you have it
or you don't." She has had at least one "heated" argument over
religion. The outcome was that the other girl "ran out of

logical arguments and began to insult my religion. I became
quite disgusted and left. The next day she apologized; hence,
I never held a grudge for her. At the time I knew she didn't
really mean all she said."

Sentiments having to do with minority groups and ethnic
prejudice were examined in a way similar to the religious sentiments: filling out a detailed questionnaire followed by an
interview. One of the first printed questions read: "Do you
consider yourself to be a member of a minority group? If so,
which one?" Carol wrote "no," then crossed it out and put
down "Yes, at times, Catholic." Her sentiments on the subject
of Jews and Negroes were largely free from prejudice. From
her religious training, she derived the principle that "God
created all men equally," and from courses and experiences at
college she concludes that "there are good and bad in every
group." A course in social psychology has given her insight
into the irrational causes of prejudice. On the questionnaire
she strongly rejected items consisting of derogatory stereo-
types about Jews and Negroes; likewise, she rejected the item,
"Though there are some exceptions, in general Catholics are
Fascists at heart." "In religion," she explained to the examiner, "the Church teaches Catholics what to believe, but it
doesn't force them to believe it. They are allowed to think
it out for themselves."

Carol has Jewish friends at college; "most of the Jews I
know are nice." But one of her friends frequently says that
Jews in business are aggressive and dishonest, and she believes
that this may be true "because they think that others are trying to keep them down and that the only way they can get ahead
is to be aggressive." She sees reduction of prejudice as calling for something on both sides: Gentiles to forget about
ethnic differences, Jews to be "less aggressive and more honest
in business." She would not consider marrying a Jew because of
the great difference in religion. "My, and his, family would
be against it. I wouldn't fall in love with him." She might
possibly marry a Protestant, though she thinks this unlikely.
But this would be contingent upon a prior agreement that the
children be brought up as Catholics. "I would have to bring
up the children as Catholics, I must have the children because
the Church demands it."

Questioned about her personal knowledge of Negroes, Carol
responded as follows:

S: I haven't had too much experience with Negroes. There is
    only one family in our town. The man is one of my father's
    clients. He raises all sorts of tropical flowers. He gave
    a hibiscus to my father. We all went up to look at his
    garden. He seemed very nice, very gentlemanly, and every-
    thing like that. My only other experience is with a Negro

girl in our dormitory. No one seems to be particularly
prejudiced against her, or tries to make it unpleasant for
her. Those that are prejudiced ignore her, or else try to
show they're not very prejudiced by being very nice. We
discuss it quite a bit at the dorm. The southern students
are violently prejudiced. They try so hard to keep the
Negro down. Which makes the Negro more hostile than ever,
so then the southerners try harder to keep them down. It's
kind of like a vicious circle (pause).

E: Talk about some of the things you've heard.

S: A friend of mine in Washington said that one night in a bus
a Negro man started to stare at her. He kept on staring
and when she changed buses, he changed too. He seemed to
follow her. She was about to make one more change when the
Negro man got off. A Negro woman then came up to her and
said, "It's all right, dearie, he's gone now." This shows
you can't condemn all people in either race (pause).

E: Do you think Negro men are more dangerous than Negro women?

S: Yes. That's what I've heard. But white men are more dangerous too. I remember something that happened to me. I
was out walking with a girl at the dorm and she was a
southerner. We had gone down to the drugstore and were on
our way back. Suddenly a big, huge Negro came out of the
driveway and he was poorly dressed. It was obvious that
he didn't belong in the neighborhood. I had visions of
newspaper articles I had read. My friend, she wasn't
frightened. I was surprised because she was a southerner.
She wasn't in a hurry, she just wanted to walk on slowly,
and I wanted to get back quickly.

E: Can you tell me some other things?

S: Not to any great length. The girl in that family that lives
in our town is a taxidriver. She ran over a little boy and
killed him. I expected that she would get it hard -- that
they would be twice as angry at her. But the fact that she
was a Negro didn't seem to enter into the trial (long pause).

E: What do you think should be done?

S: I don't know. It seems hopeless. Can't see anything. If
more Negroes were better educated, they might be helped.

E: Why?

S: Because most people consider the Negro as being ignorant.

E: Why?

S: Partly because of the way they're treated. People tend to
generalize. They say Negroes are lazy, ignorant. The
movies have helped to raise the Negro a bit. People realize
that they have talent in many ways. The radio has helped
also. My father lived in Washington for a while. He was
telling us about the Negro spirituals that he heard there.
How amusing they are. The singing is very good.

E: Can you tell me more about the Negro girl in the dorm?

S: A friend of mine says she doesn't like her. She's silly
and insipid. It's hard to be one out of seventy-two. She

probably goes out of her way to be nice because she is
slightly inferior. She is silly, but because she is trying hard. Her voice is bad, and she asks dumb questions.
She talks in a whiny voice.

E: Has she been there long?

S: No, this is her second term.

E: Do you remember any discussions about her when she came?

S: A few people commented. No, not any real discussions.

E: How would you feel about going out with Negroes?

S: I don't imagine I would go out with a Negro. I wouldn't
want to marry one.

E: Would you if everyone else thought it was the right thing
to do?

S: If everyone else thought it was all right, it would be all
right with me.

E: How do you feel about marrying a Protestant?

S: If I were really in love, yes.

E: Jews?

S: I don't know. The religion is really quite different.

E: Frenchmen?

S: No.

E: Have you thought much about these problems?

S: Not to any great extent. Last year a girl married a Japanese boy. A lot of people thought it would be unfair to the
children. There would be trouble in their social relationships.

E: Would you marry a Japanese?

S: If I were in love, but I wouldn't fall in love.

Carol was given a standard test on values, the Allport-
Vernon Study of Values. This test consists of comparisons between different quite specific lines of interest or action;
the subject is asked to indicate preferences. Taking her
choices as a whole, Carol gave a strong first place to religious values, second to social values, a close third to aes-
thetic, fourth to political, fifth to theoretical, and a weak
sixth to economic values.

6.   TESTS AND ESTIMATES OF ABILITIES

Carol was given several standard tests, starting with the
Wechsler Adult Intelligence Test. Her I.Q. calculated for the
whole test proved to be 128, and she had approximately equal
scores on verbal and performance items. She was not nervous
or tense during the test; indeed, the examiner's impression was
rather the opposite, that she took the whole thing in a casual
spirit, not seeming to exert herself more than was absolutely
necessary, and in consequence making occasional errors that
seemed merely careless. It follows that her scores might have
been a little higher had she cared to make a greater effort,

but in any event an I.Q. of 128 on this test suggests abilities
entirely sufficient for college studies and is consistent with
her good scholastic record in high school.

Of a somewhat different nature was the Vygotsky Test,
which involves classifying a large array of blocks which differ in size, shape, design, and color and do not easily lend
themselves to the required grouping into four categories.
Some subjects attack the problem by moving the blocks around,
as if in this way the correct classification could be made
to leap to the eye--a perceptual approach.   Others proceed
more in their heads, as if trying to find a rational hypothe-
sis--a conceptual approach.   Most subjects are somewhat frustrated by the unexpected length of time it takes them to find
the solution, which is by no means easy.   Carol had taken the
test the year before but did not remember the solution.   She
cooperated in a passive way, without enthusiasm.   Her procedure was almost wholly perceptual, and she found it hard to
state the principle even when she had made the correct grouping.   Asked how she had liked the test last year, she said,
"Oh, I hated it.   It made me very angry because it took me
every bit of three quarters of an hour."   Told that this was
not unusual, she said, "Yes, but my girl friends did it in
twenty minutes.   Then the next day I read about it in abnormal
psychology and I thought maybe I was a manic or something."
Her time on the second performance was twenty-five minutes.

Carol was better pleased with the Rorschach Test, which
required her merely to say what she saw in the ten examples of
inkblots.   She appeared to feel comfortable and agreeably entertained by this imaginative task.   There was nothing unusual
about her performance, certainly nothing to suggest any form
of mental disorder.   Her behavior was calm, her productions
well balanced, orderly, not especially original; imagination
was good though not striking, and there was little that would
suggest lively emotions.

Another test taken by the subject was the Allport A-S
Reaction Study, a scale in which she was called upon to rate
herself as to how she behaved in a large number of specific
situations.   In all of these situations behavior could be considered ascendant (dominant or assertive), submissive (yielding or avoiding), or somewhere in between.   Carol's score on
the form for women was slightly, not markedly, toward the submissive side (-7).   Inspection of the individual replies showed
that she was highly submissive toward people whom she regarded
as superiors, hating, for example, to speak up in class or to
take leadership at a social gathering, but she had no difficulty in dealing assertively with tradespeople and returning
unsatisfactory merchandise, and she represented herself as
sometimes opposing people who were annoyingly dictatorial.

In an interview on abilities she rated herself above
average (in comparison with other college women) on only four
of the fifteen listed abilities.   These were observational

ability, memory, entertaining ability, and artistic sensitivity. These were not, on the whole, the abilities to which
she attached high value. Rating the list on how important the
abilities were to her, she chose as her first four, in order,
social ability, erotic ability, intuitive ability, and leading
and governing ability, and she placed herself only at the 30th
percentile on them all.

   An attempt was made by means of an interview to throw
light on certain temperamental or emotional qualities that are
likely to be important in personality. Carol was questioned
especially about anger, fears, and excitability.

E: Do you remember in your childhood whether you used to lose
     your temper?
S: One time I was very angry at this girl I used to play with.
     Her mother was always taking her part in arguments and I
     didn't like that. She was very selfish. Selfish with her
     playthings. Once I touched something of hers—just
     touched it—and she got very angry and so I decided to
     scare her. I picked up a pair of scissors and pretended
     I was going to stab her, and she got frightened and ran
     home and told her mother that I had stabbed her.
E: Any other incidents?
S: Sometimes I used to get angry at my mother. (Doesn't re-
     member specific events.)
E: Did you ever feel angry but manage to control it?
S: Sometimes when I was punished I used to feel angry but it
     never lasted. It used to turn into shame very soon.
E: When was the last time you lost your temper?
S: I was slightly annoyed tonight. My girl friend was an-
     noyed with me and I didn't think she had a right to be.
E: About how often do you lose your temper nowadays?
S: Little things sometimes bother me, but not as a rule. I
     don't lose my temper very often.
E: What kinds of things bother you?
S: There's a girl in my dorm who's always borrowing things.
     She bothers my roommate, too. She never returns things—
     not very dependable.
E: When you feel angry, how do you control it?
S: Sometimes I make a sarcastic remark and sometimes I don't
     say anything.
E: As a child you were afraid of certain people, places, or
     things?
S: I was afraid of the dark and the ocean.
E: Were you afraid of any situations in general?
S: No, unless it would be connected with the dark. Oh, and
     ghosts. I used to be afraid of ghosts, too.
E: And the ocean—was it anything particular, being in the
     ocean or on it?
S: I was afraid of swimming in the ocean or water of any kind.
     I used to like boats, though. That didn't bother me. I

wasn't afraid of it (water) as long as I didn't have to
swim . . . I remember once I wasn't supposed to play with
these children because they had whooping cough and we
went up to this house that was supposed to be haunted.
There was an awful slimy old pond, and these boys made a
raft and we went out and started to sink. I jumped. I
was near enough shore. I was afraid Mother would find
out. Maybe that had something to do with it.

E: What situations are you most afraid of now?

S: I don't like to ride on the subway. They've had a few
accidents lately and it rattles so--you'd think it was
going to fall apart, and I have sort of a fear of high
places, that I might fall, and so forth.

E: As a little girl you were sort of a tomboy, active and
energetic, and later you became quieter and afraid to do
some things like talk in front of strangers.

S: And yet with people I know I'm the same as I was when I
was little.

E: How do you think this came about?

S: I don't know. I used to be afraid of boys. I didn't know
how to act, and I felt rather inferior in high school because there were so many other girls more popular than I.

E: Did you used to get excited as a child, so that you would
shout and scream?

S: Yes. Most of the time.

E: How old were you?

S: I'd say I was like that most of my life at home, and if I
knew people quite well, I mean if we were out playing.

E: You were sort of a tomboy?

S: Compared to my sister I was. I played mostly with boys
until I was 6. My father got me a trapeze set with rings
and bars. We used to swing on the rings.

E: How about when you were older?

S: It depended on who I was with and where I was. If I knew
the people, I was inclined to be enthusiastic and boisterous. If I didn't know them, I didn't say very much and
was quiet.

E: Was this true when you were younger?

S: Not so much so. I gradually became more self-conscious.

E: Are you much stimulated by a group that is wisecracking?

S: Does it make me want to do it too?

E: Yes.

S: You mean sarcastic? or witty?

E: Just witty.

S: Yes--my girl friend and I have a good time pretending we
are other people and saying witty things. We know this
boy who is very stable--the boy scout type, and we were
pretending what our life would be like if we were married
to him.

E: Do you get lively at parties?

S: Sometimes. If there are just girls there I do, but sometimes I've been at mixed parties and there's dancing--I've
been rather lively but not when people just sit around.

7.   THEMATIC APPERCEPTION TEST

In one of the last interviews to be given, Carol said
that of all the procedures she enjoyed most the Thematic Apperception Test; she found it fun to tell stories. This is by
no means the universal response to the test. Not uncommonly
subjects find it difficult to use their imaginations and tell
stories, and the procedure is often a subject of complaint.
In interviews Carol was not easily communicative; some examiners spoke of real difficulty in getting her to say more than
a few words. It was therefore something of a surprise that
she liked this test and told rather long stories. Because of
this, five of her twenty stories are given below, for whatever
light they may throw on her personality.

The Thematic Apperception Test is conducted by presenting
pictures and asking the subject to construct fantasies around
them. The subject is instructed to compose a story, giving
the incidents that have led up to the situation shown in the
picture, describing what is occurring at the moment--the feelings and thoughts of the characters--and telling what the outcome will be. The pictures selected for the test generally
show one or more characters, but the nature of the action is
somewhat ambiguous, and there is little detail to influence
the choice of plot. Under these circumstances the story that
is told has to spring largely from the subject's own mind;
neither the test materials nor the instructions encourage him
to be descriptive and literal.

In the stories that are told, the characters are placed
in various situations; they act and think and feel in certain
ways, and their behavior leads to some kind of an outcome,
frustrating or successful. The test is based upon the assump-
tion that a substantial part of what a storyteller ascribes to
his characters, especially to the character with whom he is
most identified, is an expression of his own experience and
motives. It must be expected, however, that other things besides the storyteller's personal tendencies will influence the
content of his narrations. He may follow certain conventions
as to what constitutes a good story. He may borrow his plots
from recent books or movies. He may try to vary his plots in
order to avoid monotony, thus presumably rejecting plots that
first came to his mind. Allowances must be made for this kind
of influence when we undertake to use the stories as a means
of studying the narrator's personality.

It is usually possible to decide with which character in
a story the subject is most fully identified. Characters of
the same sex and age are most readily chosen, and the identifi-

cation figure is apt to be mentioned more often and described
more fully with respect to inner life and feelings. The tendencies ascribed to the identification figure are likely to be
those of the storyteller, while the attitudes and behavior ascribed to other figures are more representative of the way the
teller expects other people to act toward him.

    Understanding can best be approached by asking oneself
(1) whether or not the principal characters in the stories be-
have differently from the Carol of the interviews, and (2)
what the differences, if found, seem to signify about wishes
and motives that are not given expression in everyday life.

    1. (A young woman is standing with downcast head, her
face covered with her right hand. Her left arm is stretched
against a wooden door.) Oh, gracious! (laughs). This girl
Sandra came to New York to get a job as a model, and she left
home much against her parents' will, and her friends all told
her she didn't stand a chance, and so she went to New York,
and she walked up and down the streets, and she didn't find
any work, and so finally she took this position as a secretary
in a newspaper office, and while she was there she met this
very nice boy who fell in love with her, and she liked him,
but she still had the old modeling bug, and wanted to make a
name for herself, and so she walked all over but he didn't
care because he loved her so much; did I just say that? And
he wanted to marry her, but she told him about her plans, how
she couldn't marry until she had made a name, so she said if
he really loved her he'd help her get ahead, and so he promised
he would, and he went to see a few . . . he had a friend who
was fairly influential in the modeling business, and he was
talking to him about Sandra, and so the man became quite interested, and so he wanted to see her, Sandra, and so he fell in
love with Sandra himself when he saw her. She was a very beautiful girl, and so one night he suggested Sandra come up to
his apartment and see his etchings (laughs) and talk business,
and Sandra had an appointment with this friend that evening,
but she broke it much to his disappointment, but he sort of
sensed she was going out with the head of the agency, so he
watched outside and saw Sandra going in, whereupon he became
very angry--uh while he was debating what he was to do he saw,
he would see into the room, and saw Sandra there, and after he
watched for a while, he saw Sandra was having a little trouble,
so he rushed upstairs and he broke into the room, and so he
said to the man, "Take your hands off that woman," and the man
just laughed, and so they started to fight, and in the skir-
mish the head of the agency began to fear for his safety, so
he whipped out a little light gun and shot Sandra's friend,
whereupon Sandra picked up a vase--no, not a vase, picked up a
sword that was hanging on the wall, and thrust it into the
head of the agency when he wasn't looking, so this is her
grief--and she realized the horror of what she'd done, and how
she'd really loved the other boy, and should have married him

and not even thought of becoming a model, and she realized what
a mess she'd made of her life and that there wasn't any use
living any longer, so she burst out of the room and--uh--ran
out into the street in front of a truck and she was killed. (E
stirred.) Wait a minute I'm not through yet. Then a crowd
gathered, naturally, and a policeman came up, and he wanted
to know if anyone could identify her, and, of course, no one
knew who she was and anyway wouldn't have recognized her in the
present mangled condition, so they picked up what was left of
her, put it in a little box, and left her in the morgue for un-
claimed bodies.

    2.   (A young woman sitting on the edge of a sofa looks
back over her shoulder at an older man with a pipe in his mouth
who seems to be addressing her.) Hum. Well, there's this
young schoolteacher who didn't play any favorites in her class
at all, and she was new in the school and all, and, I mean,
there was the son of a very rich man in her class, and all the
other teachers had always favored him and let him have his own
way, but she didn't, and the teachers all told her she'd better
be careful or lose her job. The little boy went home and told
his father that the teacher had been unfair, and so the man
asked to have the teacher come and see him, and he told her he
could have her lose her position, and she became quite angry,
and she said she wouldn't want to work there, and he realized
she was quite poor, and he threatened to blackball her with all
the other positions in the state, and she said that wouldn't
make any difference, she wouldn't play favorites in her class,
just because his son was in it, and he was wealthy and influential. So then she went on to tell him how she thought he
had spoiled his son, and the man began to admire her spunk
because everyone else in town cowered and catered, and so he
began to realize he had made a mistake, and he let her keep her
position.

    3.   (An older woman is sitting on a sofa close to a girl,
speaking or reading to her. The girl, who holds a doll in her
lap, is looking away.) Uh--this little girl is the daughter of
very wealthy parents. They love her and all that, but they
don't pay her much attention because they're too much absorbed
in their own world, and so on her birthday her mother and
father planned to be home to dinner but they forgot, and the
little girl was very sad, and even though her nurse played
dolls and read to her, she was very sad and she read of other
little girls like herself which even made her sadder, so she
began, little by little, to resent her parents, and she finally
succeeded in amusing herself, and she grew up to be a very
independent person, and so when her parents were too old to
enjoy their social whirls they began to realize their daughter
didn't need them in any way and had grown up without them. And
so she left home and received a position, an interesting position quite a way from her home, and she ended up by marrying
this very nice and successful man, and he was an explorer, so
she traveled around with him, and very rarely had a chance to

go home, and her parents were very lonely in their old age, and they wished they had seen more of their daughter and had been more interested in her.

4. (The portrait of a young woman. A weird old woman with a shawl over her head is grimacing in the background.) Uh--Emily was married to the only son of this old woman--and the woman resented her from the beginning. I mean, in her own little way she kept trying to get Emily in wrong with her husband, whose name was Gregory, and the old woman kept plotting one against the other because she was jealous of her daughter-in-law. Uh--finally, trouble went on for such a long time that Emily and Gregory decided to get a divorce, and the old woman supposed that her son-in-law (sic) would be the way he always was before she found he had changed quite a bit, and without Emily he was very unhappy. He began to drink and gamble, and finally all their money was gone and the old woman had to sell flowers for a living. Uh--one day Emily, who wasn't much better off, came by and saw her there, so she bought a flower. The old woman was very angry to see Emily, the cause of all her trouble, so she--uh--planned, planned a way to kill Emily. She --uh--got ahold of some poison and saturated a beautiful rose with it because she knew that Emily always bought roses of that type, so the old mother-in-law went out to sell her flowers the next day, and she was going to her stand with her flowers when she slipped and fell, and ah--without thinking, of course, her nose became buried in the rose that she had poisoned, so--she died.

5.   (A young man is standing with downcast head buried in his arm. Behind him is the figure of a woman lying in bed.) Uh--(half gasp, half laugh). This poet--fell in love with the daughter of a very rich banker--and the banker threatened to disown the daughter if she went away with the poet, but she did, nevertheless. The poet really didn't make too much money, and they had barely enough to live on. His wife became very ill with a strange malady, and she suffered very much and no doctor could cure her. She pleaded with her husband to kill her by giving her too much dope, but he refused to. However, finally she was suffering so much and in a moment of weakness he gave her an overdose and she died--and he felt just terrible about it--and he began to write poetry in her honor, in a very melancholy tone, and he became very famous because of the poems about this wife who had died. He didn't feel right about accepting all the fame because of his wife's death, when he knew he had been the cause of it. Finally, it got so that everywhere he went he was haunted by his wife's face, so he went to the authorities and gave himself up.

QUESTIONS ON SECTIONS 1 TO 7

1. In an interview Carol said: "I think the fact that I was a younger child tended to make me stay younger than I should have." But Solomon Kompten was also a younger child, and

the effect on him was different. How do you explain Carol's
having "stayed younger than she should have"?

2.   Carol describes her relation to her sister as one of
affection, admiration, and imitation, free from rivalry and
jealousy. Have you detected any evidence that suggests unrecognized resentful and rivalrous feelings toward the sister?

3.   In what roles does Carol cast parents in her stories
for the Thematic Apperception Test? What differences are there
between these fictional parents and her own parents as described
in the interviews?

4.   The passivity and dependence noticed in Carol by several of the interviewers seem at odds with her earlier reputation as a tomboy and her interest in sports. What explanation
do you find for her increased self-consciousness and docility
in later childhood and in high school? Is she currently quiet
and well behaved with everyone?

5.   A survey of the initiative and assertiveness displayed
by Carol's heroines in the Thematic Apperception stories suggests an interest in such behavior that goes well beyond what
she expresses in everyday life. What unrecognized urges and
desires do you detect in these stories?

6.   Carol speaks of strong guilt feelings connected with
childhood punishments. In her Thematic Apperception stories
there are several instances of behavior leading to guilt feelings and punishment. What do you believe to be the urges in
Carol that led to feelings of guilt?

7.   Carol describes her satisfaction with life at college
as being more social than intellectual. What does she seem to
value most in her relations with other young people?

8.   Would you predict that Carol's religious faith would
crumble during her remaining two years at college and afterwards?

9.   As a sophomore in college, Carol reports no interest
in a career, and hopes to get married after graduation. One of
her Thematic Apperception heroines gets into bad trouble by
putting career ahead of love. To what in her experience thus
far do you attribute this attitude on her part toward career?

8.   SUBSEQUENT EVENTS

Twenty-eight years went by before contact was renewed by
letter with Carol O'Brien. Indications were given of the kinds
of information that would be pertinent to bringing her life
story into the present. She responded with interest, saying
that she had often wondered what use was made of those old records. The foregoing materials were sent to her, and before
long she sent in a long history together with a story she had
written fairly recently. The life history has been slightly
condensed for this workbook, but except where indicated it is
wholly in the subject's own words. From the story, excerpts
have been taken that seem likely to contribute to understanding.

As I read now what I wrote so many years ago, I am amazed
at how little life had touched me at that age, or, more honestly, I am amazed at my immaturity. It seems that I was quite
unaware of the world around me--whether close in or far out.
Maybe this is because nothing much had really happened to me.
The three major tragedies in my life up to that point had been
my dog's death, my high school beau asking another girl to the
junior prom, and my brother-in-law's death. The latter was
real enough and affected me quite a bit because of my affection
for my sister and for him, because he was the first adult in my
family who treated me as an adult.

For the remainder of my college life, I continued to have
a good time socially and garner most of my education from talking with the other girls in the smoking room rather than delv-
ing deeply and with any sense of real commitment into my studies. I managed to get through college pursuing this course of
action, but now I feel I would have been a more serious student
had I been a few years older. On the other hand, the smoking
room converstions were probably equally important to my development, and I would not have wanted to miss them.

The courses that I enjoyed most at college were some of
those in my major (psychology); art and music appreciation
courses; geology, because it was completely new to me; and last
but not least, comparative drama.

In my junior year the parade of people that I thought I
was in love with began. Actually, there were only three, and
of them only one who had a marked influence on my attitudes,
interests, and development. I don't know whether I assumed his
interests and attitudes as my own or whether he confirmed the
ones that I already had. His feelings for me went a long way
toward my developing more confidence in myself and accepting
myself.

The dating years before marriage were difficult in a sense
for me because there was a conflict between my feelings and what
I regarded as right and wrong behavior. During those years I
never solved this conflict in any satisfactory way.

I worked for eight years before I married. First I lived
in Boston with three other girls who went to college with me
and worked in an advertising agency. I liked the field, but my
job was menial and not satisfying in any way. I was ill a lot
that year. Actually, my friends and I had a hard time adjust-
ing that year after college. We went from belonging to a group
to belonging to nothing, and into a world which was not in the
least impressed with us. Many of the fellows we dated were
still in college, due to the interruption of their studies by
the war--but we felt definitely passé, and they seemed surprised
that we were "still around." My roommate and I and quite coin-
cidentally twenty-five other girls I had known in college went
to Washington, D.C., and worked for the government. Life was
more pleasant there, but became boring after about a year and a
half. The job was OK, but I was interested in a fellow in the

New York area and wanted to get into the field of advertising
and publishing. At that time I was not at all interested in
politics, and I am sure that feeling this way I must have had
a certain sense of isolation while in Washington. I kept trying to get interested, but it just didn't come. Now and for
the past fifteen years I have been intensely interested in political affairs (more about this later).

I lived with my sister and her two children in a suburb of
New York for the next three years. I loved New York and still
do. I feel it is a place where one can really be free, and I
enjoy the very thing that most people dislike about New York--
the anonymity of the place. Also the variety and excitement
of the city have a good effect on me. I used to get a real
thrill being a part of the stream of humanity walking home on
Fifth Avenue from work. There was always so much to see and do
in New York and so many interesting contrasts.

While in New York I was a secretary in the art department
of a publishing house, then a secretary in a small editorial
consulting firm, and finally a secretary in an advertising
agency. I enjoyed the work and general atmosphere of publishing and advertising, but I couldn't break out of the secretarial
mold. I managed to do more than a secretary ordinarily would,
by getting involved in photo reproduction, layouts, trainee
programs, preparing manuscripts for printing, but always I
stayed in the secretarial slot. This was a frustration for me
because I felt, and so did all my friends, that I should have
a more important job, but I lacked the push or know-how to get
there. I was confident that if someone would pick me up and
put me in an important position I could do it, but I just
couldn't seem to get there on my own. Most of my friends had
better jobs than I, and this made me feel worse about my own
situation.

About this time I developed an interest in painting--an
interest that has grown and deepened over the years. Painting
is something that I do in which I can forget where I am--what
time it is--I am grateful I have this absorption--many people
would like to have something like this. Unfortunately, I go
through periods when I don't paint at all and I try to figure
out why. When I am pregnant, for one, and am creating inside,
I have no need for external creation. Maybe it's because I
progressed in painting to a point where it has become work, and
I really care how the painting turns out. It frustrates me to
have an idea in my mind's eye and not be able to execute it--
but this is a rigidity I should try to overcome--I should go
where my painting takes me--I'll have to work on solving this.
I have developed a certain talent in the area of painting, won
a few prizes and sold a few. Right now, I am in a nonpainting
period. I suppose it's because I am too busy doing other
things, but I am not sure that is why. I am sure I will go back
to it. If I didn't have other responsibilities, I believe I
would paint all the time. It is also a source of getting ap-

proval--which I know is important to me.

About the age of 27 I began to get depressed--when I would
visit married friends with children I would come away with the
keen realization that I was not the center of anyone's life--
that I was not important to anyone or ones. A girl friend and
I used to joke and say that we would have children even if we
did not find spouses--I don't really know about her, but I was
not really joking.

I had also begun to realize that I was not going to make a
big splash or even a small ripple in the world of business. It
is incredible to me now to think that I managed to whip up a
fervor working in an advertising agency, having spent my married life being barraged by ads and commercials. But the feeling in the agency was almost religious, and everyone was loyal-
ly devoted to the success of this agency. Also, it seemed to
me that everyone enjoyed working there. There was almost a
party atmosphere, which I never found in any other place of employment before or since! One fellow I worked for was my age
and tried to help me progress. He had me writing copy. I kept
submitting pithy and witty material. He kept telling me that
this sort of thing was not what they were looking for; but if
I were going to write that was my style and, actually, I had
never been a consumer and had no conception of what it took to
encourage a person to buy a product. I would not have liked to
write anything less than I did. I would have felt untrue to a
value or ideal. I felt if I were going to write at all--it had
to be more literary or worthwhile. It was a surprise to discover that copywriting was selling, not writing. Took me too
long a time to figure that out.

Perhaps a word about my parents and sister here. I notice
in my autobiography a lack of understanding of my parents, and
I remember one of the psychologists at the time asking me,
"What are your father and mother really like?" I attempted to
describe them physically. "No, no, what kinds of people are
they?" I remember with some embarrassment that I really didn't
know. At age 19--that's incredible. Over the next six years I
began to look more clearly at them--tensions began to develop.
As I became more independent, this seemed to threaten my sister
(our roles were changing). Although she was always kind and
motherly to me, it became apparent that our values and attitudes
were quite different. I was more democratic and trusting of
others. Her husband's death may have influenced her attitudes
to life. Since I have been married, she seems not to want to
be too close to me.

I realized that I was always seeking my parents' approval,
which I had always gotten by doing well in school in my studies.
I realized that they preferred my sister, and she seemed to be
more their idea of what a person should be. This bothered me.
I did not feel that I could legitimately resent her because she
had always been good to me. The harder I tried for my parents'
approval about this time of my life (19-25) the further away

the possibility seemed. My parents and I seemed to have different values also--I have always felt that my mother and I
were alike in temperament and my father and I were alike in attitudes and values--whereas my sister and father had similar
temperaments and she and my mother shared similar attitudes and
values. My father and I began to argue in these years, and
although he was kind to me, I felt we disagreed on issues that
were important to me then. He seemed to be self-conscious and
very much aware of what people generally thought of him. Sometimes I think he felt he had to be more dignified than he would
have liked because he was the "judge" in a small town. Perhaps
it was valid for him to feel this way, but I am sorry he gave
in to it and was self-conscious and he wanted me to fit into
this image when I would breeze in from New York. I think I embarrassed him when I wouldn't. They were small things, matters
of dress and small social actions, but we would have angry
words regarding them. (Also he wanted me to register as a Republican and was quite annoyed when I informed him I was a Democrat. He then persuaded me not to register at all in our home
town. I think he felt his clients who were mostly Republicans
would think it strange for me to register otherwise.) Finally,
at age 26, I realized that no matter what I did, I would never
have my father's approval and that he would always think more
highly of my sister. So I said to myself, "Who needs his approval?" Coming to this conclusion was a big help to me as a
person--it freed me from trying desperately and futilely to get
his approval. Actually, years later when my father was dying,
I realized that he was fonder of me than I had realized even
though he had not been able to approve of me in the way that I
needed. I realized, too, that instead of someone to fear, my
father was really a kind and sentimental man. I sensed that my
father was pleased when I married, and, in addition, he liked
my husband.

     Another truism that struck me about this time was that if
I wanted to get married, and I did, I was going to have to break
a certain chain or pattern of not liking those fellows who really liked me and only liking those who did not like me. The for-
mer group bored me and the latter fascinated me--but never led
me to the altar.

     About this time, I met my husband, Dan, on a blind date.
He was the first person that I had met who really liked me that
did not bore me and seemed to want to get married. We became
engaged in three weeks and married within three months. Dan
and I share the same attitudes, interests, and intensity of
feeling toward these attitudes and interests, which was very
important especially as this related to religion. We also had
the same backgrounds religiously, ethnically, socially, and
economically. Sounds great, doesn't it, but we had different
temperaments--Dan is an extremist and I am even keeled. There
were, of course, differences to work out and differences not to
be able to work out. Our first marital years were stormy--

problems from without and those of our own making. Even though
I was 29 and Dan was 30 when we married, we were both immature
and also self-centered and dependent. We had the usual problems of not enough money, Dan's mother (his father had died and
he is an only child), and at first Dan's trouble in finding his
niche in the "system." He had been in two wars, spent a total
of five years in the service, and was off to a late start
careerwise. We both seemed to have a lot of repressed hostility, which didn't stay repressed too long; we both wanted to
make our marriage work and had the New England "stick-to-it-
tiveness" or tenacity. We both entered marriage with a feeling
of permanency formed by religious and cultural standards. Also,
we had a lot going for us--the similarity of interests and attitudes that I mentioned--we both had had lots of good times
before marriage and had a need to settle down and lead quieter
existences (which was good because our economic status dictated
this course)--but more important, we both had a gut feeling
that we had something important between us; we knew we were
really alike in the secret soul of one's self where such questions are asked and answered. When I have to put it all in
one question, "Why do I love my husband?" the answer is "Because he knows how and wants to make me laugh."

     In order to solve our differences we have talked and talk-
ed and talked and once in a while communicated.

     We had three children in the first five years we were mar-
ried: Paul, Scott, and Katie. I guess life would have gone
along as usual and we would be more or less the same people we
were when we married if something tragic had not occurred to
make us stop and think.

     Our oldest child, Paul, died suddenly at the age of seven
(cardiac arrest caused by an unknown virus). Paul was a sweet,
sensitive, witty, creative, and gentle child, and this was a
terrible blow to us. We went through a period of grieving that
involved every imaginable emotion from shock, sadness, to eventually an actual physical ache inside me.

     This event, for lack of a better word for it, was the be-
ginning of a turning point in our marital relationship, parental handling of children, outlook and actions as human beings
as part of a larger society

     At some point in college my religious beliefs were chal-
lenged, but I managed to work out the doubts either myself,
through discussions with others, or by asking the opinion of
different priests. I thought I had my faith neatly in order,
a sort of fait accompli. Needless to say, when our son died
and my thoughts turned to afterlife, and I had to try to place
my dead son somewhere, my whole faith began to shatter. I was
filled with doubts. I began to look again for explanations in
books and started to read the New Testament over and over.
This reading helped a lot, and for the first time my faith had
some back up and substance. It took a while to accomplish all
this reading. Dan and I were not much help to each other in
this time because we were both suffering in different ways.

But we were helpful in the fact that I tried to get him to talk about it, and he made me carry on as usual and would not encourage me to wallow in pity and grief.

We joined religious discussion groups. This was about the time of Vatican II and Pope John. We joined a combination religious discussion and action group and also an ecumenical group of people who were searching like ourselves for a deeper religious experience. The topics in the latter group usually were on religion or politics. We were all people struggling to be better Christians, and, more important, to know what this meant in the U.S.A. in our time, These people are still our closest friends.

Rebuilt Faith

My faith was slowly rebuilt, and this time had new strength because I was more mature and explored questions more thoroughly. God had brought good out of evil (from the loss of our son some good things did come). One of these good things was somehow the fact that I had survived my son's death and kept on going, gave me a sort of confidence in myself--I knew I could take anything having done that.

Paul's death was an unusual one, and because it occurred while he was taking a bath many people disbelieved us and assumed he drowned. An autopsy showed that death was caused by cardiac arrest due to an unknown virus. Both Dan and I felt a lot of guilt in connection with his death because it was so vague. Dan had found him in the tub and blamed himself for not being able to revive him, and I blamed myself because he had been sick the week before and I pushed him into a week of day camp without making allowances for his previous illness. We also felt that we had been too strict with him and generally hard on him.

Years later my husband became involved in a T group at work and was able to freely discuss his feelings about Paul (he had always found it hard to talk about, even though I used to try to get him to). As a result of this group, Dan went on for psychotherapy and got a lot out of it. I was pleased, as I saw myself the principal beneficiary of this endeavor. When our relationship became worse instead of better, I went to the same therapist to discover why. I didn't get too much out of it, a few rewarding insights, but I left after four months. I was not desperate enough for the full personality overhaul. Dan wanted me to continue, but at this point we had assumed a large financial obligation and I went back to work part time. Now that I am working I can see that I have a few hangups with authority still, which would have been nice to resolve, but I am hopeful that the passage of time and the fact that I am aware of them will see me through. Our marital relationship did improve remarkably in the last five years.

If it had not been for my faith and closeness to Christ and friends, I would not have been able to adjust to Paul's death, but it helped me put guilt in its proper perspective. All my life I had felt vaguely guilty, and this developed into a religious scrupulosity from time to time, and when my son died and

Guilt

I had to face real guilt that maybe he had died because I had
not taken good enough care of him, I realized that this guilt
was real and different from other feelings of guilt I had had.
I felt there was only one to answer to--God--so I said, "God,
I'm sorry--You know how sorry." Strange as it may seem,
because I had to face the possibility of real guilt, all the
various guilts I had felt or been feeling all my life fell into
perspective from this time on. I still feel guilt about some
things I do, but I can cope with it now and it doesn't over-
whelm me.
       Dan and I pursued our interest in a deeper Christian com-
mitment from that time until this. I began to think of myself
as more of a Christian than only a Catholic. The fact that
some resented the Catholic Church at this time (the sixties)
did not bother me, for all my life I have regarded the Church
as being a body of laity and clergy with all the human failings.
I keep all the main rules, however, because I want to enjoy the
freedom this gives me--a peace of mind--which is the motivating
force in my life, I believe. I am not happy if I don't have
this and eventually do whatever is necessary to achieve peace
of mind. There are certain ritualistic rules which I do not
pay heed to anymore. I have given them some thought and if
they don't make sense, I don't follow them. For example, it is
still on the books that one should fast an hour from solids
before Communion. I usually ignore this. Christ has become
the central force in my religion and, of course, I feel now He
always should have been. I think Vatican II has renewed this
emphasis on Christ and ecumenism for most of its Church members.
I do not believe that any of the following are moral--birth
control, abortion, capital punishment, or war.
       Dan and I became involved actively with a new movement for
Christian renewal. This movement is a new and different
approach to old truths. It enables one to see Christ in others,
the loving Christ, the suffering Chirst, the joyful Christ, and
so forth, and so to love others more. It begins with a retreat,
after which the people in the area meet on a fairly regular and
not at all organized basis. The people in this movement develop real bonds of feeling and love, and I believe this Christian
community is an attempt to get back the feeling that existed in
the early days of Christianity. It must be sort of like a
commune except people do not live together in groups. There is
nothing magical about it, but everyone seems to get out of the
experience what he needs most. It is a spiritual growing over
the years; people go in different directions, some perpetuate
the movement by conducting retreats, some spread it when they
move to other parts of the country, some become activists.
When members of the group meet regularly, it would remind one
of a T group or sensitivity group. In fact, it is a sort of
group confession except it is apt to be more on the positive
and joyous side. People tell the good spiritual things that
happen to them as well as discuss failures in this area. The

The difference is, though, that these groups are more loving,
more supportive, than sensitivity groups. The hostilities just
aren't there, and yet people aren't being insincere but honest.
     Unfortunately, as with anything human, it doesn't always
work just right. Dan and I were much heartened to see Protes-
tants and some Jews making the retreat in the beginning and saw
this as a real instrument for ecumenism; but in our area, some
people began to be real uptight about everyone receiving Communion together, and these people finally had their way.
Therefore, a Protestant version was set up, which is essen-
tially the same except for the liturgy. Dan and I have become
active in this Protestant version along with other members, and
I still hope for unity among Christian churches. I remember
that the first time I received Communion with some Protestant
friends of mine I cried. I had not realized until then how
very much I wanted this. Our age has done some exciting things
religiously. I am delighted to be alive in it. When I remember as a child how my spine would tingle with apprehension when
going into a Protestant church, not for a service even, but
maybe to practice for a piano recital, then I say we have all
come a long way.
     Since coming to our present home fifteen years ago, I have
been fairly active in the community. When the children were
small I went through the club activity stage. Later on I got
interested in politics and worked for liberal "dovish" candi-
dates in primaries, and so forth. I guess this period of my
life dovetailed the Vietnam War! About this time, too, Dan and
I did a lot of one-to-one work with parolees who came into our
community from various prisons under a rehabilitation program.
I found this work (volunteer) the most satisfying of all I have
done in the social action field. I have tried to figure this
out but can't. I did some civil rights work and a few other
things. I tried teaching, didn't do well at it at all!
Couldn't discipline the kids and even though I was intensely
interested in the subjects I taught (religion and social stud-
ies--this was a paid job) I failed to engender much interest on
the part of the students. So I didn't really feel I wanted to
work to help Negroes, or to deal with the various problem areas
involving children, but I did feel a real sympathy and desire
to help prisoners. I still am involved in this volunteer work,
but on a much smaller scale because I have a full-time paid
job now.
     I'll have to backtrack a little here. Just as I emerged
from the four months of therapy I mentioned earlier, we found
a house at the edge of the ocean in Maine. We had always
dreamed of having a beach house because we both love the ocean.
I have a real mystical feeling about it; it terrifies and fasci-
nates and comforts me. Anyway, we were lucky, it was for sale
very reasonably and we were there. We couldn't afford it but I
wanted it so much I said I would get a job. That was four years
ago and I have been gradually creeping back into the job market
until my job this year (which was necessitated by our sending

our oldest boy to prep school). I started with substitute
teaching where all mothers begin. It has been difficult to get
into the "system" again. Dan thinks I had a tough time because
of discrimination (middle-aged woman). I think it is just hard
to get back into the system after being out of it for so long
and not having had a very good job when I was young. I had an
equally difficult time when I graduated from college finding a
job that I liked.

I always knew I would have to go back to work when the
time came to educate the children. Dan and I are not savers or
planners but I made up my mind that if I were going to work the
next ten to twelve years I would do something that was interesting, not secretarial, and that would in some way help
alleviate the social problems of our society. First I thought
of continuing with my painting, but I knew I would never make
enough money selling paintings without further training and a
lot of luck. Somehow it seemed frivolous or selfish to spend
the next twelve years painting when there were so many problems.
I was afraid when it was over I would not feel I had done much
for others or with my life. I kind of had to force myself to
make this decision because without too much persuasion I would
have tried to go on with my art. I realized in order to get a
good job I would need further education or a degree of some
kind. I investigated teaching but it would have taken me years
to get certified in anything I wanted to teach and also I could
tell I was not ever going to be good at it.

About this time, a psychologist I had met socially insti-
tuted at a local college a graduate program in community psychology. This seemed to be the direction I should go in because psychology was my major and I could start in without
taking undergraduate courses, and also the word "community"
caught my fancy because of the involvement I had had over the
years and my desire to work in the field of social action. I
enjoyed being back in the academic atmosphere immensely and
discovered that I really enjoyed studying for the sake of
learning. I signed up for one course in the evening and worked
all day as a teacher in a parochial school where I taught
religion and social studies. It was hectic and I got two A's
in the two courses and I got fired from my job. It certainly
was a year of contrasts!

I was extremely lucky looking for a job and finally landed
a good one. I am project director of a senior citizens' volunteer program in our county and I enjoy this job very much.
Also, I am dealing from more strength than in teaching. The
best training I had for this job, believe it or not, was all
the club work I did about ten years ago. Our agency places
people over sixty in volunteer assignments in non-profit organizations throughout the county. I have four people working
for me, and so a lot of the job is administrative and not so
much people oriented as I had hoped. But it is open-ended,
one can be very creative, the people I work with are much like
myself, and I am getting to know our community extremely well.

I can pretty much do as I please, which is another nice feature.
I am terribly busy, and there is not enough time to do everything because there are no limits to where the job can go.
Needless to say, I am not going to graduate school this year
and I sort of miss it. I don't know if I'll return; it really
depends on the future of the job. It sort of looks as though
I got "there" already.

Dan is a college graduate with a degree in industrial
engineering. He started in sales but did not do well and went
back to industrial engineering. He was in World War II and the
Korean War, so it was with much soul searching that he finally
became a "dove" during the Vietnam conflict. This was quite a
change of attitude for him. For several years he has worked
for a large industrial corporation, first as a manager in manufacturing and now in personnel research, where he is happier
and better suited. He has developed a program for the industry
to promote "job enrichment," helping employees to be happier in
their jobs and cajoling management to do its part.

What is he like: creatively intelligent, articulate,
charming, very witty (when in a room full of people, everyone
listens to every word he says), dependable. He has some not so
nice qualities, too, like all of us--cranky, selfish, and over-
anxious. He is quite strict with the children, which is good
because I do not seem to be able to pull this off, although I
believe in it. The children feel more comfortable with me, but
they respect him more. He is loving to them. When they are
sick he is the one who really takes care of them, and when
their toys break, I fix them. Dan does much of the cooking
because he is better at it than I and likes to do it, and I fix
the plumbing and handle the money. Needless to say, we have
come up with our own arrangements!

We are a close family and enjoy doing things together.
Both Dan and I would just as soon have our children with us most
places we go. Occasionally one prefers the company of one's
peers, but most of our leisure-time activities are now spent
with our children. The beach cottage has been a good thing for
our family. We are together there, apart from the rest of the
world and TV, so it affords the opportunity to talk. We all
enjoy it very much.

I would say that in comparison to our neighbors and friends
Dan and I are more strict and do not allow our children the same
freedoms that other children their age have. We are sort of
anxious parents and were so even before Paul died; perhaps we
are overprotective.
We have tried to impart our sense of values to our children, but it is difficult to figure out a way to do this, so how
successful we have been, only the future will tell. So far, I
would say we have been successful in this, but our children are
15, 13, and 8, so it is too early to tell if they will continue
to accept our ways or rebel in any salient ways. I feel guilty
sometimes because I feel our insistence on their adherence to
our values has meant that our children are sort of strangers in

the environment in which they have to walk; but I would do it
no other way. This may sound snobbish to say that I don't care
to emulate most of my neighbors, but my feelings toward them
are based on their lack of grace and taste, not on any other
lacks. To make up for this, in my mind at least, we have sent
our oldest boy to private school, where I feel he will at least
know there are others who feel as we do. I am not explaining
this very well, but the hostility, conformity, and materialism
of most of the people in this area is disturbing, as it affects
your children. At least, Dan and I can seek out people we like,
but our children are stuck with what they find around them.
Here again, though, I have some really wonderful neighbors, so
I speak generally.

We have always stressed honesty, good manners, telling the
truth, and not being afraid to be different. Also, we have to
pass our faith along to our children as well as some sense of
their Irish heritage. Of course, our children are often not
honest, not good mannered, and so forth, but for the most part
they are nice people to have around and have a sense of other
people's feelings.

Our oldest son, Scott, 15, is very mature morally for his
age. He has always had this quality; for example, in the fourth
grade he read a child's version of Moby Dick and said later,
"It is really a story of good and evil, isn't it?" He is bright
and has an analytical mind; he tries to figure things out. He
is steady, affable, happy, sentimental, and private (hard to
know what he is really thinking). Sort of shy with a good sense
of humor. We are now trying to have all the children develop
inner discipline with some success.

Our daughter Katie, 13, is very lively and enthusiastic;
she has a real sweetness and sensitivity and perception of other
people and their feelings. She is domestically inclined and
much more maternal than I. She has always had trouble in school.
We have had her tested for everything under the sun. No one has
come up with anything. It was probably a combination of things.
She is anxious and fearful (we feel her brother's death had an
effect on her--she was only 3), and she had some difficulty
learning to read--doesn't like to concentrate for too long and
really is just not interested in academic affairs. I must say,
though, this year she seems to be changing in this regard and is
trying much harder in school and tells me this is the first year
that she can read quickly. She loves to be one of the gang and
have the latest record and wear the latest style. She is high
spirited and very good to all the rest of us, helps me out
tremendously, and loves to take care of her little brother. He
liked this at first but is now feeling more independent, and so
Katie is caught between two brothers and sometimes they give her
a hard time! Katie is musical.

Peter, 8, is the youngest and was a real gift of joy to our
family. He was born three years after Paul's death. The eerie
thing is that he looks exactly like him, which I usually put out
of my mind. He is an attractive child and very bright and quick

thinking. Very musical and creative, excellent sense of humor,
but the most important thing about him is his charm; he has
always liked people and instinctively knows how to approach them
(notice I didn't say manipulate, because he is not like that).
To give you an example, when his mother is reading a good book
and doesn't feel like making the old peanut butter for lunch
even though she knows it is past due, almost any other kid
would say "I <u>want</u> my lunch, <u>gimme</u> my lunch <u>now</u>," but Peter comes
up and says, "Say, Mom, what do you say we have some lunch."
He never comes at you front on, and as a result he usually gets
what he wants. I've learned a lot from <u>him</u>. He too likes to
be with the gang and doing what everyone else on the street
does. He seems to be well coordinated. Dan and I have been
able to be more loving to this <u>child and it shows</u>.

    A word about prejudices, I believe I was not prejudiced to
any great extent in college against minoroty groups, but I
realized that my parents were a bit, and this seemed out of
character for them. Also, my mother did not even know any
Negroes; there was only one family in the whole town. In college I began to think that prejudice must increase with age,
with the sense of one's physical frailty in the world or something like that. I am more prejudiced now than I was. I always wondered if this would happen to me, and it has to some
degree. I wonder too if it isn't just a way of coping with all
the facts one learns in a lifetime. As one goes along, the mind
tries to assimilate and make more sense out of all these facts,
so I think people begin to think in a compartmentalized fashion
in order to make some sense out of what they learn. She has
blue eyes, red nose and is a nurse; oh, then she must also have
poor handwriting (to give just one weak example). I would
prefer to think that this is true rather than that I am getting
prejudiced. I do fight against it.

    I believe that I have more confidence in myself now than
was evidenced in my autobiography. That is the understatement
of the week! I am much crankier now than I was and argumentative. I had a nicer disposition then, but I suppose that is
true of everyone.

    I think I am a happier person now than I was in college.
When I was that age I had a fascination for things gloomy and
sad, which seems to have left me for the most part. Although I
always had, and still have, a cheerful outlook, and little
things in life seem to please me more than most people. I get
a kick out of little things--a sunset over the ocean, certain
musical selections, and funny things people do and say. My
husband is this way too, but lots of people I know are not. By
the same token, I suppose sad things hit us more emphatically.

    One thing in my autobiography which I found interesting,
and is definitely a similarity between the me then and now, is
the order which existed on my Allport-Vernon <u>Study of Values</u>.
I had not known of the results when you first tested me, but
the order of preferences is the <u>same</u> today as it was then.
Remember the decision I made about continuing with painting or

here working in the social action field? And I chose the latter, and I see by this test I took so many years ago, that same
order prevailed. I guess this means my values were the same
then as now. I believe this to be so. My goals are essential-
ly the same too!

I believe attitudes toward women in general need changing,
and I believe women should be allowed to take jobs they wish to
and to earn the same money as men. I believe that men should be
the ones liberated, for they are the ones I feel who have it rough
in our society. But someone, man or woman, should take ten
years or twenty out to have and raise children. There is always plenty of time to work later, when they are older. The
most worthwhile thing I have ever or will ever do is have and
raise children. This brings the most satisfaction when one
thinks about it. I think there should be more exchange of
roles between men and women, which each couple will work out,
and hopefully society won't set down hard and fast rules and
images to make people nervous about what they want and don't
want to do. When my children were young I was dying to get out
of the house; now that I can, I am dying to stay home. I
really do like my job, but I am not bored at home because I can
always amuse myself with painting or reading or playing the
piano. I keep getting expensive ideas, which is one of the
major reasons I am working. Don't get me wrong, I really do
like and enjoy and feel that my job is worthwhile, but still
and all working every day is a grind. I guess it is still too
early to tell how I really feel about this.

This ends Carol's account of the twenty-eight years of her
life since the original study. She also submitted a story written a few years before, not long after the death of her father.
The story, which is entitled "Made of Marble from Tara Itself,"
consists of a series of reminiscences that appear to be frankly
autobiographical. The opening scene finds the narrator sitting
in her father's room shortly after his burial, unable as yet to
begin packing for the return to her own home. Idly she looks
into the top drawer of his highboy.

Part of my father was in the drawer--at least, things
he had worn or owned. Next to a dozen or more black balls
of socks was a stack of precision-pressed handkerchiefs.
My father enjoyed the neat and orderly world, which he made
for himself, so thoroughly that he never felt the need to
impose it on anyone else. On the other side of the divider
were numerous tiny boxes and cases. Some were leather cuff-
link cases that were so hard to open and yet sprung shut
with such swift force that very young fingers were often
guiltily caught. I smiled as I remembered making earlier
forays through this highboy. My fingers could cope with the
spring cases now, so I went on looking. There were many
Knights of Columbus membership pins, Red Cross Selective
Service pins, and other indications of a community's grati-

tude for service, plus countless ornate cufflinks, which
must have represented a quarter century of Christmas disappointments. I opened a small rectangular box, removed the
top layer of cotton, and there it was--a gold stick pin.
Its head was shamrock-shaped gold, inlaid with green "marble from Tara itself," as my father used to tell me every
St. Patrick's Day when he proudly stuck the pin in his tie.
As I twisted the pin between my thumb and index finger, I
began to feel better. The happy memories of past St. Patrick's Days began to live again for me.

        Usually St. Patrick's Day began with my father present-
ing himself downstairs for breakfast wearing his splendid
satin green tie with the shamrock stick pin from Ireland
sitting in it. Then it was my turn to ask about the stick
pin and his to tell me anew that it was made of green marble
from Tara itself. In all those years I never thought to ask
him how he happened to have the pin. I know he never visited Ireland, although he had always wanted to. Had another
worn the pin before him? I find that hard to believe. The
pin was my father's; a real bit of Ireland in our house.
Next, my father would whistle an Irish tune and self-con-
sciously start to dance a jig. He never did more than a
few steps before he remembered that he wanted to present
himself as a more serious and dignified figure, being father
to me and the judge in our town, so his last step would dis-
integrate, leaving him standing in front of of me sort of
embarrassed and momentarily out of context. It always delighted me to glimpse this face of my father, and how I
wished he would continue the dance. I remember only my father and I playing this scene over and over--where could my
sister have been? My mother was usually in the kitchen getting breakfast; she was not inclined to revel in her Celtic
origins and always wistfully expressed Anglo-Saxon aspirations. No, these moments belonged to my father and me and
set the mood for the rest of the day.

    The narrator reflects that one of the nice things about
St. Patrick's Day was the relief it offered from the strict
discipline of Lent. Attendance at mass, however, was an essential part of the day's observances, the more so because the
narrator sang in the choir and helped produce the music which
caused her to hope that God was deaf.

        At the end of mass, the whole congregation, led by the
choir, erupted into a rendition of "Hail, Glorious Apostle
Selected By God." It was a roistering tribute, and everyone
put all of himself into this vocal expression of love for
St. Patrick. A sort of spiritual patriotism filled the air.
As everyone filed from the church, ebullience and good will
were reflected on their faces and in their greetings to one
another.
        Regarding church music, Miss Clift, my piano teacher,

presented me one day with a copy of "The Irish Washerwomen"
to learn. I told her, of course, that I was already familiar with the music, since we sang it in church on St. Patrick's Day. I demurely suggested to her that the correct
title was "Hail, Glorious Apostle. . . ." For further proof
of this, I started to sing the hymn and only stopped when
she gasped, "You mean, you actually sing the 'Irish Washer-
woman' in church!" I was momentarily hurt and stunned by
her reaction, but a fierce loyalty to something that even
today I don't quite understand came to my rescue and made
me sing even louder the next year. After all, what did she
know; she wasn't even Irish.

There follows a detailed, entertaining description of the
amateur dramatics that occupied the afternoon and evening.
The narrator recalls with special joy the year in which her
parents took her to the evening performance instead of to the
afternoon one intended for children.

Concluding her story, the narrator relates her distress,
during her father's last illness, that she was about to lose
her chief link with her Irish heritage. No one else would be
left to remember his side of the family history.

I realized this with panic and tried to press him for
detailed information, but I had waited too late; his memory
had gone. Like the jig my father used to dance--it sort of
trailed away leaving me out of context.

I have an urge to pass something of our Celtic origins
on to our children, but every time I try, it just doesn't
take. Over the years, my husband and I have tried rather
unsuccessfully to make something special of St. Patrick's
Day. Our children have been tolerantly polite, and so I
thought it would all end with us.

However, recently I was going on a trip. I didn't
talk much about it because the trip had been postponed a few
times. Suddenly, it was on again, and I was going to be
gone for eleven days, the longest time I had ever been away
from the children. The reality of my going stunned the
children. On the eve of my departure, just after the children had gone to bed, I was seized with some sort of domes-
tic guilt and started doing a bit of dusting in the living
room. Accidentally, I hit a couple of piano keys, and my
son, Scott, hearing this, misinterpreted and thought I was
about to indulge in one of my evening piano-playing sessions. He called from his bedroom, "Mother, play some
Irish songs--play the one I like about the wearing of the
green." I was sad to leave them and would rather play the
piano than dust anytime, so I played the request and many
more Irish songs. The children would not let me stop and
kept yelling from their beds, "One more time!"

FURTHER QUESTIONS

     1. In contrast to Solomon Kompten, who submitted his relatively brief follow-up information after a long delay and two promptings, Carol produced this detailed material fairly soon after the initial invitation. This may seem surprising in view of Solomon's greater interest in the original study. As both subjects currently lead busy lives, free time does not seem a satisfactory explanation of the difference. What do you believe to be the most probable explanation?

     2. Carol's story, "Made of Marble from Tara Itself," describes her childhood relationship with her father. What differences do you notice between this account and the one given in the original interviews?

     3. Carol describes two major insights achieved at about age 26: the impossibility of having her father's complete approval and the self-defeating results of her preference for young men who showed little interest in her. Do you think there is a connection between these two insights?

     4. Would it be possible to conclude from her description of the marriage relation that Carol is still something of a tomboy?

     5. In describing the consequences of her son Paul's death, Carol indicates a serious shaking of her religious faith, but then describes a lasting renewal of religious activity. What differences are there between her religious life before and after the child's death? How are her later beliefs related to her personal growth?

     6. In the light of subsequent events, would you say that Carol predicted correctly when as a college sophomore she rated her interest in marriage and family ahead of her desire for a career? She reports various difficulties with career; why do you think she had these difficulties?

     7. What values seem to be most prominent in Carol's description of her children? How do these differ from Solomon Kompten's values (see Question 3 in "Further Questions" in his case)?

     8. Carol describes herself as having become more prejudiced toward groups other than her own. It can be argued that at 19 she was more prejudiced than she knew, and at 48 less prejudiced than she thinks. How would you yourself describe and explain her history as regards prejudice?

③ Frederico Gomez

Contents

Introduction

    The third case in this series adds a new set of challenges
to understanding. Ramon Federico Gomez, Fred, as he chose to
be called, comes from a background decidedly unlike those of
most college students. Born in New York of Puerto Rican parents, he spent most of his first eighteen years on the streets
of Spanish-American Harlem. Schooling was spotty and of little
importance to him, so that in talking about his experiences
Fred does not place them in a school-year framework of time;
only gradually, by repeated questioning, did the interviewers
establish the order in which events occurred and construct the
chronology given below. Readers who were not brought up in a
similar environment will need to exert themselves to grasp
this subject's outlook and picture to themselves how he per-
ceives the world.

    Furthermore, there is likely to be initial difficulty in
making sense of the seemingly wandering conversations. Unlike
Solomon Kompten, who responded to questions with logical, well-
formulated answers, Fred gives the impression of feeling his
way in a situation he really does not understand. The whole
idea of being interviewed, and of expecting by such means to
understand another person, seemed foreign to him; he expressed
bewilderment that anyone would give money just to hear him
"rap." Especially at the beginning, he frequently paused and
fell silent or changed a sentence he had begun. He constantly
repeated "you know," "ah," "hmm," and a sigh when beginning to
answer a question. The text at first illustrates these speech
characteristics in an attempt to reflect the diction, inflec-

tion, and rhythm of Fred's speech; later, they have been edited out for brevity's sake. Fred's sometimes unconventional grammar has been changed only when necessary for understanding.

The study of Fred's personality rests on five lengthy recorded interviews held when he was between the ages of 20 and 22. By this time he had moved to the West Coast and had begun the semester of college work which brought him into contact with teachers interested in life histories. The first two interviews, when Fred was 20, were carried out by a man who was doing advanced graduate study in psychology. The remaining interviews, at 21 and 22, were conducted by the woman professor of psychology who was in charge of the study project. In his own way—a way rather different from Solomon's and Carol's—Fred makes an honest and patient effort to communicate what he had experienced.

Fred is of average height for a Puerto Rican man, roughly 5 feet 6 inches. He appears rather slight without seeming skinny, and his walk and manner are very graceful. At the last meeting the interviewer was impressed that he could easily be mistaken for a black: he was now wearing a full Afro haircut, moustache, and goatee. His large warm eyes and relaxed face invited conversation and closeness. His mood for the most part was calm; occasionally he seemed pained with the content and at times chuckled with real pleasure. His voice was always soft, fairly monotonic, and average in pitch.

APPROXIMATE BIOGRAPHICAL FACTS
Reviewed by Fred

Birthplace	Spanish Harlem (between 103 and 125th Streets, New York City).
Siblings	Carmen (oldest), Maria, Irma, Fred, Rita.
Age 2	Rita born; father left home
Age 5	Started first grade; mother ill; family split; lived for one or two years with lady downstairs.
Age 6, 7, 8, 9	Grades 2, 3, 4; held back one year; played "sick" often; no friends; mother hospitalized at end of this period for 8 months (?); Fred lived with aunt.
Age 9	Some loose gang activity; took long walks alone; turned on to pot; met Peggy from Village.
Age 10-11	Grades 4 and 5; gang life; school truancy
Age 11-12	Court for truancy; 6th grade in a day reform school; "took violence of the school to the streets"; beat up Juan; became president of first gang, the Young Boss Kings; mother ill; lived with grandmother (or a "little old lady") out of Harlem.
Age 13	By age 13, gang using using guns, stealing, drinking.

Age 14   Complete involvement with gang; onto heroin;
                  out-of-state reform school for one year.
Age 15-16   Drugs replaced gang fighting; socializing with
                  dances; introduction to white society.
Age 16   Kicked heroin; formed Rescuers--theater group
                  with Roberto.
Age 17   Lived with George; went to high school two years;
                  AWAKE program.
Age 18   Lived with Peggy (the second), age 30; two-month
                  trip to Orient.
Age 20   Interviewed for first time, after living 4 months
                  in California, by male graduate student
Age 21   Interviewed for first time by female psychology
                  professor; had completed high school and one se-
                  mester of City College; studying meditation and
                  doing odd jobs. Not living with Peggy. Recent
                  move to country commune.
Age 22   Interviewed for last time; on welfare; into mu-
                  sic; living in a "closet" alone in the city.

FIRST INTERVIEW (NOVEMBER 1970): AN EMBATTLED HARLEM CHILDHOOD

(The abbreviation (P) in this record signifies a pause; (LP) a
long pause.)

E: I think we should start with you just talking about what
    you think is important for somebody to know about you if
    they really want to know you.
S: . . . (LP) . . . That's a very broad question and, ah, hard
    thing to answer. Ah . . . it depends on what the person
    wants to know. 'Cause there's a lot that makes a person.
E: Why don't you start where you feel like starting?
S: (A sigh-type laugh) O.K. . . . (LP) . . . (Another sigh-
    type laugh and LP) Ah . . .
E: Pretty hard, huh?
S: Yeah.
E: There's no hurry. I don't want you to pressure yourself.
    We can wait for it to come to you. That wouldn't be too
    uncomfortable for you?
S: Oh, no. (LP with a couple of sighs) I guess very honestly
    I wouldn't know what to tell a person. I would sort of
    find out what that person is like, by just talking to that
    person, and then, ah, seeing what that person is interested
    in, and then, talk about things I know in that sort of
    line. (Clearing throat) For instance, ah . . . (P) . . .
    they may be interested in politics and then somehow I have,
    I know something about politics and how it affects me, I
    would be saying something about how I am, and who I am . . .
    (LP) . . . It doesn't really tell about a person. Because
    a person is more complicated than that. To me, there's a
    lot of undeveloped sensitive feelings, which, ah . . . (P)
    . . . which he sees in himself every day, and every day as

he discovers these new feelings in himself, changes happen.
I am not through being what I . . . oh, I don't have a
full understanding of myself to know exactly what I am because of these new . . . (P) . . . feelings.

E: Well, listening to you, I've had this notion--sort of how
it all depends on who you are with.

S: Uh-hmm.

E: What if just maybe I wasn't looking for anybody in particular?

S: Well . . . (LP) . . . (A few sighs and half-laughs) I can
say my name is Ramon Federico Gomez. I am just a human
being just like everybody else. Ah (LP, sigh) I am searching for answers.

E: To the question?

S: To who I am.

E: I hit you pretty heavy. I walk in here and ask the question that you're asking.

S: Hmm. There are times when I think I know, and there are
times when I don't. Hmm. The times I know, I'm afraid
. . . (P) . . . (clearing throat). When I am really depressed I can see that, or I have a feeling inside . . .
(P) maybe a religious feeling, or I don't really know what
it is. But it's a feeling in the form of accomplishment
in the sense of knowing who I am. . . . (LP) . . . Well,
hmm . . . (Sighs, clears throat). Well, hmm, I, I guess
the difficulty lies in, ah . . . (P) . . . not having the
words or the shapes or forms to be able to explain. Every
now and then . . . there's a struggle within myself, the
difference of being in situations like here, and I know
why I am here, and I know what I'm doing, ah . . . (P)
. . . and I know who you are, and I know this whole situation but somehow, deep inside, there is something that
says (P), "What's going on, man?" like, you know, ah . . .
It's like being you were drifting. . . . Or, ah, there's
always a doubt in many situations, this constant battle
that goes on inside of me is the same battle that goes on
in people with the same misunderstandings of not being able
to convey and say, "Man, this is what I am." . . . Ah, um
. . .

E: Wondering about, like who I am, and what the situation is.

S: Yeah (whispered) . . . (LP) . . . Oh, wow. I'm not really
wondering about who you are, 'cause you're just a human
being just like I am. Ah, I think basically the only differences are that we have different hangups (slight chuckle). . . . (P) . . . But . . . um . . . (LP) . . . hmmm
. . . (LP) Obviously, I am not doing very well in thinking.
. . . What if someone were to ask you who are you?

E: I would sort of drift for an hour or so. That's a very,
very, very difficult, hard question to answer.

S: It's a pretty difficult question, and I'm kind of avoiding
it, I suppose.

E: I had the sense that you've been answering what was very
difficult for you.

S: I was answering, but not to my fullest, I would say. I
just can't <u>find</u> words so that I can't express it. I know
that it is a <u>very</u> difficult question. I can't be candid.
Even if I had the words, I would say that it would take me
quite a while to say who I am. Yeah, because, ah, it can
be answered . . . (P) . . . I can, you know, give you an
answer . . . (P) . . . I was once down, and I was asking
myself that same question. I supposed I phrased it very
differently. Many times I was depressed, and I don't remember what I was depressed about. I guess I was looking
for an answer. Ah, and, um, and somehow I saw myself as
being a part of everything. Part of the chair, rug, lamp,
table and shoes . . .

E: Oh, I see. How was it?

S: The feeling?

E: Yeah.

S: Fantastic! I can't explain it again. It's just that I
felt part of everything. Everything was just me, and I
was everything.

E: In getting to know somebody, as it has been my experience,
it is helpful to know about the past. Maybe you could just
start with the first thing you remember and just rap on and
talk about whatever direction you go in.

S: Lead on.

E: So can we start with your earliest memory?

S: Sure. Can I turn my chair around the other way? It's
going to be a long time.

E: You just keep me posted as to what age we're at. OK?

S: Huh (sighing and laughing) OK. And also . . . the ages,
it's very, very mixed up. I don't quite remember certain
ages, what certain things went on, ah . . . because I kept
moving from places and different experiences and many
things that happened, that, ah, I can't really recall at
certain ages. I'll try to.

E: If you can't remember things perfectly, that's the way it
goes. Who does?

S: Hmm. Well, I guess I'll start talking about family situation. I was brought up in Harlem in New York City in Man-
hattan, ah. . . . There was Puerto Rican and black Harlem
--like a mixture.

E: You were right on the edge of Spanish Harlem?

S: Yeah, yeah. Right on the edge. Ah . . . (P) . . . four
sisters, ah, no brothers, three of them which are older
than I am. Father left when I was very young. I vaguely
remember him. I see him in a wedding picture with my mother, but I don't recognize him, and I don't know him.
He's a stranger to me.

E: Apparently you are a mixture of Spanish or Mexican heritage
with American black heritage. Is that correct?

S: Spanish-American, I'm sorry? (Wants clarification)

E: Spanish or Mexican or what heritage? Could you tell me
what your grandparents were like?

S: My grandmother is Puerto Rican and my grandfather is
Puerto Rican.

E: So there's no American Negro in your . . .

S: I don't know. Maybe way back there. Somehow the family
keeps saying that my father was German and was brought up
with Puerto Rican people. He does have kind of German
features but, ah, who knows? (laughs)

E: Yeah. Now your grandparents were from Puerto Rico?

S: Yeah.

E: And was your mother raised there too?

S: Yeah.

E: So you're the first generation of American.

S: Yeah.

E: You were born in Harlem?

S: Yeah. (Both laugh) OK. Ah . . . (P) . . . let's see,
where was I? Oh yeah, my father left us when we were
young. Mother got ill, and I think she had . . . (P) . . .
ah, well, I never quite understood exactly what she had,
what was her illness, except that I've heard doctors and
her family talking about all heart trouble and asthma.

E: How old were you then? five or 4?

S: About 4 or 5, yeah.

E: Do you remember what you were doing, what it all meant to
you? all those things?

S: Hmm. I don't know, except that there was a lot of fear in
the family . . . (P) . . . Mother was always afraid. We
lived in a four-story building . . . (P) . . . roach and
rat infested. It was a very dark, dark building, old with
holes in the wall, no heat, no hot water. All I can remember is Mother's always in that bed, in a tiny little
room, moaning and crying.

E: Pretty rough for a child.

S: I don't remember what my sisters were doing at the time
. . . (P) . . . there were times when Mother would get out
of bed, feel better and . . . (P) . . . We never talked;
we never said anything. There was never any affection.

E: Not at all?

S: No. . . . (P) . . . That as I remember, getting older, my
sisters would take me to school. We would all go to school
with the next-door neighbor. . . . (P) . . . In school I
had a very rough time.

E: When did you start school?

S: (Sigh) I don't remember. I guess elementary school.

E: Were you 6, 7 years old?

S: Or 5, probably.

E: Do you remember what school you went to?

S: (Names exact street location in Harlem)

E: What kind of school was that?

S: It was mix, Puerto Rican and black.
E: And you were Spanish-speaking?
S: Yeah. I spoke Spanish at home.
E: Did you have trouble with English?
S: Always. I always had trouble. And these strange women
   would come up and during recess hours they would buy us
   cookies and milk. I would just sit there. Any many times
   I would cry in class.
E: What did you cry about?
S: I don't know.
E: Just cry. Did you have money for cookies and milk?
S: No.
E: How did you feel about that?
S: I don't know. I didn't have any feeling about it.
E: I thought you did.
S: . . . (P) . . . No, see. There was so much fear in our
   family. Mother was always, even today she's still afraid.
E: Of what? Do you know?
S: No, I suppose afraid of changes. Maybe. Afraid of . . .
   (P) . . . when I was going to the Orient, when I told her
   I was going to the Orient, she just cried for weeks.
E: Afraid of losing you.
S: Yeah. More than that, I think mostly afraid of the un-
   known. What's in the Orient, you know.
E: What might happen to my son.
S: Yeah.
E: Right. She cared about you!
S: She cared about me.
E: But there was no affection.
S: No.
E: Then I guess, well, I'm going to do a lot of guessing, so
   I hope you'll correct me when I'm wrong. Will you do that
   for me? She was afraid of showing love to her kids?
S: . . . (P) . . . I think she didn't know how . . . (P) . . .
   Ah, she wanted to show us love, I think. There were many
   points where she wanted to give us something for Christmas,
   and that's a way of showing love. When she got very ill
   and was committed to a hospital, ah, the, ah, doctor was
   very young and insisted that we be put away and put up for
   adoption because she just couldn't take care of us. There
   was five kids. We lived in that cold apartment and, ah,
   and she would have to spend a long time in the hospital and
   who would take care of the kids?
E: Yeah.
S: Ah, so she, she cried and she, uh, this is what I've heard,
   I, ah, haven't . . .
E: You don't remember very well yourself?
S: No. She wanted us. She loved us.
E: And you knew that.
S: Yeah.
E: You knew that then.

S: Yeah. Otherwise she would have gave us away and said OK
   put them up for adoption.

E: Yeah.

S: Well, she wouldn't have given us up. She said that she'd
   rather die than give us up. She wanted us and loved us.
   For a selfish reason? an unselfish reason? I don't know.
   But she wanted us. She loved us, and she wanted to bring
   us up and give us a home, motherly love, or whatever. I
   don't think she was a woman capable of giving us emotional,
   physical, mental love or understanding.

E: So it was just a rough scene all the way around. Well,
   you've said there was a lot of fear around, and to me that
   sort of means that your mother was afraid, but that some
   other people in that house were afraid too.

S: Yeah. I was afraid because my mother was afraid. I was
   afraid.

E: Do you remember attaching your fears to things?

S: Yeah. I remember. One time Mother went out to the hospital for something, and my little sister and I were home.
   My sisters were in school. We woke up in the morning.
   Mother wasn't there. No one was there. So we crawled
   back into bed together and we hid under the sheet and just
   stayed there all day until Mother came back. We were
   afraid . . . being in the apartment alone, nobody there,
   afraid to go outside, afraid somebody, a stranger, might
   come in, ah, may kill us or something.

E: Do you remember that somebody might kill you?

S: Yeah.

E: Your sisters would walk you off to school, and like you
   said, you'd cry in class. It sounds as though it must have
   been a very difficult time for you.

S: Uh-hmm.

E: Maybe you could describe what went on in school.

S: . . . (P) . . . Hmm. I can vaguely, vaguely remember, because it wasn't so long ago except (laughs) that so many
   things happened. But, um, just little things like being
   shy and being afraid and . . . (P) . . . just being withdrawn and not participating in anything, anything that went
   on. And things had to be brought to me and someone had to,
   somehow, sit there and try to give me individual attention
   in building blocks or painting, and put the brush in my
   hand.

E: Hmm. You didn't have any particular friends?

S: Um, no.

E: So it was really just your family.

S: Um-hmm.

E: So you go to school, and it sounds as though you just sort
   of cringed there all day. And then got home as quickly as
   you could. You didn't stop off on the way home ever?

S: No.

E: And that went on for how long?

S: Well, for the first, second, third grade, and the fourth.
    Then by the sixth, the fifth and sixth, I started to some-
    how walk around the streets and, you know, open my eyes to
    the neighborhood.

E: I'm sort of hunting for the time when you ran across some-
    body who wasn't in your family who maybe was a friend,
    that something happens with.

S: Um . . . (P) . . . no. I simply cannot. Ah, maybe it
    might have been next door, where we lived. There was a
    black family, and I think there was a Puerto Rican family
    next door also . . . (P)

E: I imagine they helped take care of your mother.

S: Yeah. I guess they came up when my mother wasn't feeling
    too good or something. Maybe the lady downstairs.

E: What was she like?

S: Well, there were several. There was this old lady, her
    daughter, and that lady's daughter (chuckles).

E: Three generations.

S: Yeah. Ah, that was it. I guess, ah . . . I don't know.
    Who did I know? It might have been Johnnie, who was the
    colored boy next door, 'cause we were very close. We kind
    of lived together, really. The black kid.

E: How do you remember him?

S: I don't remember exactly when I met him and what happened
    then. But it seems that I can't remember when was the
    first outsider or the first person other than my family
    that I had any contact with. Yeah. I started meeting
    friends. In the fifth grade I started playing hooky. I
    started not going to school. All along that line I started
    staying home and playing sick, in third, fourth, fifth
    grade.

E: Um, a lot?

S: Oh, yeah.

E: The truant officer didn't catch up with you, did he?

S: Uh-hmm. No, not at all. They didn't catch up to me until
    I got to the sixth grade.

E: What did they do?

S: Well, they took us to court or something. Well, not a
    court, but some building where they scared us or tried to
    scare us.

E: Did they?

S: No.

E: Why not?

S: I just wasn't afraid by then. I had no fears. Mother was
    afraid. She cried and cried, and she covered up for us
    . . . (P) . . . But ah, I wasn't afraid. 'Cause by then
    I'd been in the street and fighting, you know.

E: Was this just on your own or part of a gang or . . . ?

S: On my own and gangs.

E: Now, by the sixth grade, you had already been in a gang?

S: Yeah. So in the fifth grade I would say I was in a gang
    already . . .

E: Well, was it like a formalized gang?

S: Yeah.

E: It had a name and a war chief and . . .

S: Well, it wasn't like that. It was just a group of kids together, you know. Just sort of hanging out together and . . .

E: You had your own territory?

S: Yeah. That sort of thing. . . . (LP) . . . I didn't really care whether they accepted me or not. That's funny. I was just pushing my way in there, you know. Just fighting and just being there. I guess I have all this holding back in elementary school. In the first, second, third grade I'd hold back so much emotion. I didn't talk to anyone. And finally I just burst. And said "fuck it all." You know. "Here I am and I don't care about anybody. And just be."

E: And just be what?

S: And just be me.

E: Do you know what came of those feelings that you were holding back?

S: I don't know. Except that . . . Maybe I was fed up with these white teachers and, you know, putting a paintbrush in my hand and telling me to paint. And, and . . .

E: And it's hard to say what that was.

S: Um-hmm. Anyhow, I was, I burst, a lot of me burst, not all of me, there was still a lot there that was holding back.

E: So at this stage you said "Fuck it, I'm going to be," and among other things, you were going to be in that gang.

S: Um-hmm.

E: What else did it mean?

S: That I was not going to be scared any more . . . (LP) . . .

E: Scared of people, you mean?

S: Yeah.

E: Physically? or just scared?

S: Just scared. Not physically. Let me think.

E: Do you remember your first fight?

S: My first fuck?

E: Fight.

S: Oh (chuckles).

E: We'll get to that later.

S: Um, no. I guess it was in school probably. Most likely. There were so many fights in school that I don't remember which one was the first one.

E: What kinds of things did you fight about?

S: Oh, maybe when I got down to, well, little things like erasers or pencils or getting in line or pushing.

E: How did it go?

S: Oh it was pretty bad.

E: A pretty bad fight.

S: Yeah.

E: How did you feel then?

S: Why did I do it? . . . (LP) . . . I don't know. They'd

never choose me in a game because I would always be fighting. I would grab somebody and push him on the floor, and
that sort of thing. And ah . . . (LP) . . . also a lot of
my child life has been, not all of it, but good parts of
it, were spent in another suburb of New York with my grandmother. Occasionally my mother got really bad, and at one
point she had, ah, pneumonia, and she was in critical condition, and we had to be split up, separated, the whole
family. So my sisters went to my aunt and some of us went
to my grandmother, and I went to school there once in a
while. But that was after sixth grade. But, ah, I remember during this change when I began to, ah, open up and,
was more free, and . . . ah . . .

E: Your opening up was around the fourth grade?
S: Yeah. I remember taking long walks alone . . . (P) . . .
just, alone. Just daydream . . .
E: Do you remember any of the daydreams?
S: No. I remember that most of my walks were done in the
ruins of buildings. There was construction, and there was
nobody working at the time. And I was just walking in and
go through these old buildings. They were falling apart.
I would climb to the top and then climb down. I would go
to the basement and just sit there and meditate. Sometimes
when I would be down in a hole for about four or five hours
I would come out feeling very very happy for some reason.
E: You mean like elated happy?
S: Yeah.
E: Would you say those were the happiest times you had?
S: No. I don't know . . . (LP) . . . Yeah, I suppose they
were! Yeah. Yeah, they were the happiest times.
E: What do you think it was? It sounds as though one of the
important things about it was being alone.
S: Um-hmm. Well, there were points where I just couldn't be
alone.
E: When did that start?
S: I don't know. I guess when I started drinking and smoking.
E: You mean smoking or turning on?
S: Smoking pot, yeah.
E: And how old were you then when you started doing that?
S: About 9.
E: Well, that's fourth, fifth grade. And so you were smoking
and drinking by the time the whole gang scene started up.
S: Yeah.
E: Was it different for you when you had been smoking or had
been drinking? Was the world a better or a worse place?
different?
S: No, it seemed the same in a way . . . (LP) . . . Let's
see . . . (LP) . . . No.
E: No difference?
S: No difference.
E: Now it was the sixth grade when the truant officer came

down and tried to give you a scare.

S: Well, actually, he did scare me when I was home and, ah,
two policemen came in and practically broke the door down.
I just felt scared and . . . (LP) . . . wondering what
they were going to do and what were they up to and what
did I do wrong (chuckles). And finally they said we're going to lock you up, and I thought . . . They were going to
take me to school, and I'm just going to run away again.
Ah . . . (LP) . . .

E: They said they were going to lock you up. I take it they
didn't.

S: Well, they didn't. No. I'm trying to think. I was just
thinking way back of my experiences with the cops and when
was I _first_ exposed to them, a cop and, um, I guess I had
pretty good experiences. My first experience was pretty
good. I remember once going to the market with Mother and
I got lost (chuckles). She went one way and I went the
other, and I got lost, and I don't remember very much what
happened except that maybe I was crying and yelling for my
mother, and looking for her, and hoping to find her, and
I kept walking up and down places. And somehow I was in a
cop car, I can remember that, and somehow two policemen
bought me a bag of Fritos and wanted me to point out the
building in which I lived . . . (P) . . . And I was too
young to do that. So maybe, I think what happened, was
this old lady who I was talking about before, she, ah,
stopped the police officer and came over and said, "I know
who that child belongs to." Yeah. That was a pretty good
experience. They didn't give me a hard time (chuckles).
Then the second experience when they came in, I wasn't
afraid. So in the car going to court they started talking
about taking us away, away from our parents, from my mother
and my sisters and, ah, locking us up in jail, behind bars
and starving us. And, ah, 'cause we've been bad and, ah,
we have to, and they have to put us away for a while.

E: It was a little scary, huh?

S: Yeah. Then it became a thing like, wow, let me see. What
do I do next?

E: Now you were smoking dope at the time? Did it ever occur
to you that that is why they were breaking down the door?

S: Ah . . . (P) . . . No. No, because at the time I didn't
think that it was a bad thing.

E: You didn't know it was against the law?

S: Yeah (large chuckle).

E: (Chuckles) All the other kids were doing it. It must be
OK. I'm sort of hanging in anticipation here, because it
sounds as though the sixth grade was a real turning point.
Something happened then. Is that true?

S: Well, a lot of things happened, and one is that I moved
out of Harlem. And I went to live with my grandmother in
another part of New York. And I had friends . . . ah . . .
Just people who I talked to. That's when I began to talk

. . . ah . . .

E: Yeah. These were people who would talk with you and
    didn't give you the feeling that you should go hide again.

S: Um-hmm. And also, let's see what else happened. Well, as
    I said, there was just quiet times and just walking into
    rooms of buildings, just being alone. All of that contrib-
    uted to the big change.

E: What was the big change? What happened?

S: . . . (P) . . . New fears (chuckles).

E: Were you able to name them better this time?

S: Ah . . . (P) . . . no, not exactly.

E: When thinking back about them, can you pin them down at
    all? What were you afraid of?

S: . . . (LP) . . . Well, when I got back from that truant
    officer scene, I told all the fellas, then I began to be
    afraid of cops. That was one thing that I was afraid of.
    Um . . . (P) . . . Um . . . (P) . . . I was no longer
    afraid of being alone in a room. Ah . . . (P) . . . so
    that's another thing that I developed alone. In my apart-
    ment, in my mother's apartment, just alone . . . (P) . . .
    I was no longer afraid of me. That sort of thing. I was
    afraid of the outside world. I'd never been out of Harlem
    except to my grandmother's place, and there I was just in
    her apartment, then maybe to a new school, and then back
    again.

E: What were you involved in?

S: Oh, relationships with friends. I started developing a
    lot of friendship and people.

E: We are still in the sixth grade now?

S: Yeah. This game was bringing me into contact with people.
    Running around and chasing someone, and holding them and
    attacking them, and fighting with them.

E: So for you it was a way of, you never felt that you were
    beating them up, but for you it was a way of getting con-
    tact.

S: Yeah.

E: Did you feel that way then or is this something you figured
    out now?

S: I felt it then. I think. I felt . . . (P) . . . I felt I
    wanted to, ah, 'cause there was so many fights going on,
    with the big kids on the block and the kids in school,
    fighting all the time, so I sort of fell into it, and so I
    felt like I'm part of them and I felt like I was growing
    up. I was communicating with them.

E: With your friends too?

S: Yeah, it was always a game, it was always, actually it
    wasn't fighting, it was just a way of communication. Yeah,
    just, you faggot, you punk. . . . Yeah. It's just you get
    together and you fly birds or smoke a joint, you know
    (chuckles).

E: Well, now, at the time, you regarded this fighting as a way

of being with people. Well, what about the other fighting?
Like when you were with a gang fighting another gang?

S: It still was a way of being with people, except . . . uh,
it's a way of being with your <u>own</u> gang, and that's a way
of ah . . . (LP) . . . of being with your own people, actually, the other gang you really don't care about . . .
uh . . . (LP) . . . uh . . . the fighting somehow draws
you closer to each other.

E: What did you fight with, fists, bottles, chains?

S: Well, it started out with fists, and then ended up with
knives, chains, and guns and rifles.

E: How long did it take to get from fists to guns?

S: Oh, uh, ah, maybe, God I don't remember . . . six . . . I
don't remember. I don't remember. It was off and on . . .
sort of thing . . . uh, oh, maybe three years before I had
a gun in my hand . . . (LP) . . . I'll give you an example
of what fighting was like then, and it continued to be that
way, I suppose. There was this fighter on the block in my
neighborhood. His name was Juan. And his father was a
boxer, an old-time boxer. And he wanted his son to be a
boxer too, so he trained him to be tough. And Juan was
known for maybe four or five blocks, and he was very good
with his hands, and nobody could beat him. So that made it
very tough. I kept running into him, and he . . . uh . . .
would, ah, kept bullying me, and taking advantage of me.

E: Yeah. Were you still not a very good fighter?

S: No. I never was. Let's face it (chuckles). It depends on
what you call good. I don't know. . . . Well, anyhow, I
used to dream, and I guess a lot of times I would just
think of how I hated this guy and how I just wanted to beat
him. Well, one day he would stop me, and he'd come over
and . . . (P) . . . ask me for some . . . pot . . . and,
uh, if I didn't give it to him, or I didn't have it, he
would, or his boys would take me and search me. And take
it. And then he would start hitting me if I had it on me,
and if I didn't have it on me, he would still hit me (chuckles). There was nothing I could do. I couldn't beat him.

E: How did it go in the daydreams?

S: In the daydreams it was things like he would ask me for
something, and I wouldn't give him any chance to ask me, I
would just punch him in the face and he would fall. So he
was really very tough. And everybody was afraid of him.
So . . . (P) . . . then I got enough courage to fight him
one day, and he whupped, he really whupped me--two black
eyes and a bleedy nose and a busted lip, and he kicked my
ribs in, he really hurt me. And, uh, when that happened,
then I really got very angry and very uptight, and all my
boys weren't friends with me, and we were just like very
quiet, and everybody was very quiet. Wasn't like it used
to be, maybe it was me, I don't know, but everything sort
of changed. My gang was still seeing each other, but not
as much. So I kept fighting Juan, and every now and then

he would come up, and one day I really punched him in the
stomach, and I really gave it to him . . . and he went
crazy. And he heaved at me again. And I kept losing. I
fought him four, five, six, or seven times and just kept
losing. And maybe by the fifteenth or twentieth time I
was already, you know, by then I knew his moves, I knew
his upper cuts, his fakes, and finally one day I got him.
I knocked him out. Gave him a black eye, bleedy nose.
Well, it's enough for maybe four, five, maybe six blocks
knew about it, and beyond! Yeah. So everybody knew what
it was. And then it was bad, because everybody wanted to
try me. To get a reputation. Because they knew Juan was
tough and they couldn't give it to Juan because he was
good with his hands. And I wasn't good with my hands so
if they beat me or lick me, then it would be easier to get
a reputation than through Juan. So then I had fights
after that like crazy. Kids would be waiting in the hallway when I'd come down and they'd all jump me (chuckles).
And that sort of thing . . .

E: So you must have been damned determined to get him to go
through all that. Why all the determination?

S: . . . (P) . . . I just hated the guy. Just wanted to kill,
wanted to just destroy him. Yeah. Yeah, I hated him, even
after I knocked him out. But I was also afraid. I was
afraid that he would come back--which he did. But when he
came back he was afraid. And his father really beat him
that night because he was licked.

E: How old were you now?

S: Maybe 13. No, about 11.

E: Oh, 11. What would it have been like to have a father like
Juan?

S: . . . (LP) . . . There were times I hated his father also
because he made Juan strong with his hands. And there
were times, because maybe I suppose I envied him and wanted
to be strong.

E: You envied him because your father was gone? maybe dead?

S: No, I just, you know, I don't know.

E: For you he's dead?

S: Yeah, I suppose so. 'Cause he's not here, and I never saw
him.

E: You haven't heard from him at all?

S: No . . . (P) . . . I might have slight little things, but
they might just be fantasy, you know, with my father and
my mother at home. With my father coming in every night,
coming from work . . . (LP) . . . That's all. And then my
mother being married.

E: Is she sick in these memories or fantasies?

S: Sleeping, I suppose so, yeah, but not sick. She was always sick. But she would be in bed . . . (LP) . . .

E: Well, so, getting back, the scene with Juan wasn't really
a gang scene.

S: Well, be the age of 13, 12 and 13, that started developing,

really close to 13 . . . (P) . . . I was never very good
with my hands, but I remember winning a lot of fights, and
we made friends that way. There were times like, well,
Juan and I became very good friends after the fight, after,
'cause after I beat him he came back and wanted more, he
wanted to fight me again. And I suppose by then he was
afraid, so he was careful not to really get licked. So we
would call it a tie or a draw.

E: On one hand, you weren't very good with your hands, but you
    were able to beat him. Were you very good with your feet?

S: (Laughs) I mean I wasn't trained like Juan. I didn't have
    any, maybe it was that, I didn't have any confidence in
    fighting. Yeah. Probably the next thing the friends that
    I had, we ah . . . (P) . . . developed a gang sort of
    thing.

E: And the regular gang scene, with the name, the war chief,
    the president, the whole schmere?

S: Yeah, well, the guys stole some money and paid this lady to
    make some sweaters for us and some shirts, with our name
    on it.

E: What was your name?

S: Young Boss Kings.

E: How many kids were in it?

S: Oh, when it started out there were twelve, but then about
    twenty, twenty-five.

E: Did you have any special position?

S: I was the president.

E: What does it take to be the president of a gang?

S: Well, I don't know. I mean I don't know how I became pres-
    ident, except that twelve of us, well I would say maybe
    about six, there were six of us who started and, ah . . .
    (LP) . . . I really don't know.

E: You really don't know how you became president, but I asked
    you what does it take to be president.

S: Ah . . . to think fast.

E: Think fast how?

S: Well, make plans, quick plans for fighting. Sort of like
    a war counselor, but uh . . . we had a war counselor.
    Yeah, Joey was the war counselor. We had two, as a matter
    of fact. Bobby was a war counselor too. Uh, and I suppose
    I would have been good for a war counselor, but they de-
    cided I was good for the president somehow, because I just
    thought very quickly, did things very quickly, and, you
    know, uh (chuckles) . . . (P) . . . I had more guts. No-
    body would have stood up twenty times to Juan. It just
    takes a lot of guts. And, uh, a lot of patience, and a lot
    of mind. We were thinking, I fought all the guys, all
    these six guys that were with me, I fought them all and
    beat them, and so they decided I was the best. You know,
    I had more birds in my coop, and that's . . .

E: Was that a status thing? How did you get the birds?

S: Steal them. Yeah. And ah . . . well, I guess I went

through a test with all the guys, they'd put me through
a test. They, uh, the six guys would go on the roof and
would blindfold me and just spinned me around seven times.
Meanwhile, while they are tapping, I'd have to go over and
touch them, and be careful not to fall off the roof--
blindfolded.

E: You know, the way you talk about it, I get the feeling
that, actually, you're pretty proud of all that, but you
sort of don't think you should be.

S: I proud of it?

E: Yeah, I mean you were a pretty big deal. President of the
gang, beat all the six guys, you could walk around without
falling, and nobody could do that. Fight twenty times.

S: Well, when I look at it now, I see how sick it was. Sick
in a way, I mean, you know, was it, you know, worth doing
that. I would have fallen off that roof--what would that
have proven? I mean, suppose this guy would have killed
me, just hit me in the right place and killed me? Now I'm
aware of that, but then I wasn't, because then I was just
proud. So I'm trying to, just trying to explain it as it
was then, and trying to feel if I felt proud. Yeah, I'm
trying not--to be the grown-up man now, I'm trying just to,
uh, to feel back actually the way it was. And occasionally
I feel a little guilty or bad, probably 'cause I realize
how sick I was--sick in the sense that I would know how
sick the world was for me. And for a lot of other people.
Sure. That's probably where the pride comes in, and how
you had to be sort of a killer in order to survive. I
mean, if you walk down the street and say I really don't
want to fight, man, you know, just leave me alone--someone
would just kick your ass every day, and it would make you
fight. And then you get to a point where all you know is
just fighting, and how to kill and hate.

E: Your life was pretty bad. Well, you know, I . . . this
question may be completely out of line. I mean, did you
ever have that in mind to kill them?

S: (Whispers) Yeah.

E: Hmm. You don't sound as though you want to talk about it
much.

S: . . . (LP) . . . So, uh, those were a . . . some tests
that went on at that time, uh, and I became president
(laughs). And uh, ah . . . (LP) . . . like I would leave,
spend hours going up to sleep on the other gang's territory. And . . . (P) . . . there was another gang that I
was also involved with, which was called the Imperial Tops.
Well, I found out the president was Roberto, and, uh, we
became very, very good friends. He was an old man to me
at the time--I was just a kid (laughs).

E: It's my notion of how gangs in Harlem function that, uh,
about as much time is spent stealing or pushing or whatever
as is spent fighting, or perhaps more so.

S: Well, my gang, uh, our gang, uh, started out just, as I

said, a little club associating, uh, we would fight . . .
uh . . . for bird coops. We'd go at night, as I was gonna
say before, to another gang's territory, and break the
coop and kill the birds, and those birds that were left
we'd take them. And that sort of thing. And then there
was drinking involved, and that sort of thing, social
things, and then it developed into stealing. We were
breaking into apartments, stores, stopping people in the
street. I was the one who planned it, and did some of it.

E: Well, you must have been out of school then.

S: Yeah.

E: When did you leave school?

S: Right after elementary school. I never <u>went</u> to elementary
school. It really was just playing hooky. And then, you
know, and after a year, the year that I was supposed to
graduate, you know I just . . .

E: And so you just hung it up then.

S: Yeah. So then, uh, that's when you know that gang got developing, I guess at the age of 13, in knives and chains.
And that sort of thing. And I think the old man--there
was an old man there who had a long alley in the block,
from one side to the other. So I was hanging around the
alley all the time. He'd say if you guys would clean up
the basement, you can have it, or . . . I think it was
like that, or . . . I don't remember . . . (LP) . . . Anyhow, I moved into this alley, into this basement-like room.

E: Oh, you moved out of your house into the basement?

S: Well, not literally, I didn't sleep at home much, spent
plenty of time, you know, out on the street all the time.
And I guess I came home and Mother was sick in bed, she
didn't know when I was missing, when I was there, just
kept on running out of the house at all hours, and she just
couldn't keep track of whether I was there or not.

E: What were you feeling about her then?

S: She was in a different world. I didn't feel much about my
family--I was just involved with the gang and the fellows.
And I don't know. Then I guess I had plans like arranging
how to get the guys jobs in stores, all kinds of stores.
And then they would come back and tell me about the situation of the place. . . . And I would figure out how we
could break in and get the money, if there was any money
available, or merchandise. So we furnished the club.

E: Yeah. This is like you were 13 at this point, and, uh,
from what you describe you are completely out of the law,
and I mean you must have had a fence, uh, for merchandise,
is that right?

S: Yeah. I had all kind of people coming over. Junkies
would come over to buy a record player or a radio for 2
bucks and go out and sell it for 5 or 8.

E: Yeah, right.

S: And then old ladies coming by and reselling stuff to little
old ladies. Very good. Cheap for that time. Uh, so

people would buy it because it was cheap.

E: Yeah, and you must have been making pretty good money.

S: Yeah, we had a lot of money. And then the gang increased
and more fellows coming in. And nobody really knew who was
the president, because I was like one of the fellows, and
I was a member of the crowd.

E: I mean it was like a secret then?

S: Yeah, I always kept it a secret, I mean everybody wanted to
know, but I always kept it . . .

E: Is that typical for a gang or . . .

S: I don't know if it was or not, but that's just the way I
wanted it. I don't know why I wanted it that way. And I
had six guys with me, and we were, you know, we'd have a
meeting, just these six guys, and so if they had to knock
any one of us, they'd have to knock all six, because they
didn't know which one, uh, and I didn't have a special
sweater or anything like that, uh, and I had two names . . .
uh . . .

E: Where did you get the second?

S: Well, I changed my name to, uh . . . Little Rico . . . (LP)
. . . Yeah, I remember . . . you see . . . Again I'm going
back to the very beginning. OK, uh, I guess maybe about
the third grade--I don't remember exactly, but there was a
girl there came over from the college, or university, I
don't know, playing guitar for the young kids, or something,
and, uh, I don't know, she just liked me or something, we
became very good friends.

E: She was a college girl. You were in third grade.

S: Maybe, yeah.

E: Did you see any reason why she should have liked you?

S: No.

E: Why do you think she did?

S: I don't know, but she offered to take me places, or something, and I said alright. And I went with her to the Village, Greenwich Village. Hippies. And, uh, smoked pot together, and that sort of thing. I met her friends.

E: You were a third-grader and you were smoking pot with this
college girl? And you must have been about 9, and I picture
this little kid walking in and lighting a joint with all
these grown-ups, it just seems a little weird, but I guess
it wasn't for you, or for them.

S: No, it wasn't weird at all, the way I see it. So, we, she took
me to several night clubs, you know that sort of thing, and
this was the first white person I came in contact with.

E: What was it like, the first white person?

S: I don't know, I was kind of removed . . . (P) . . . like I
sort of let everything happen. Like I didn't have any con-
trol--I did, I could say, "Look, man, no," but, uh, I just
let it happen. Whatever happened, I just, it was just flow-
ing, floating with whatever went on. And I didn't trust
them, you know, in a way.

E: How was it that you didn't trust them?

S: I don't know, they just, they didn't speak slang, they
   didn't speak Spanish . . . (P) . . . they, uh . . . A lot
   of the times like they would just sit there and rap and a
   lot of the times I would say what the hell. I felt insecure in not knowing what these people were talking about.
   And every now and then they would mention Little Rico,
   which was what she called me, because she was in love with
   this cat whose name was Rico, and she wanted him, and she
   couldn't have him because he was in love with another
   chick. And I guess she called me that, and she called me
   her son--she called me Little Rico. And, uh, this Rico
   was white, and Peggy was white. Rico had a car, and every
   now and then we'd drive around the Village and smoke pot
   in the car.

E: And that apparently all came to an end or something?

S: Yeah, we had plans to come to the West Coast and go to
   Mexico, and they were going to smuggle me in the car, and
   just before it was going to happen, I guess she was on
   heavy drugs then and I didn't know about, but she wasn't
   getting along too good with her parents . . . (P) . . .
   I keep making these grammatical mistakes, but I guess you
   get the general idea of what I'm trying to say.

E: I understand all right (laughs).

S: Ah . . . (P) . . . one day I came to her house and her mother said she wasn't home.

E: Just like that?

S: She went to the hospital, she wasn't feeling well. And I
   still have some letters of her. And I never saw her after
   that.

E: Did you love her?

S: Uh?

E: Did you love her?

S: Yeah. Very much. She was concerned.

E: Must have been pretty awful, then . . . for her to disap-
   pear like that?

S: She had some mental breakdowns. It was really bad for me;
   my sister was helping me write some letters to her, she
   wrote back, every year she would say I owe you two Christmas presents and birthday presents.

E: That's what she'd write to you?

S: Yeah, among other things. She loved me. She wanted me to
   read, and keep reading. She was, I remember, she was very
   sharp, she could read . . .

E: Hmm. And you were like 9 years old.

S: Yeah. We would go on the subways. I was blind, I'd never
   gone on the subway before, I never went to any place other
   than Harlem. I just, I don't know, you know, with my eyes
   closed, I really trusted her.

E: Did you really close your eyes?

S: Well, not literally, like, you know.

E: Just like if you trust her, she'd take care of you.

S: Yeah. I saw her five years after that whole thing, sitting

in a park with friends and . . . (P) . . . somehow I saw
this kind of old man walking with this oldish but not old
white-haired lady with a white robe, kind of loose, kind
of nightgown sort of thing . . . (P) . . . and like a beam
of light around her, a halo.

E: Like it was really there or was it?

S: I was projecting it on her, that sort of thing.

E: You saw it or you felt it?

S: I guess I saw it and I felt it.

E: And you knew it was her?

S: In a way, yeah, I wasn't sure, I didn't trust my feeling
so much. I looked and saw her, she was just walking,
everybody was sitting down, and she was just walking
around, sort of gazing at this fellow. And then I dropped
everything and I went over and I followed her. I kind of
walked, and then I stopped and I kept watching her. She
kept walking slow, I started running a bit, 'cause I was
sure, I was really sure. And then I stopped, ran up in
front of her, and I said, "Peggy?" . . . (P) . . . She
looked at me sort of . . . she shaked her head. She was
bewildered, she didn't know who I was, she didn't recognize
me. "Remember me, Little Rico." She just couldn't figure
it out. And I kept staring at her, and I was determined,
'cause I knew it was her, but by then I just knew I looked
into her beautiful beautiful eyes, and this face . . . (LP)
. . . and I just looked at her, and finally, her eyes
opened and she saw me and she hugged me and kissed me and
we held each other for a long time. And she was among
friends then, and she stopped. Her group of friends was
trying to figure out what was this guy doing, and I just
didn't care, I was just like really into her (long sigh)
. . .

E: You still miss her, don't you?

S: Yeah.

E: How long ago was that, when you saw her that time?

S: It was recently, I . . . (P) . . . I mean, about a year ago,
after I hadn't seen her for five years, and she grabbed my
hand and she said, "I have to go to the bathroom." And we
skipped to the bathroom in the park and I waited for her
outside. She looked at me and she hugged me again, and she
told me she was taking some yoga classes at a museum. She
said that I could find her there, just ask anybody where
the yoga classroom was, she'd be there in the mornings from
9 to around 11. And, I don't know, she was with friends
. . . (P) . . . she just had to go. She said goodbye, and
she just left.

E: Did you go see her?

S: I went three times, and they said there is no such thing
as yoga classes there. And she sounded pretty serious, I
don't know. She wanted to see me. Then I remember that
night; I was living with a man then. I came home and told
him about it; and I went to my room and I just started

crying.

E: What kind of crying? There are lots of different kinds.

S: Well . . . (P) . . . I just felt very, I don't know what I
    felt. She was like a mother to me, and in a way we thought
    . . . I felt very close to her, and I felt like I really
    want to be with her . . .

E: I guess she gave you some pretty important feeling.

S: . . . (LP) . . . That is, I felt very attached to her, very
    close, close . . . very wanted . . . because she was such
    a nice person, I suppose, I carried on the name that she
    had called me.

E: So since the first time you saw her must have been when
    you were like 9 years old, you were with her for like five
    years. Is that right?

S: I didn't spend much time with her.

E: Well, I mean the relationship continued.

S: Yeah.

E: So what I'm wondering about now is, by the time you were
    14 you must have become, you know, a sexual creature, and
    here was this woman you loved; what would you do about it?

S: There wasn't. . . . I didn't have any sexual feeling for
    her. It's kind of like Peggy, the girl I have now. You
    know, there are times when I don't feel like I want to have
    sex with her. I don't have this stimulus, and there are
    times when I do. There are times when I see her as my mo-
    ther, as a mother. And there are times when I see her as
    a girl friend.

E: Yeah. You don't think of your mother as you do a girl
    friend?

S: Yeah, I guess not. Mothers, you know, take care of you
    and see that you have the things you want or need, and
    food, and that sort of thing, and you sit down and rap, you
    know, about, I don't know what mothers and sons are sup-
    posed to be like, but I know that I have the feeling with
    Peggy, the Peggy I'm with now, that I had with the other
    Peggy. (Both of these girls in real life had the same
    name.)

E: Well, what was it like with your mother? What was the mo-
    ther-son thing? Between you and . . .

S: Well, it was neither sex nor motherly . . . uh (laughs)
    . . .

E: What was it?

S: I don't know.

E: She was sick, she was afraid . . .

S: Yeah, she never gave me affection, and I suppose that's
    what I needed . . . you know. Not physically, but you
    know, in an emotional and mental thing.

E: Yeah. Well, how did you respond to her, I mean that she
    didn't give it to you?

S: I just lived without it. I mean, I don't understand, there
    was no response. I suppose it was just after all these
    years, I met this girl named Peggy and this feeling of what

a son was supposed to be like just came out on her, and I felt like she was my mother. She was the first woman practically that came out and said, "Hey, man, you need a mother (chuckle). And you're, I'm your mother, and you're my son," and it also happened with George, this fellow I lived with for a while. Ah, he became a father image. He was a homosexual, and he was a producer and director of shows, and one night we just hit it off.

E: It was a homosexual relationship?

S: No, it wasn't.

E: So it was a special relationship for him, too?

S: Um-hmm. Might have, it might have not been. I mean I don't know the guy, where his head is, except that, you know . . . (P) . . . he treated me as a father, in a sense, as he saw a son should be treated.

E: Is this the guy you were living with when you met Peggy (the second)?

S: Yeah. Well, I sat there when I told him I had seen Peggy-- I remember sitting in the chair for hours, just gazing at the floor, and ah . . . (P) . . . and at one point he came over and put his arms around me and . . . (P) . . . and said, "I understand."

E: Did you believe him?

S: . . . (P) . . . No. I mean, how could he feel what I feel? How can he understand when I haven't explained? Except, I mean, he hasn't lived through what I lived through. I can believe that he can see how I'm feeling--he can see now that something has, had happened to me. That day that I met someone and something happened--because I wasn't my usual self. But I don't think he can understand the feeling that I had.

E: Well, how did that make you feel about him?

S: It made me feel, you know, nothing, actually. I just accepted it because I knew that he was a human being. And that's the way we all are. I mean, I can't actually feel your pain, because I haven't lived through your pain.

E: (Softly) That's true.

S: Ah, so that's how I got my name Little Rico (laughs).

E: Well, now that we've settled that! (laughs)

S: And ah, so anyhow, I had two names, it was . . . people used to call me Little Rico and Ricky (Mother called me Ramon, Ricky) in the gang. Ah . . . (P) . . . we had kind of a lot of members, and a lot of money, and a lot of . . . hmm . . . ah, sure I'm skimming a lot of things.

E: That happens; that's my job to help try to get back to them, if we can.

S: I remember, as time went by, we had fights, like . . . well, that's when I had to do a lot of thinking and arranging for new situations and things. 'Cause I had to spend nights kind of going up on the roof and looking around and trying to figure out how we could make our club safe. We got two clubs then, and then three clubs. We had one on one end

. . . of the block and at the other, and the main one was
in the middle. So what I did was I put two guards at the
main entrance. And anybody from any other territory had
to go through the guards, and usually we had at least a
rifle or a gun at each place.

E: Well, in your mind . . .

S: And the people, getting back to, excuse me, the people in
the neighborhood, they looked out for each other, for us.
. . . And there were a lot of people there that were just
afraid of us. There was this old man once, partly Jewish
and partly Spanish, somehow. But, ah, he moved in and he
called the cops one night because we were shooting it out
in the alley. And somebody got hurt and started yelling
for help, and somebody broke a leg or an arm or something,
got shot, I don't remember. But he called the cops, and
the next day, I just told the guys to take care of him.
When he came back from his job everything in his apartment
was burned. And then he moved out. And the next person
who moved in just knew what was going on.

E: So you pretty much ran the neighborhood.

S: Um-hmm. And ah, you know, people just kept quiet if anything happened, because, you know, they knew what was good
for them. So they didn't . . .

E: Yeah. You were hauling in a lot of bread. What did you
do with the bread?

S: Well, a lot of bread, I would say the majority of it went
. . . weapons were hard to get at the time. To get a gun
you had to shoot a cop. Ah . . . (P) . . . so we had to
buy guns with the money, and ah, refreshments and all that
kind of thing for the dance and the sweaters and the jack-
ets we got. . . . And the, ah, we had to pay rent for the
two clubs, I suppose.

SECOND INTERVIEW (NOVEMBER 1970):
PROBLEMS OF PREJUDICE AND LOVE

E: I'm actually uncertain as to where we should start. You
might just go ahead and start where we dropped off last
time; you might just sort of start talking about the things
that interest you.

S: (P) . . . We got onto many, many fields. One was . . . hmm
. . . how I felt about being black or Puerto Rican . . .
hmm . . .

E: Yeah. I was of the impression that you were glad--that you
had, at some point, ancestors whom this racist culture finds
as black.

S: Hmm . . . well . . . (P) . . . I guess the reason why I said
I was Puerto Rican, because I am. I mean, that is my na-
tionality. I was brought up with Puerto Rican people in
the neighborhood, and black people. Ah . . . (P) . . . when
I'm in the presence of a white person I'm always considered

black. Ah, not Puerto Rican. How <u>would</u> you consider a
Puerto Rican in this society?

E: Puerto Ricans, I guess, are sort of like people from Mexico. But that's apparently not quite the same way they
get regarded in all parts of the country.

S: Hmm . . . no, really. I met a lot of Chicanos, who have
somehow been treated as Chicanos, whatever this being
treated is. . . . But my experience has been just a black
man. I don't know, maybe I have black features . . . (P)
. . . maybe 'cause I pronounce certain words with black pro-
nunciation or whatever, if there is such a thing.

E: Well, there are a few black dialects, but you don't happen
to have one, as far as I can tell.

S: I certainly don't have any Spanish accent.

E: It sounds sort of general New York accent to me.

S: When I say "whitey" I certainly don't mean it in, in a vicious or resentful way, or . . .

E: Perhaps a little bitter?

S: Well, you may, well . . . if I'm bitter . . . (P) . . .
(laughs) . . . (P) . . . hmm   I don't know. Maybe I am
bitter. And if I am, I'm sure I have a reason. And whether the reason is valid or not, who knows. No, I do believe that there is some bitterness in me. And that there
is some, I wouldn't call it <u>prejudice</u>, or anything, but
just . . . (P) . . . not at all <u>for</u> what the white people
has and the way that they've set up the society. Not just
because they're white, but just because they've ruled the
society. And that seems to me the main reason that I may
have some bitterness in me. And yet, now and then I feel
that it's silly to be bitter, and it's foolish and absolutely senseless to be, ah, affected by the mistakes that
mankind makes. Because he himself has no way out, because
. . . let me just mention one thing. Somehow I may be getting off the track, but it will tie in, I suppose. Way
back, I remember going when I was a kid to the zoo with a
friend and we kind of snuck into the zoo. We were in front
of the gorilla and just looking at him. And it was funny
how that gorilla looked at me. I could <u>see</u> in his eyes and
the expression in his face that he was saying, "What the
fuck am I doing here?" you know. And ah . . . (P) . . .
and that made me think . . . (P) . . . I'd say to myself,
"What the fuck am <u>I</u> doing here?"

E: Do you have this sense about yourself still?

S: Well, it's a thing that everybody feels; it's not just me.
Nobody wants to say, you know, "What's going on here?" Nobody knows <u>why</u> they're here.

E: Yeah. The Black Panthers are saying, "What the fuck am I
doing here? And it wasn't <u>me</u> who built the cage; it was
somebody else."

S: Hmm . . . (P) . . . I guess the thoughts that run through
my mind is not blaming people or accusing them for the presence of this cage. But rather looking at it and saying,

"We are all in a cage." And if I look at it in a way that
"Gee, it was the white man who built this cage," then I
have to ask myself, "Who built the cage for the white man?"
And not just seeing one side of it. I mean, does that explain it?

E: Yeah, it's a fine answer. That is one of the really nice
things about interviewing you. We don't end up caught in
my categories; we get how the world is for you. So, thank
you (laughs).

S: Well, that's, ah . . . (LP) . . .

E: I was thinking after the last interview, you must be pretty
well known around Harlem.

S: Um-hmm.

E: (Chuckles) Are the Panthers or any political groups pursuing you?

S: Well . . . when I was in New York, my mind was somewhat politically oriented. I wasn't so much into this black-and-
white thing. I was basically concerned with the present
situation, which was addicts, gang fighting . . . (P) . . .
and better life for everyone who was around me. Not politically, but more socially and financially, and emotionally.
And I managed to start all kinds of, you know, social
groups and . . . (P) . . . they were directed in those
areas. And when I came to the West Coast . . . (LP) . . .
I met a fellow much older than I who used to live in Harlem
with me. We knew each other, vaguely; I must have been
about 13. I mean, he wrote some really beautiful, beautiful poetry when he was there. And they had an effect on me.
And I guess his poetry was not like the poetry you read in
Shakespeare. Just plain, simple, Harlem life; all he knows
is Harlem. And when I met him up here his mind had changed.
He was into a Black Panther thing, which he introduced me
to, and I went to several meetings . . . (P) . . . and it
was so sad to read his new poetry, because it, it wasn't
the original him, it was somebody else. And it was more
like, hmm . . . (P) . . . "Black must live, Whitey must die,
pick up a rifle or a knife and stab him in the back." Just
a lot of hate, a lot of violence . . . (P) . . . and it
struck me when he was in Harlem, he was in worse condition
than he was here, and here he seems to be more frustrated,
more intense, and . . . (P) . . . and just angry at the
world, and at the white society. So that this was my first
introduction of political fighting. Going to several meetings and going to several clubs, and seeing that the young
kids are being prepared to kill. Opening up chains of restaurants, black cooperatives, and this sort of thing kind
of turned me off, because it gave me the feeling that we
are picking up the same disease that white society has.
They are actually trying to change the system in which they
can be on top and Whitey can be at the bottom . . . (P)
. . . And it would be a thing that would repeat itself from
generation to generation. Pretty soon, then, the white

people would try to conquer the black and it would just repeat itself. And I certainly don't like the system the way
it is, and I just don't believe that violence is going to
solve anything. I certainly do want to bring up kids in
this world, and if I can't, then I would like to adopt some
children and give them a chance to learn something. But I
don't believe that I should do it by means of violence, to
bring about this change this way. Or bring about the
change by separatism, because obviously separatism brings
about violence. And it seems like the Black Panthers are
striving for separatism and trying to establish a new society where they are on top, they are no longer on the bottom . . . (P) . . . And I just haven't found the right
group, or haven't because of that introduction. I am not
at all enthusiastic about taking the initiative and doing
something to help this matter politically. Because I don't
feel with the times today and what's going on, I don't feel
that I'm much help.

E: I was wondering whether you see something in your life
    that's leading toward a solution?

S: At the moment, I could say that . . . that I certainly
    wouldn't, ah . . . take either side . . . (P) . . . And I
    would say that I'm not preparing myself for anything . . .
    (P) . . . I'm sure there's something I can do. As a matter
    of fact, I'm doing a lot now, by just being me. And when I
    come in contact with any one of these particular groups in
    my life, I'll just give 'em the honest opinion, which is
    that I am me. That I am not Black Panther, that I am not
    in this society, and that I'm not going to contribute to
    this.

E: Yeah, I was just sitting here thinking, "That's a damn hard
    thing to pull off."

S: Yeah, it's kind of silly, because how can you say you're
    not going to live in this society when you are part of this
    society? I mean, if you don't swim you're just going to
    drown. It's a hard situation, to meet black people, and
    they treat me like brothers and they want me to help, and I
    just have to tell them that this is my head, that I'm just
    me. And it's pretty hard to walk in a white restaurant and
    not be served, and not being able to marry a white girl.

E: Can you tell me what that's like? I've never had that ex-
    perience.

S: I went in for a cup of coffee, with some white girls that
    were with me. The guy said, "I'm sorry but we're closed."
    So I went into another restaurant alone. And I sat there
    in the restaurant. And I sat, and I sat, and I sat, and I
    sat.

E: And how did all that feel while you were just sitting?

S: . . . (P) . . . I felt sorry for those people. I felt
    sorry for their lack of understanding of human life. I
    felt sorry that their love of life was so limited . . . (P)
    . . . And on the other hand, I understood that people who

don't know themselves react this way to foreign things.
And I couldn't blame them for what they were doing. So
the feeling in me was not a feeling of hatred or a feeling
uptight, but only feeling hopeless.

E: At age 13 you've got your gun in your hand, you must have
    been angry at some point in there. But maybe I'm wrong?

S: . . . (P) . . . Sure I was angry, I was angry at I don't
    know what (chuckles). And just . . . (P) . . . I know
    that when I had a gun in my hand I was out to kill a mother-
    fucker. I was out to hurt somebody . . . (LP) . . . I
    don't know what the fuck I was angry at, man. I was angry
    at everything, man. I get so angry so easily. Even with
    girls, I should be gentle and sweet, you know, but like
    when I dated girls and you know the girls would do some-
    thing that, that I don't know . . . (P) . . . wouldn't
    please me, I would smack her and give her a bloody nose,
    or just beat the shit out of her, you know, I just . . .
    And I remember so much _anger_, you know. It wasn't directed
    at one specific thing, I know that. I remember one time
    my mother said something to me and I picked up the chair
    and threw it at her. I could have _killed_ her; luckily, it
    didn't, you know . . .

E: And how did you feel after that?

S: I don't remember, I just felt like, _lost_, man, you know.
    I went up the hallway of the same building, I couldn't
    leave the building for some reason or another. I kept
    wanting to leave the building, but I just went up to the
    roof. And it was cold. And I collected all the garbage
    that was out in the hallway, and I started a fire in my
    building, the building my mother lived in. And I slept
    there. It was kind of a stupid thing--I could have burned
    that whole house. I could have burned myself to death.
    But I was just, I don't know, out of my mind, I suppose.

E: I'm wondering whether you said to yourself, "I'm grabbing
    hold, I'm taking over, I'm going to change things."

S: Hmm . . . (P) . . . (chuckles)

E: Oh, you're smiling, what's that about?

S: . . . (LP) . . . The time in which I . . . grabbed a hold
    of my life, and said, "Man, there's got to be a change" is
    yet to be determined . . . (P) . . . I mean that I'm chang-
    ing constantly; we are not aware of our changes because
    every environment influences me in many ways. And you're
    just not aware of it. Every people you meet. When exactly
    was it that I felt that I wanted to give love to people and
    in terms I wanted to accept love--is something that I've
    always asked myself. That's where I stand now, you know,
    that I'm just doing my thing--I don't believe in violence,
    I don't believe in prejudice, I just do my thing. When I
    was young, it was just _hate_, destroy, I mean the hell with
    love. I guess when I was a kid I never knew what love was,
    or I never knew what compassion was, and I never knew ten-
    derness for other human beings. I'm trying to think of who

was the first person who--I think Peggy . . . (the first
Peggy) . . . (P) . . . Funny, why I don't mention my mother
. . . (P) . . . There's a lot of things about the relationship between my mother that I want to know about and I don't
understand. Anyhow, that's something else, I suppose. But
Peggy was like a mother image is supposed to be . . . (P)
. . . And I was, like hurt, in many ways with her. She hurt
me because she developed a sensitivity. She made me look
at my . . . (P) . . . possibilities of being affectionate,
thoughtful . . . and yet maybe she didn't, because you
can't make a person . . . (P) . . . I felt hurt when she
left. I felt hurt every time I went to her mother's place
and she wasn't there (sighs) . . . (P) . . . I got on a
train maybe for the first time and went all the way out to
this strange suburb and find out she's not there. I did
that over and over and finally I just gave up. So I learned
that, one has to be not depending on somebody for love.
Just loving people and not expecting it back in return . . .
(P) . . . And George like . . . (P) . . . he needed me, I
can see that, and I also needed him. I suppose a father
figure. So we kind of, gave a lot to each other. Ah . . .
he was a very vicious man with his tongue and his mind. He
was a jealous homosexual . . . or a jealous father.

E: Like, how is it that he's a father figure?
S: I really don't know, man (laughs). Except, maybe, I just
. . . (P) . . . I wanted to learn more about the white society. And we were very close friends, you konw, and . . .
(P) . . . (sighs) . . . and I told him I wanted to learn
about the white society . . . a father helps you learn.
And there were times when he was like, I mean, a real father
--the cat went out and bought me clothes. When I had problems we sat down and we discussed them. When he had problems I listened to him. This bothered me . . . I was a son,
you know. I went to school; he made lunch for me. Ah, he
introduced me to all his friends as his son. He was a director and producer of plays. And he knew a lot of theater
people. (Fred assumed George's last name while living with
him.)

E: And then you changed again--you said, "No, I'm not going to
go that way either."
S: So I don't know what happened. You see, the relationship
was nice with him. And he was supporting me. And at times
I would get a job and support myself, 'cause I felt kind of
bad taking the cat's money. He comes home and argues about,
you know, our living situation and our financial situation,
and I saw him working too hard for money, and all he'd
talked about was money . . . (P) . . . And I was taking
dancing classes and a science course in school which I liked.
And going to psychiatrists and that sort of thing . . . (P)
. . . And then, I just grew out of that whole situation.
We argued a lot frequently, and he was very stubborn, and I
was very stubborn. I would say I'm going out to see a girl
. . . (P) . . . sometimes he would say, "It's OK," you know,

fine. And sometimes he would say "No." When girls were
in the apartment with me . . . (P) . . . I can see that he
just didn't like it. I was never doing very good in school
since I started. The first year at school, I wasn't dating
anyone, not going out. Occasionally I would go to see
one of the plays he produced, or I would go out to dinner
with one of those rich people that he knew . . . ah . . .
and I didn't have any friends. And it just got too much.
I started to just fall asleep on the books, and couldn't
keep my head straight, and I kept doing every conceivable
thing I could think of doing other than studying. Started
dating girls, and seeing more girls, and getting into
dancing and everything else. And the first year when I was
failing all my courses I was really depressed for a long
time . . . (P) . . . I got tired of him supporting me, I
got tired of . . . of being given an allowance, and being
told when to go out and when not to go out . . . (P) I
just got tired of school, of studying and not getting anywhere . . . (P) . . . So I kind of used George, in the
sense that he let me know what the white society could be
like. My first introduction, living with white people,
and mingling with them, and with money, theater people,
and a very, very materialistic world. And . . .

E: And, was it Peggy that was the next step?
S: Yeah, then came Peggy (the second). Somehow, it all seems
to happen the same way, you know, when I first met George,
it was because I had an argument with Roberto. And when I
had an argument with George, Peggy came into my life. Actually, I had known her before that. What happened was
that . . . ah . . . I was going through the halls of the
school when I heard the guitar of a friend of mine. I went
over into the room and I noticed she was playing. And I
didn't know it was any class. It was a teacher, but I
didn't notice it too well--I was more concerned with the
guitar, the sound. And then I started playing. Sort of
improvising something, putting my own words to it. And
suddenly the teacher and I started staring at each other
spontaneously.

E: And the teacher was Peggy?
S: And wow, yeah. She was really, really beautiful . . . (P)
. . . it was just the time for it to happen, I suppose.
And I was seeing a lot of other girls . . . hmm . . . but
that was just really wham, you know, just looking at Peggy
. . .

E: How did things get going between you after that?
S: Well, I didn't see her for a week after that. And I was,
you know, with George and still not getting along . . .
(LP) . . . There were times also, way back in the relationship, where I threatened to leave . . . (LP) . . . And I
didn't want to go back to Harlem. If I was that uptight
about the situation, I would just leave. And there was
one day way back when I just packed up all my suitcases

and said, "This is it, I'm going back."

E: Was it a nasty scene?

S: Yeah, we barked at each other. There was never any violence. Well, anyhow, I hadn't seen Peggy for a week, and
then one day she just happened to walk into the school going
the same time I was. And she came over and she said, "That
was very nice playing on the guitar." And I don't know
where my head was at, but I said, "I'm sorry, you've got
the wrong person." I didn't recognize her, I didn't know
who she was. Literally, I just couldn't remember her.
Ah . . . 'cause we never spoke, you know, it was just that
we just looked at each other, or I looked at her . . . but
anyhow, she stood there a half hour nagging me (chuckles)
about trying to recall the whole thing (chuckles). Because
so many things had happened that week, you know. But inside of me I knew that there was a person in that building
that I had had an emotional experience . . . (P) . . . And
then somehow after that half hour of, you know, going back
to the songs, I said "Oh yeah," but not meaning it, you
know, not really meaning it. I just got tired of listening
. . . (laughs) and then . . . (P) . . . Somebody said,
"Fred, there's trouble in the office," 'cause I had my own
office in the school, the Awake office, the narcotic group
office. And I said, "Why don't you come into my office, you
know, when you have the time, and we'll talk about it. Ah,
I have to leave now." And that was it. And she came back
later, and said, "Is there anything I can do for your work?
I'd really like to help?" I mean, she wasn't going to give
up (laughs). And I looked at her again, and she kept talking, and suddenly I felt that same feeling.

E: Oh, it just sort of hit you, like you had the experience
again?

S: Yeah. I wanted to just put my arms around her. And suddenly she stopped talking and we just stared at each other . . .
a long time . . . (P) She's so beautiful. Ah . . . (P) . . .
then I had to ask her to leave because I had a meeting with
some young addicts, and I thought it would be a little too
rough for her to be there. And I didn't see her for a week
again. And then one day I was giving a speech to the facul-
ty, parents, and student body . . . and some important
people from different Awake clubs, and . . . (P) . . . I've
been in the theater before, I've been on stage, so I don't
get that feeling of shakiness talking to a lot of people.
So I just got up there, and I felt, ah . . . (P) . . . somehow she was out there, and I looked at her and I freaked.
I really freaked. Like, ah, I forgot what I was talking
about. The whole room was silent for maybe seven minutes or
something . . .

E: What was going on with you? (Chuckles)

S: I didn't want to feel that now, whatever it was, because it
wasn't the time to feel. You know, like I stared at her,
and it was, I felt good and yet, you know . . . it threw my

whole chain of thought away. I didn't know what I was doing, and what I was supposed to say, and what these people
were doing here, and why the hell was I up there (laughs),
and yet it was a good feeling because I saw somebody I
liked. I don't think she was controlling me, I've met a
lot of girls that have tried to start a relationship by
certain looks, certain come-ons, that sort of thing. But,
you know, this time I felt it wasn't that way. So, after
I finished my speech she came out, and . . . (P) . . . and
we just looked at each other. And she gave me her phone
number. She said she was sorry she can't stay because she
has an appointment, but she would like to speak to me . . .
(P) . . . Anyhow, five days went by after that, and I did
want to see her, so I called her after school, and she said
that we can make a date to see each other after school the
next day. And the next day, I didn't come out in time.
She wasn't there. So I called her at home. It was going
to rain, so she said, "Come on over" to her place; she had
some kittens, and, you know, we can talk. And I asked her
to dance. All the while I was feeling kind of, you know,
like here's a schoolteacher and, ah, what am I doing,
'cause it's, you know, kind of strange. But I embraced her
and it felt so great, you know. And suddenly I just turned
her face and I kissed her. That sort of feeling . . . (P)
. . . And then before you know it we were in bed. It was
just all in a matter of minutes. And then I stayed over
that night . . . (P) . . . And I stayed over the next night
. . . (P) . . . And I stayed there forever, and I didn't
have sex with her, I mean when I said we went to bed. I
mean we just lied in bed together. And I kissed her . . .
(P) . . . and went through a lot of physical things, but we
didn't have any sexual contact, and I was living there for
maybe three or four days . . . Then, like after not seeing
George for a while, you know, he was worried, 'cause every
time if I would stay out one night he always wanted me to
call. And I never stayed out during the week. So . . .
(P) . . . (sighs) . . . he notified the school counselor
and told him to give me a note if I was in school or not.
So . . .

E: Let's see, this was last year, right?
S: It's not even a year ago--four months, maybe . . . (P) . . .
And then one day I . . . (P) . . . I asked Peggy if she
could lend me some money so I could get my own apartment
and get a job, and then pay her back . . . (P) . . . 'cause
somehow I sensed that I wouldn't, I couldn't, see her again
if I lived with George. And I wanted to see her because I
loved her very much, or I felt I loved her at the time.
And so I went over to George one day and I told him that I
was going to move. And as I was saying it, I noticed that
tears came to my eyes. I started crying. And he gave me
a whole lecture about "You're going to go back to Harlem,
and it's going to be the same old, it's going to be this girl

you say you like, it's going to just destroy you, and she
probably just wants to marry you, and she probably just
now and then needs someone. That's a way of escaping from
reality. You don't want to go to school. You'll avoid
the responsibilities of growing up and facing life." . . .
(LP) . . . And he says, "You're not ready to be a man yet,
but if you want to leave, I can't hold you." . . . (P)
. . . I knew he was hurt, and I know that he wanted me to
be there. So I came by occasionally to see him . . . (P)
. . . 'Cause I, I guess, I did like him. 'Cause he . . .
and . . . (P) . . . he made me feel like I owed him something. And I guess I did, you know. He supported me. He
helped me to learn about this world. I guess I never
thought of the fact that I have to give him something . . .
(P) . . . Anyhow, it was sad. Going to see him all the
time, and then I didn't see him after that. He kept saying
that the door was always open for me, that I can still live
there if I wanted to, and I didn't have to go to school.
He said the reason you're going to school was because you
wanted to go to school, and if you stop going to school tomorrow, it's fine with me. You just have to go out and get
a job, and be a man and support yourself.

E: Sounds like it makes you sad when you think about it.

S: One time he was really flustered, I suppose, and upset. I
told him who the teacher was and I told him what was happening; I just wanted to be honest with him. And he went
to school one day, and . . . and found out where Peggy was
teaching. And he went up to see her, and ask her when she
has time if she would talk to him. He told her that she
didn't know what she was doing. That I was a very immature
boy, and I needed help. I needed help desperately, that my
psychiatrist said to him that I was a very sick boy. And
that I should see him right away. You know, I was going
through some heavy, heavy changes and that I needed to see
him. And I stopped seeing my psychiatrist. And, ah, it
went on and on, and I suppose it got to a point where she
said to him that she loved me. She said she didn't bend my
arm and . . . (P) . . . and he said, "Well, I want you to
tell Fred to come back and to stay with me, because I can
help him, because I know him better than you know him. I
know he's trying to avoid responsibilities." And she said,
"I can't tell him that. It's not up to me. I think Fred
is old enough to know what's right and what's wrong, and if
he runs away from responsibilities, I can't tell him not to,
I'm not his mother. I just know that I love Fred." And he
said, "Well, OK, if you don't give him back to me, now,
this very moment, if you don't promise to me that you'll
throw him out of your house, then I'll go to that school
and tell the principal what you're doing to him, and I'll
see that you lose your job." And he marched right into the
school and told the principal that he should have that
teacher fired, because she was not helping me. You know,

I had a very good relationship with the principal, because
they made an exception, and they treated me with care.
They knew that I was too old for that school, and I was
far behind; I was not even junior high school material,
and I was in a high school. They were giving me special
attention in the school, special help, and I was in the
College Preparation Program, and they were helping me.
Peggy came home, just terrified. And for hours and hours
she was just crying in bed. And she said he destroyed her
whole career, he destroyed her whole life. She said,
"This is what I always wanted--to teach school," and he
just came over and just destroyed it.

E: So the principal had fired her?

S: No, no, but she knew that that would happen. You know,
because teachers are just not supposed to do that. I felt
really mad, and really hated him--not hated him, but I
pitied him, I supposed. You know, 'cause he just hurt this
girl that I loved. I suppose he was jealous, you know,
that was why. But I just didn't like the way he handled
that. And the next day the principal sent for me. So . . .
(P) . . . ah, I was honest and I said, "Yes, I did. I am
living with a teacher. And . . . (P) . . . and I'm in
love with her." What could she say? Something about,
"Well, you know, that's not a very good thing for a teacher
to do. You could get kicked out of school and she could
lose her job." And I said, "Yeah." I said, "Well, I want
to see her and I don't think she will." And she said,
"Well, you know, it isn't that bad, actually." She was
very good about it. She even said, "I can understand your
situation because I fell in love with my professor in
school. And I married him when I was a student and I married a teacher. So I can see how it's possible" (sighs).
And on the last day of school, Peggy and I saw her. We
were leaving the school together for the first time, 'cause
she had never seen us together, you know, in school. We
kind of hugged her and had a very warm moment together,
and she said, "I wish you both the best of luck for your
life." . . . And I never saw George again, never spoke to
him, just never wrote to him, just never called him . . .
(P) . . . So Peggy and I one day were just talking, and
she said something about she's always planning to go to the
Orient. For ten years she's been studying the culture.

E: She was into Zen?

S: Yeah, I guess she had a special interest in Oriental culture. She had a lot of books and things, and she was studying the language, and she was going to a tea-serving
school. She listened to a lot of Oriental songs. And this
is all a whole new thing for me, you know. I didn't know
anything about this whole thing. She said if I would like
to go. And I said, "Gee, I would have to work." I'd have
to get some money. So I went looking for jobs, and I
couldn't find any. And one of her friends told her about

S: a charter plane that was going to the Orient round trip
    for $400, or something like that. And she had some money
    saved up, and she said she would pay my way, she would
    loan me the money and we could go together. And I said,
    "OK!" You know . . . (P) . . . And we went to the Orient,
    and we had a horrible time.
E: A horrible time?
S: I don't know exactly how to explain it. Except that we
    were nagging each other and getting in each other's way.
    And arguing a lot, real arguing. She's always been the
    jealous type, for one thing, and I seemed to be attracted
    to a lot of Oriental girls while I was there (chuckles).
E: You were attracted to them, or they to you, or both?
S: Both. They were pretty, and I was just, you know . . .
    they would look at me and smile, and they wanted to take
    photographs with me, and things like that . . . and I
    couldn't say "No." And many times she resented, like we
    would split up. And Oriental kids, they just wanted to
    practice their English. And I seemed to attract a lot of
    the girls, and she seemed to attract a lot of the boys.
    I just never got uptight about it, but she did. And maybe
    there were times when I just looked too much and made her
    feel that she was not there. That could have been possible.
    And anything that went on, she would and I would bitch
    about it. But it was a very good, a very important point
    in our lives. Because it helped us to know about the
    bitchiness that we can have toward each other. And that
    brought us closer to each other. Because I can see that
    with her friends she's not like that with them. This
    bitchiness and this stubbornness never comes out with her
    friends, but it came out with me. And I, maybe I triggered
    it.
E: When did you make the decision to come to California?
S: (Sighs) . . . Well, somehow, I didn't want to come back to
    New York . . .
E: Was that Harlem you're not going back to, or New York in
    general?
S: New York in general. And she also, I guess we looked at
    the chart and the plane was landing in California. And so
    somehow we both said, "Gee, I guess it would be nice to
    stay in California for a while." . . . (P) . . . And I
    was kind of scared, because it was, you know, a foreign
    place, and I didn't know what it would be like. But I
    said the hell with it, I'll try it, you know. 'Cause there
    was nothing going on in New York, anyhow, except my parents
    were there, my parents--my mother and my sisters (sighs).
    And ah . . . she said, you know, I can stay with her at
    the Zen Center. And we did for the first day, and I stayed
    there for three weeks. And her parents had come into Cal-
    ifornia on a vacation and . . . (P) . . . Peggy went with
    her parents, and I stayed at the Zen Center alone.
E: How is it with you and Peggy now?

S: There's the parent situation. I certainly don't want to
    make her life miserable, because her parents can disown
    her, and her parents mean an awful lot to her. And I
    don't want to make her choose between her parents and my-
    self. Because that seems like that's a very hard decision
    to make--being so attached to your parents. I guess at
    times I become very selfish, and I say, you know, "You're
    going to have to marry your parents. But don't worry, you
    know, you're still young, there's possibilities (for other
    men). You're only 34 or 33, or what is it . . ." (chuck-
    les).

E: That reminds me, in the first interview I said "fight" and
    you said, "You mean fuck?" And I am interested in when
    sex started for you.

S: Sex started, I guess, maybe . . . (P) . . . when I was 13,
    14? Any physical thing like that started at that time.
    And I guess I was in the alley with a bunch of friends,
    guys, and somebody started masturbating. Is that how you
    say it--masturbating? Ah, and I tried it, and I thought I
    was going to die. Man, all that stuff coming at me, God I
    almost freaked. And then I started thinking of girls,
    "Gee, I wonder what girls do!" And there was this colored
    chick that lived next door, and one day her mother wasn't
    home. And I just started touching her body, and she was
    just sitting there, scared. She was liking it, but she
    didn't know what to do--she was too young. So I did it
    with her, you know. That was the first time . . . (P) . . .
    And it felt good. I didn't think much about it, it wasn't
    a big thing. I was so involved with fighting at the time,
    I didn't care so much about it . . . . So every now and
    then, I suppose, there was a chick that was drunk, or some-
    thing . . . (P) . . .

E: It's my impression that you regard yourself as a man, with
    your interests in girls.

S: I also had homosexual experiences, and I didn't care for it
    . . . . It was something I was curious about; it just didn't
    impress me. There were times where, a lot of George's
    friends, and a lot of other people around then whom I met
    gave me the eye, the come-on look and phone numbers and all
    that. No, not for me . . . (P) . . . and I just told them,
    we just don't have anything in common. I just feel that,
    because, sure, I like men, but not sexually. I can hug a
    man, and I can kiss a man . . . and love a man . . . but
    not sexually. . . . (P) . . . That's the way it went.

E: This is switching to another track, but it's something that
    I had intended to ask you about: religion. I take it that
    you had some relationship to Catholicism at some point.

S: What is Catholicism?

E: The Catholic Church.

S: Oh, yeah. Why do you say that?

E: Because you're Puerto Rican.

S: . . . (P) . . . My sisters went to school, and I guess a lot

of friends were into this Catholic trip, you know. My mother was never into it. She was into a hallelujah trip,
whatever that is, Spanish church, or something.

E: Oh, it was one of those little churches?

S: Yeah, where they play some, what do you call it, tambou-
rine, or something, and then they get up and have fits
. . . (chuckles) weird trip . . .

E: Did you ever go with her?

S: I went there a couple of times with her, when she felt well
enough to leave the house. She got very attached to it for
a while. And I didn't like it.

THIRD INTERVIEW (APRIL 1972): SEARCHINGS FOR IDENTITY

(This interview, occurring a year and a half later, was
the first of three carried out by the woman professor of psychology who was in charge of the study. Asked for his views on
resuming the study, Fred expressed a continuing feeling that it
was somehow "unreal" and "funny" for her to pay to listen to
him "rap." He stated several times that he would like to see
the manuscript. He enjoyed inventing pseudonyms for his family
but thought disguises unnecessary: "What could happen?")

E: The last time I saw you, you were thinking about finishing
high school.

S: Yeah, I went through an adult high school, and I was not
accepted to a regular high school because of my age.   I
was carrying a lot of classes, and I did very well: A's
and B's. I was accepted at City College and spent a semester there. This summer I just decided that I was not gonna
go through it.

E: You mean . . . ?

S: . . . (P) . . . I don't know what I mean by "go through it."
I guess I just reached that peak where I've just had enough
education of that nature for a while, and there's so much
other education that's in my mind, curiosity is going elsewhere at the time . . . just mainly that they stress job
security or also for status security in the society.

E: You said you found some other form of education that meant
more to you.

S: Ah . . . (P) . . . well, I don't know if it means more,
it's just that I guess it's where my curiosity lies at the
moment. But, this other thing that I mentioned, this nature, the country, people from that environment . . .

E: Who live in the country and who are close to nature.

S: Yeah. I've never seen very much of the ocean. So I'm
spending some time near the ocean and studying what a star-
fish is and rainbow trout and fishing . . .

E: You are fishing?

S: Yeah. Caught one fish just last week (chuckles). But,
anyhow, there's just so much beauty and so much to discover

and learn about and the people who have been doing it for
a while, who live their lives just by growing things on
their land, not going to the local drugstore or supermarket
or whatever, and milk their cows . . . build their houses
and communes.

E: Hmm. So are you in a commune with people?

S: Well, I'm living in several communes, actually; I go back
and forth for almost a month now. The one I'm staying in
is a very small commune. It has a sort of a religious
orientation to it, but there are others. In another commune people constantly moving in and out and experimenting
with drugs. And sharing a lot of what they find somewhere
else and bring it back. And it's sort of constant change
of people, whereas in the commune that I'm staying in,
there's a set group there that stays for a while. And then
there's a musician commune there . . . where a lot of musicians go and express themselves through music.

E: I hadn't heard much about your interest in music before.

S: I've always been interested in music and not been able to
express anything with an instrument. Maybe it's just I
haven't had the time, busy doing other things. Occasionally I've met people with a guitar, and I'd pick up the
guitar and strum here and there and I've enjoyed it.

E: I am wondering about the religious part of this commune that
seems to be meaningful to you.

S: . . . (LP) . . . (Sighs) . . . The things that I've discovered through visiting those communes, there are a lot of
communes there that are just total chaos. In organizing
things, there's just no way of doing; the people are not
cooking or not taking care of gardens or not milking cows
or not feeding goats . . . (P) . . . And a lot of people
that I've encountered say, "Well, that's freedom"--not doing, you know, doing whatever you want! And . . . that
philosophy is beautiful, but I also see where somehow
there's no communication within that freedom because they're
all speaking different dialogues and somehow trying to say
the same things in different ways. And not being listened
to. Whereas, in a religious commune there's some form of
discipline, in a way. There's some unity. There is that
freedom where if you don't feel like milking the cow you
just don't do it; if you don't feel like cooking supper you
just don't do it. Somebody else will do it. But at least
you know that that's what you will do--generally . . . (LP)
. . .

E: So that even if you don't feel like milking the cow at that
moment . . .

S: Someone will come by and see that the cow is not being
milked, and they will do it. Well, everybody knows how to
do basically everything on the farm, and everybody's teaching each other. There's not one person that specializes in
one thing--carpentry, or gardening. We all are learning
together. And as you wake up you feed yourself, you think

of the chickens (laughs), and you realize that they need to
be fed, too . . . (P) . . . It's sort of oriented in a Zen
religion way. It's sort of the same thing, which is to
become aware of your environment so that you become aware
of yourself. And I think this is what they're doing there.

E: Thinking back about it, where did the idea come from to go
from city school life to the ocean and farm?

S: . . . (LP) . . . I had a friend, who I met in . . . (P) . . .
in the city, a girl friend named Deanna, who was doing
meditation. And I think she went to somewhere like a farm.
She met a group of people who just did meditating without
speaking for 100 days, and just . . . (P) . . . And she
wrote back and told me about her experiences and I just developed a curiosity. Some who go to City College have been
out in the country for a while.

E: Had you been into much meditation and Zen before you went
to this commune?

S: Ah, yes, I have . . . (P) . . . Me and Peggy in New York,
she sort of introduced the way of Zen into my life. It's
all a different thing than I never heard of. And for the
longest time I couldn't understand what she was talking,
what Oriental culture was all about. Until I went to the
Orient and finally understood.

E: When you and Peggy came back from the Orient, you continued.

S: Yeah, we continued sitting at the Zen Center in California.
And we met people who were interested in Zen, and so we
lived in a Zen commune house in the city for ah . . . (P)
. . .

E: When you first came back from the Orient you got into this
Zen Commune. What was that like?

S: I don't know. I didn't stay long. I was looking for a job,
anything that was available. I needed food and shelter. I
figured it would be much easier to get a job in the big
city, and sure enough, I found a job painting houses.
Scraping paint off these old houses, painting them for people I know. People at the Zen school. I got an apartment;
I lived in the Spanish district. It's kind of like a . . .
(P) . . . a Spanish slum, sort of, but very suburban
(laughs), Spanish suburban. All the Mexican people go
there, and Filipinos.

E: Now that's the first time you'd come back to a Spanish-
speaking area?

S: I moved in with a woman who was Puerto Rican, ah, and we
had a few talks about her life and my life and her family
and my family.

E: When you talked about your past and your family with someone who could really dig that, how would you describe your
mood?

S: Well, by then, actually, having moved away from that Harlem
trip, and having gone to the Orient and having to experience
different cultures than my own, gave me more an open mind
that there are other worlds than just mine, my own little

culture, my own little Puerto Rican gang, there are other
gangs. And I was able to adapt to their ways. So when I
spoke to this lady, I was not identifying with her as she
is Puerto Rican, and, wow, that she's my race or my blood
and that she knows something that I know. But it was rather, you know, talking a tongue that I once spoke. And
it was good to hear it again. I remember times when I
was using certain Spanish dialogues, and I would get flashes
of the places where I used it in Harlem, and . . . but ah,
somehow I just through all of this Zen, and through all of
the Orient and through all of Peggy and California, I was
able to detach myself from all that. I was able to realize
that I was different, that I was not, that I was a changing
being. So having spoken to her was interesting, because I
learned that about myself. I learned that "Gee, there's a
race I once knew, and I still know, but at one time I would
say, 'My race and my people.'" And now I just see it as
people. And not as a security thing, not as a way of identifying myself with them to protect myself as I used to.
Accepting ways, accepting all ways, accepting all kinds and
all things without, without labeling wrong or right. Without expectations . . . (P) . . . or rather just looking
. . . (P) . . . and accepting by looking, listening, and
feeling. If I see someone in the street who is in pain or
in the desperate need for something, it's not as though I
would stand by and watch him die and say, "Well, I accept
you dying, man," you know. It's not that I'm separating
myself from what is in front of me. It's not that I'm not
having any feelings when I say I am just looking at things
without forming an opinion . . . (P) . . . It's just that
a lot of suffering is caused by mind, and people's minds
. . . and uh . . .

E: I wonder what you would do, say, if the people in your
    house are angry about something. You wouldn't label it as
    right or wrong? How do you decide what you want to do, or
    maybe you feel that you don't have to do anything?

S: Hmm . . . (P) . . . Ah . . . I first, I thought, that when
    I went there I didn't know what it was all about, and I was
    just a lot of the time observing, and now . . . (P) . . .
    I am getting into conversations with anyone. People would
    ask me, you know, when a crisis was up, you know, what do
    I think; was he a bastard or was he not, you know?

E: Yeah (chuckles).

S: Ah, some of them were upset because I didn't give them an
    answer . . . (LP) . . . There's not much I can do because
    I was there part of learning how to accept.

E: And so, in the position of learning how to accept them, you
    decided you didn't want to give an opinion?

S: Yeah . . . (LP) . . . I decided that I didn't want to . . .
    even though I did have an opinion.

E: So, right now there isn't any particular person that you
    are very attached to?

S: No.

E: You say, Peggy moved out of the commune. And how was that for you, personally--you two going your different ways?

S: We were always, I guess, in different ways. I was kind of attached to her in a way, but it was kind of, it was a very romantic thing at the beginning, as most relationships start off to be at the beginning, very romantic and extremely poetic in every sense. Sexual, emotional, and mental satisfaction. But . . . (P) . . . gradually, as time went by, I, not that I'd lost any feeling that I had at the beginning, it was still there, but I was learning to live with a new person other than myself, you know. Who was a lot older, in age and experience.

E: How much older?

S: She was 12 years older than I was.

E: And so that, learning to live with another person . . .

S: It was always, well, I'd lived with others . . . I did live with someone before Peggy, but it seems like living with another person, with different people, it's always different, it's not the same to me. There's so much that, the neuroses are so different that we have to adapt to each other's neuroses in different ways and share our what we are learning day by day. And I would go through a period of asking myself, "What am I doing with this other human being, what am I sharing, and what do I expect from her, what does she expect from me, and where are we going, you know, together?" She would talk of marriage, and I would be puzzled, because I don't understand what marriage is, to be; I don't, I just never considered it. And when I began to consider the possibility I knew that I was not ready for that at this point, or didn't even think that I would ever be--it just never interests me. Maybe eventually it will.

E: Yeah, but not for now. You spoke earlier about each other's neuroses?

S: I meant sharing each other's childhood anxieties, you know, and ways of looking at things . . . (P) . . . like, I would consider a neurosis something that someone would, cannot, well, different cultures--I don't know what I'm thinking of --well, what we would consider hang-ups. You know, my hang-up at the time was that I was very . . . (P) . . . aggressive with her--with Peggy. I had a very masculine attitude, wanting to be a master of women. And I didn't see her as an equal . . . (LP) . . . an equal in terms of mentality or whatever, you know, emotions. And it took me a while to be able to understand that she could do what I could do, I mean, that we could share our things together, that I didn't have to be dominant. And her background was that her father was very, very strict with her, and she has always been running away from any man that's strict. And so to her history of men, she has somehow gone through an awful lot of what you would call passive men that would allow her to always suggest and create the mood and take the initiative. And so

that neurosis, that sort of thing, crash or clash between
us, that was what I meant by neurosis, that we had to sort
of somehow deal with these neuroses to learn to live with
each other.

E: You learned to live with the clash?

S: Yeah, there are so many things I learned about that. My
. . . it was hard at first, but somehow I let her take the
initiative, and somehow it just worked out, and, you know,
where her suggestions were fine, and she realized that I
was very pushy at times and she accepted when I would somehow come out a little too strong because she realized that
where I was at from the beginning, before I met her, and
that's a thing that gradually she'd have to understand.
So that simple things like cook together, I would find that
as a woman thing, in the kitchen, and "Me, kitchen, cook?"
"Apron?" No way. But you know . . .

E: You did learn about each other that way, and made some
changes. What separated you?

S: I think what separated us was that we were growing in different ways . . . (P) . . . What made my curiosity go elsewhere, not in other women, it wasn't that, or that she was
interested, I guess, no, she wasn't interested in other men,
it wasn't that, it's just she was interested in school, in
psychology. And I guess . . . (P) . . . marriage, children,
and a stable life, but basically I think she was just doing
it to learn about herself through psychology. And applying
whatever she learned about herself. And also for credits.
I think she had been working on her California credentials
to teach at high school.

E: When she went that way, you went . . . ?

S: Ah . . . (P) . . . I went, I found a group of, well, I guess
that's when I gradually started moving out to the country.

E: Did that leave a vacuum in your life when you stopped living with her?

S: Ah, a vacuum?

E: I mean in the sense that you were living together, and then
she went her way and you were changing in different ways.

S: Oh, yeah, it created feelings to her. I was . . . we were
both completely emotional and physically shaken, shook, or
. . . (P) . . . moved in some way . . . (P) . . . We never
expected it. It was a gradual thing that was happening,
but yet when it happened it didn't seem gradual, my feelings were I met a beautiful person in my life, you know,
and I'll always respect her . . . (P) . . . But I wasn't
torn apart. I didn't lose control of self.

E: Your self-esteem didn't go down. I mean, you can accept
yourself in this?

S: It was just another thing to learn about myself. Yeah,
learning to accept that, breaking up with people. And in
her mind, I think basically, she was more upset than I was,
because I think she thought about a long-term relationship.
She spoke about marriage and children and security and home

and a job for myself, and . . . (P) . . .

E: And you're not thinking about that. Were you thinking
   about that then?

S: I <u>was</u>! I, actually, at times when I went to school I was
   thinking, "Oh, wow, I'm going to (laughs) probably make a
   lot of money some day and buy some land and buy a little
   house, and Peggy and I will retire and have lots of babies."

E: You thought about that briefly (laughs). So you realized
   that wasn't yourself?

S: Yeah, but somehow I tried to be careful not to accept and
   to . . . ah . . . (sighs) . . . shall we say commit myself
   to something that I would eventually make myself unhappy
   and make her unhappy because I couldn't meet the expectations that she created.

E: Yeah. I think I can understand that. Now you met Peggy
   when she was teaching in your high school. You had some
   kind of a special role in that school, you had an office,
   something called AWAKE. What was that?

S: That was, well, it was one of the dreams that I had. I
   was using drugs, and I was strung out for a while.

E: What were you like then?

S: What was I like? Hmm . . . it's hard to remember, different kind of life. It's kind of a nonreal vegetable kind of
   thing.

E: Nonreal, yeah.

S: No feelings, it's very cold . . . (P) . . . frustrated all
   the time. No, just, no feeling about the outside world,
   no awareness of anybody else existing other than myself.

E: And what were you aware of inside you?

S: Actually, just aware of my physical needs, but not of my
   sex needs and my habit needs, but not any feelings about
   . . . (P) . . . me as a leader or me as a punk, or anything
   like that. I was just being whatever happened.

E: You got really strung out, and you mentioned that that led
   to a dream, about AWAKEness . . .

S: Well, I guess I went through changes in meeting Harlem. I
   didn't want to go through the same thing I went through before, but anyhow I left drugs, and I changed my environment
   and changed my perspective and scene and went into different worlds, totally different worlds.

E: You mean down in the Village, was it? Was there any person
   connected with this moving and getting off heroin?

S: Yes and no. There was a girl named Peggy, another Peggy
   who had adopted me as a spiritual son, kind of thing; she
   introduced me to the Village; she was into heroin at the
   time, and she knew this guy I knew who I used to cop my
   drugs from, and she used to get drugs from him, too.

E: Yeah, what is the sequence here?

S: OK, the people I was living with . . . (P) . . . I met this
   old guy who had done . . . five years in prison for murder,
   and somehow we had similar backgrounds. His name was
   Roberto, and he was a gang leader, too, an old-timer. I

had left Peggy, and I had kicked the stuff cold turkey.
And then most of my friends were either shot or dead or in
prison or strung out, and well . . . (P) . . . people, some
people wanted me to go back into the same situation, and I
didn't see that I was the same person any more. And this
man who had come back from prison, somehow we happened to
meet in the street, he had a lot of money occasionally.
And he was very interested in working with the community.
He started talking about his community trip on me. And I
was very influenced by his talk. And that's when I started
doing something. About changing something, about expressing
other than through drugs or through violence. So I got a
few guys, a few people together who were not doing stuff
and somehow tried to control them and found it hard to influence them to join me in general in working in this new
gang called the Rescuers.

E: This new gang still had a sort of ganglike structure, but
it had other aims?

S: Yeah. So we went around to all the war counselors and all
the different gangs to see if we could sign a peace treaty.
And we had a big, big meeting one time--there was a lot of
hostility in the air, and it was hard to communicate; we
had frequent meetings, and gradually people would be there,
their rifles and guns on the table and not touch them
during the meeting--it was pretty good for them at that
time to do that! There was no way we could search anybody,
so that if there was ever any killing, you know, that could
have happened very easily. So there was that trust, eventually. And then gradually we got rid of the weapons somehow; we'd drop them in a box so we didn't have to look at
them on the table all the time.

E: This is a new gang called the Rescuers. What about your
old gang? Was the Imperial Tops still in existence?

S: At the time I was doing this, a lot of them were dead, or
in prison for robbery or for murder. A lot of them were
just strung out on dope.

E: So that your old followers were gone.

S: They were gone, yeah. But, then we formed a theater group,
eventually after that. We had meetings and we had dances
on weekends; it was kind of peaceful and social. And in
the theater group was, it was a lot of young kids were
there. I think what we started to do was to get the young
kids that are growing up, before they get into dope, before
they get into murder or robbery and bring them into a different environment, orient their minds in a different way
by introducing them to a theater group--something that they
can let out themselves, express themselves without using a
weapon or a gang.

E: How old were you at this time?

S: This was just about the time I met George, which is about
16.

E: So, when you were talking about "we" in the new gang, you meant you and Roberto?

S: Yeah. So we got the parents involved, and so the parents
would come down and watch the kids perform in theater
games. Or if any of the fathers had a car, they would take
us all on a drive somewhere around the block. So it was a
community thing, more or less, everybody had to take part.
We used a lot of forcing on the parents, a lot of demanding
from them . . . (P) . . .

E: Where were you living at the time?

S: I moved back to Harlem. I would go to my mother's occasionally, but I had a place where we had a sort of the club
house.

E: Roberto had gotten interested in this type of work after
his time in prison? Is that where he got his head turned
around?

S: During prison and during his probation time, when he came
out and had to go get jobs and things like that, and he had
to go out working with construction . . .

E: So Roberto was kind of getting old and settled. Was he
fatherly to you?

S: No, actually, he wasn't. In a way he was; he looked at me
as a little boy, and I resented that; I resented being
looked down at. But somehow I looked up at him, that's
probably why he looked down at me. He had a lot of scars
and a lot of anger and a lot of bitterness, and somehow it
seems that he had more than I had, not that he killed somebody and I killed somebody and that made us even, but . . .
he killed a lot more than I did, and he got away with it.
And he did some time, which was more time than I did. And
experienced a lot more. And I guess at the time age meant
more than the experience. So I looked up at him to his age
and through his experience.

E: Where were his bitterness and anger directed at this time?

S: It was directed in wanting to take an initiative to doing
something, actually. He just wanted to control something;
he wanted to become a leader again, but it wouldn't work
with violence. I think I could relate to what he was going
through because I had the bitterness and I had the anger
and I could see his uneasiness or his wanting to do something and feeling hopeless because there was nothing to do.
He knew that if he picked up a gun again that was it, because he's going to kill somebody again. And he would probably get the gas chamber or something, you know . . . (P)
He knew that there was no way out. He very much felt trap-
ped, and I felt trapped, and we could relate to that feeling of being chained down and not knowing where to go, and
either jail or fighting, or, you know, what else is there?
Drugs? We tried everything; we both did. And we just
couldn't get it on. There's just no way.

E: And so you got into a new kind of gang.

S: We hadn't really tried everything (chuckles). He decided
to put away his weapons and try to use his mind in reorga-

nizing the community. We tried that, which worked out;
that's the way it was.

E: Your interest in the theater, and improvisation, was that
something that Roberto brought about?

S: Something that came about from meetings. Actually, Roberto
didn't have any ideas of what should be done, but he did
have that feeling of frustration, of feeling trapped. So I
guess that came out of the meeting of consulates and presi-
dents of gangs. Why don't we just sit back and watch what
we can do other than what we're doing? And somehow we just
got tired of sitting back, and somebody got very comedian
one day and started making fun of somebody. Somebody
smacked him in the face, and they started fighting, and
that got to be very funny. And there was a lot of blood
and a lot of teeth knocked out, but actually it was a beautiful thing, because after it was finished everybody was
laughing and they enjoyed it. And nobody picked up rifles
or guns, and it built up a very theatrical thing where
people were expressing themselves. It was just kind of an
encounter group; they were encountering their feelings, and
expressing their feelings without completely destroying
themselves.

E: That violence can be funny! Yeah, it's a funny thing.

S: Yeah, once you can get them to laugh at what they are doing,
and see the humor in it, not take it all so serious, they
somehow detach themselves from it. And enjoy it, and realize that it's just all a joke. And that their whole life
is just a joke. That they are just playing this gangster
role (chuckles) and that they can change and become come-
dians!

E: So there became a kind of comedy theater?

S: Yeah. Basically that's what it was. A comedy theater.
Well, it originated from comedy, but we did a lot of heavy
drama, too.

E: Um-hmm. Where did you fit into this?

S: I played parts helping to stimulate ideas and sometimes
encouraging people that I felt had some problems in expressing. Yet they could, but they felt they couldn't. And I
would play roles in any part that anybody thought I could
play. I'd sing and dance and play an instrument, too.

E: Have you continued with any use of improvisation?

S: Ah . . . through my daily encounters (laughter by both).

E: But not in a theater!

S: No, but that's how I met George. He came by to watch the
group one day, and I figured that George had an Off Broadway
theater and it was available. We rented the theater and we
was doing plays there. It was available on certain nights,
and he liked the idea that maybe he would like us to come
over and perform for him.

E: So you were now on Off Broadway.

S: Yeah. And we had a lot of our family coming, leaving Harlem
and coming downtown and visiting the theater world. We

found a lot of people didn't go; there were very few families that would go out to see their sons and daughters
performing, but there were some.

E: Did you get some money, or was this just a chance to be in
theater?

S: Yeah, well, actually, it was a donation thing; people
would come in and give whatever they can. We used the
money for props.

E: And then somewhere along the road you moved in with George.

S: Yeah, and the . . . (sighs) . . . ah . . . (P) . . . then
somehow I just felt there was no need to be there any more.
I got to talk to George and went to plays. Roberto and I
and a couple of the other guys started rapping to him and
. . . (P) . . . and there was a lot of, a millionaire came
over and offered some money and, uh, to build a building
for us, and there was a lot of exchanging thoughts and
ideas with these newcomers and some financial deals. They
never worked out, I never felt that what I had done was
enough, I guess. That from there on they would take in
people from that one world, so they saw the world that I
had seen, but there was nothing more that I could show them,
because that was all I knew. A lot of them are still having
problems in expressing themselves. We all gradually started
going into different . . . the older ones got married, the
younger ones just continued on. Roberto continued with the
young ones.

E: So it stayed, but you moved on with George. You must have
been 18 by now?

S: Yeah, I was 18. I went back to school, and it was George
introduced the idea that he had a summer stock theater on
Long Island, and he offered me a job working there as a
production assistant doing miscellaneous things, as usher-
ing and occasionally stage managing. He had this big house,
and he offered it if I would like to spend some time with
him and I said "fine." One day I decided to go out and see
what it was all about.

E: Were there other people living in the house?

S: No, the house was used for actors when they came in, but at
the time it was empty, 'cause it was just about the time
the season for it to be occupied by the actors, so I went
there before the summer stock theater opened. Maybe I went
in with the intention of bringing the group out there. Actually, I don't know what the feelings were when I went out.
I don't question this, kind of very spontaneous, the offer-
ing of a job and it was a job.

E: Was that one of the first times that you got paid for something?

S: Well, I got paid for selling guns.

E: Yeah, I know (chuckles).

S: Yeah, that was the first time I got paid for doing that kind
of work. And . . . (P) . . .

E: George was a homosexual; you knew that from the very beginning?

S: Yes, yes, he was. It didn't bother me, because, you know,
    I was aware of it, and I think he was aware that I was
    aware.

E: And he didn't push you into any sexual activity?

S: No, he didn't. At times I was amazed, I was surprised, I
    was waiting. Like, any moment I knew it might happen, he
    might offer some . . . we lived together and we lived in
    separate rooms, shared the same rooms, sometimes cooked
    together and shopped together, and went to see plays to-
    gether. It was like a homosexual relationship basically
    without sex.

E: When you thought about it might come up, were you wary
    about it?

S: No, well, yeah, I was; I didn't know how I would react, I
    didn't know how I would tell him, "That's not my trip"
    without hurting. And there were times when I would ask
    him, "George, you know, why are you so like, kind, why are
    you doing this?" Because there were times when I found he
    would go out of his way to try to please me, like buying
    me material things, and offering me a lot of love and af-
    fection. But then gradually I understood that he needed
    to care for someone, he needed to let out this feeling of
    love and affection toward someone. And I guess he can
    find sex somewhere else, without having to care for some-
    one, and I guess that was one of his hang-ups, not being
    able to find them both in one, but he was able to find
    them separately, and I guess that made him function.

E: So you didn't feel that he was laying a trip on you at any
    time?

S: Uh-huh; actually, we were both needing something from each
    other. Because I was buying that experience of being able
    to live in a different environment, and being able to try
    to understand somebody with a different culture and values
    . . . (P) . . . And someone caught up in the theater busi-
    ness and with hang-ups, sexual hang-ups, and . . . (P)
    . . . just sharing his life for a moment. Yeah.

E: Did you think at the time that you'd like to be an actor?

S: I think that's what I was, at that time, actually, an
    actor. It's nothing that anybody, I mean, I guess we
    could all do that. A lot of junkies go through a lot of
    acting trips. When you're a hustler, you're a hustler;
    you play any role to get your bread. But George intro-
    duced a different type of acting, and once I realized what
    it was, I realized I didn't want to be that. I didn't
    become it, it really didn't interest me at all . . . (P)
    . . . And I remember George also saying at times, "That's
    really not your kind of life," and I'd say, "You know,
    that's right, it isn't."

E: Yeah. What did he think was your kind of life?

S: Hum . . . (P) . . . He didn't know. I knew that that
    wasn't it. I knew that whatever . . . (sighs), whatever
    happened that made me curious, that was my kind of curi-

osity, my kind of life, where I came from and looking at
the past and examining the past to where I am now, that
was my kind of life.

E: But not learning a role and performing it.

S: No. There was one time where he took me to a very, very
expensive private school. I think this is where I first
got interested in school. There were a lot of white kids
there who studied hard. He'd say, "Don't you want that
kind of life, isn't it nice to study, to learn so much from
books"; he would say, "So much you can do expressing yourself in writing," and he would emphasize that a lot. And
so I guess I kind of became very influenced by that, and,
thought of it as . . . well, ah, well, not trying the idea,
but I knew all the time that that's not where I was at.
Sure, I could go through high school, and get you A's and
B's. Is it going to teach me to deal with me? Eventually
talking to a lot of teachers in school where I went to high
school, and when I visited these university psychologists
that George took me to, I realized that a lot of these people were very shallow in what they had to say, that they
sounded very mechanical; they were all being somebody they
were not. They were all playing a part, taking a role, being an actor. Yeah. So anyway, I went to a school eventually when I moved into the city with George. Because I was
going to school, I was being his boy, in a sense.

E: What was it like?

S: Well, I was interested in biology; I was interested in
dancing . . . (P) . . . which I did very good, very well,
and performed in a couple of Off Broadway theaters with a
group of professional dancers, but I was just taking little
parts, and . . . the teacher at school helped me into this.

E: And that brings us to the high school where you had your
office called AWAKE?

S: Yeah. Spending a lot of time there, I realized that there
was a lot of heavy drugs there. See, the school was located between a section of minority groups and a white suburban section of New York. And a lot of the kids would get
hooked and then came to school, and sell their dope so that
they can keep their habit. And somehow I just developed
this dream that maybe there would be something that I could
do about it. So I decided to say fuck my classes and spend
my energy on that, on my dream . . . (P) . . . And . . .
(P) . . . I went and consulted the principal, and I told
him I was going to take over a room for that purpose. I
didn't tell him that I was dropping my classes, but that
gradually happened. And at the time the principal just
didn't know what to do about the drugs. And there were
kids who died at the school of overdose. So I took over
the building, not the building, the office (laughter), and
with the help of a couple of students from my dance class,
we bought some buttons that we pinned on our coats, saying
AWAKE. And we drew a lot of posters, and again I applied

my acting method of improvisation, acting heroin drug problems and how people start to use drugs and how the teachers
are, how the parents are, the pushers are, and the students
are, and all playing their roles. I got introduced to a
lot of people who had been working in rehabilitation programs, and they introduced me into ideas of encounter
groups and other methods of methadone and information of
where they can go.

E: Did the groups help the kids you were seeing?

S: Well, I thought it could be helpful, because I found that
a lot of people couldn't express their feelings. And again,
it also worked out in the theater thing, some people do
find that an encounter is a situation, and they have to
deal with them. And it helped because there were a lot of
kids who couldn't talk to each other and couldn't say "fuck
you" to each other and "I hate you" and would accept each
other, and some would break out and cry and feel all these
feelings, and . . . (P) . . . and then when it's over they
realize they got something out of it--they got moved in
some way. To be able to learn that that's what reality is,
that people are always knocking and how are you going to
react and if you can truly answer without being fucked up,
without panicking and without being destroyed. And a lot
of kids really broke down, completely broke down. Their
little games and fantasies were destroyed, because everybody, because everybody realized that they were playing a
game, and they told them that they were playing a game.
There were a few that the groups really helped their idea
of using drugs, so they went into some other form of cre-
ativity of expression. When I got involved with this AWAKE
thing I had broken up from George, because I was losing
interest in my studies. I had created a conflict in his
mind, because I thought that he thought that that was losing him, because that was what he had built me up to be.
And I guess maybe that's what I kind of built up for him,
by accepting.

E: And you met Peggy at that school and finished the year with
her. Did you start back in the fall at the same school?

S: There was no need in going back, since Peggy had lost the
job . . . (P) . . . So I was very much involved with her
life. She introduced me to Zen, and then I started meditating and . . . so I guess, my life was her life in a way.
I was experiencing something different again as I had been
doing and leading my life through experiences while adapt-
ing to new changes and new environment and so meeting new
changes again, and so did she--she couldn't find a job in
the city. The summer that I worked with George I had saved
a lot of the money. So we took off to the Orient on a charter flight, and spent some time there, and then we came
back here.

E: I guess you had a lot of understanding and ability to help
these young kids in the program AWAKE, because you'd been

through the drug scene. What did you think was going on
with you, how you got into heroin?

S: Yeah, I see what you mean.. . . . (LP) . . . well . . . (P)
. . . hmm . . . I don't know, actually. I mean, what I
was going through at the time that led to heroin was a lot
of fear and a lot of violence, basically. I couldn't relate to anything; I couldn't live up to an image. I
couldn't see any images of who I was or who anybody was,
except loneliness. And what was loneliness? At the time,
nothing but running and fighting from it, and fighting
with it, and . . . (P) . . . heroin was there before I was
there--so that was an image that I could live up to, to
those who were feeling what I was feeling.

E: Yeah, so there were real people you knew who were on heroin.

S: So I would have to play that act, at the 13-year-old stage.
I guess subconsciously what I was doing with the AWAKE
group was that--I was aware of myself. I guess I was, but
maybe not. I wanted to show them what the whole school
was about, so that they were able to look at it and could
laugh at it. At 13 years old, I was acting, but not aware
that I was acting and I was caught into an act.

E: You didn't have the perspective on it like you were showing
the kids? And yet you kicked cold turkey?

S: Yeah. There was this little old lady, where I lived in
Harlem . . . (LP) . . . a little old lady and a little old
man, wow, they were nice. They had a candy store. They
always liked me as a kid; I don't know why, and I hated
them. They were very nice people. I used to to and steal
their candy all the time. I remember hating them in the
sense I would tell everybody that they were horrible people,
and say, "Hey, let's go," you know, and somebody said,
"Well, don't steal from them, you know, they are your people," or something. So they caught me one time when I was
in a hallway, in the back alley where their candy store
was, and I was just going into a heavy stage of overdose,
and I was almost dying--God, I was, really, just whew!--
just really drowning in darkness it was--and they came over
and poured some cold water on me and dragged me into the
store and locked me up in the room upstairs and didn't let
me out. And I fought to get out, but they wouldn't let me
get out--they were smart. So they just let me kick there
for . . . I stayed there for about three weeks, actually.

E: How did you keep away from drugs from then on? You were
still a leader in the gang?

S: At the time, no, I wasn't. I couldn't handle it at that
time. I left and I went to the Village with Peggy--I was
dealing some drugs, too . . . (P) . . .

E: Peggy was helpful in staying off drugs?

S: Uh-uh! She was really strung out; she wasn't very cool
about it at all. She was very sloppy with her way of dealing with it--a very greedy little girl . . . (P) . . .

E: And what activity did you get into next?

S: I don't know, I didn't do all the things that I preached!
. . . (P) . . . Well, I had other girl friends in the Village I used to go see at the time, quite a few, just for
sexual purposes. Seems like I got into a heavy thing with
white chicks, you know. Just appealed to me, and I could-
n't get into a black chick or a Puerto Rican chick, or
Chinese, or whatever, you know.

E: You haven't really been with Spanish-speaking people for a
long time?

S: Yeah, and I'm amazed that I can still understand it. I
went back to New York this Christmas to visit my mother and
my sisters. And I was amazed that my sister would say,
"That's my mother and that's my sister," and she would
translate, word for word. And some translating was going
on some of the time when we got into discussions.

E: What is your mother like now? She was sick when you were
a little kid.

S: Yeah, she was sick, she spent most of my youth time in
hospitals . . . (P) . . . She had asthma and heart trouble
and double pneumonia, stuff like that, a lot of sickness.
It was all originally started from being in a different
environment and losing her husband.

E: You mean, coming from Puerto Rico?

S: Yeah. And then coming to New York and then separating and
not speaking English, and not having any jobs. She completely collapsed.

E: She lost her husband. He left after the last child, you
think, you were just 2? And she got sick from then on?

S: Hmm. From then on she was just ill.

E: At what age were you when your family was split?

S: Oh, God, I don't know, 'cause it was an on and off thing
when she'd go in the hospital and then she'd come back.
We'd get back together again and separate again all the
time. And finally, there was a state, I guess, maybe I
was . . . 5 or 6, something like that, I don't remember,
yeah, about I guess 5 or 6, where my grandmother couldn't
put up with me, 'cause I just didn't do anything she wanted
me to, and neither could my aunt. And there wasn't any
place for me to go! (Chuckles) So they wanted to put me in
a home. So the little old lady downstairs, who used to
take care of us when my mother was sick, she took me in.

E: For long?

S: For about two years.

E: But you were close, you were downstairs from your sisters
. . .

S: No, no, no, my sisters were in Brooklyn, and some of them
were in other suburbs of New York. So I didn't see them
after that.

E: And where was your mother?

S: She was in Harlem in the hospital.

E: What do you remember about your sisters? I know nothing
about your sisters.

S: Either do I! Just beautiful. When my mother came back to
Harlem, that's when it all started again, and I was more
able to deal with a sister and brother thing, I mean, when
we were young we were never together that much, so we were
never expressing or growing together. See, my own aunt
had four kids, and they were about our age too, and my
grandmother had two kids too, but they were a lot older.
So when I went to my aunt's house and stayed there for a
while, my cousins were just like my sisters and there was
nothing . . .

E: Um-hmm. Nothing really special about your own sisters because you hadn't been around them when you were very young?

S: And then they came back--two years later, around 7, around
8, I guess, and we started to fight a lot!

E: (Laughs) You fought, and you went to the same school.

S: No, I didn't go to school; I went, but they couldn't keep
me there. They sent me to an elementary school 'cause I
was a discipline problem. They put me in a reform school,
and they couldn't keep me there, so I ran away from that
(laughs).

E: It really was a state reform school?

S: No, it was in a city, a day thing. They had policemen as
teachers. You have to stand at attention in a line and
march all day, that kind of thing. It was a weird school
. . . whew!

E: So again you were separated, and you were in one school and
they were in a local public school. About discipline, you
mean running away; what else went into what was called a
discipline problem?

S: Well, beating teachers up, and what were the other things
I used to do? Taking fire extinguishers, or whatever you
call those things, and spraying them all around and taking
kids' food away and eating it up, and . . . (P) . . . starting a lot of fights during the gym times, and I was never
quiet during the time, and I would never salute the flag,
and I would always sit in the back and never let anybody
touch me.

E: I don't suppose there was anybody to touch you. Do you
think that was because you didn't let them? Did your grandmother and aunt want to hold you some?

S: I don't think so, no . . . (P) . . . They had their own
kids, and my aunt and my grandmother were sort of, they
were really strange about my mother's kids, you know. I
guess they had a thing; my mother had a battle with her
mother, you know, "That's not the right man, I told you so,
so it's your responsibility!" So she says, you know, "Well,
I've got my own kids to worry about, you had your own trip,
if you laid your eggs, you gonna have to sit on them, baby,"
you know, that kind of thing, which was cold. It's funny,
but then later on I became very affectionate with my sisters, one of my sisters, the next to oldest, Maria.

E: Where are you in the family?

S: I'm next to the baby, Rita, then Irma, Maria, and Carmen is the oldest. It seems like Mother had one every year.

E: And you and Maria could be affectionate with each other?

S: Yeah, we had sex together, actually, at the age of . . . 13? Oh, no, well, 12. I guess I didn't know what I was doing, but like I was experimenting with her body, you know. And the first time when I ever noticed a girl's body, I guess every boy sees his sisters.

E: How did that go over with her?

S: We still have a tremendous closeness, a tremendous tie. She's always writing. Because somehow I share some common bond that I can't really explain. Spiritual existence sort of thing. It's just too bad that she's married and has a child.

E: How do you see her? I was wondering if you see yourself as like any of your family?

S: Like Maria, I guess, very much like her. I guess that's why we have some kind of very close ties. She ran away off on her own. Well, I guess Carmen (the oldest) went too, the only two that went off on their own.

E: Maria writes to you about your life; what is her life like now?

S: She used to be very deep, but now she's very shallow with her life. She somehow wanted to follow in my steps. She bought a gun one time, and she didn't know what to do with it, and she was asking me what to do with it, and I turned her on to drugs, you know, to small drugs, cocaine, and stuff like that. She was around me a lot, you know, at the time, when I was dictating most of the meetings. Everybody there was sort of dating each other, that sort of thing. She was very, very attractive. So, a lot of the guys would just come up and want to spend some time with her.

E: When other guys came up, what did you feel?

S: I didn't feel anything. You know, it's her life.

E: It's her life?

S: At times I guess I would say, "Go away, sister," you know, (chuckles). Something like that, you know. And she probably prevented a lot of opportunities for me with other girls.

E: Yeah (chuckles). Any of the other sisters hang around the club?

S: No, well, Irma, the one who comes right after me . . . (next oldest). The youngest one, Rita, and Irma usually stayed at home with Mother. They would always do the cooking and baking and washing and bathed Mother when she couldn't move, fed Mother in bed, that sort of thing.

E: So, let's see, the one who actually did the cooking and taking care of mother was the youngest?

S: The youngest was too young for that, actually, but that was the one that Mother would give the affection to, and she needed to give affection to somebody, and there was nobody there but the youngest one, the baby. And Irma was the one

that was able to take care of Mother when she needed to be
fed and bathed. Carmen, the oldest, she was . . . I don't
know about her problems. She was always very withdrawn,
like Irma, in a way. Maria was very open-minded and ready
to do anything anywhere, and wanting to go out and see the
world and very curious. And Carmen was, but at the same
time, she wasn't very sure of it, I mean, she'd want to
stay home, that kind of thing. And then when she did go
out and got hurt or she somehow didn't find a place there,
she'd alienate herself in some way, and she went back home.
But then she'll come out again . . .

E: You say she had some problems but you don't know why?

S: Yeah. She still has them, a lot of withdrawing, you know,
a lot of . . . (P) . . . she withdraws a lot, she was never
open, she was never, you know, she never let anything hang
out, she never did . . .

E: Was she expected to, as the oldest, was she expected to do
more around the house?

S: Probably, I don't know. I don't know what trip my mother
laid on her, but I was never there . . . (P) . . . ah, I
guess I kind of influenced Maria and Carmen, actually. I
used to come home for meals, when they were having meals
(chuckles), and I would talk different from them and they
would learn everything from me, and they would, always
girls, you know, be curious, because my mother was always
keeping them around. But she couldn't do that to me, because I was always throwing chairs at her when she did,
and I almost hit her once with a chair . . . (P) . . .
Well, I don't want to get into that . . . (P) . . . I had
sort of influenced them in going out eventually because I
invited them to all the dances that I had with the clubs.

E: So in a way, you were their older brother? You were out
there, you at least had a little more experience under your
belt.

S: Not really. They had their own separate ways. They started going where I was going, which was my club and dances,
and until eventually they got involved in the Drama Club,
and . . . (P) . . . found other neighborhoods, other gangs,
other dances and other clubs, and met other boy friends.
That's when they started running away, meeting all these
other boys.

E: And so they finally left home for good?

S: Yeah. And then they got caught, and, ah . . .

E: As runaways?

S: Yeah. And school truancy, too, and got sent to the out-of-
state . . . women-young kids institution, or something like
that.

E: Was there any time you were locked up?

S: Yeah . . . (P) . . . used to have a lot of shoot-outs with
other gangs, and . . . (P) . . . one time I had a dance in
the club and once this guy from another gang got in. I

don't know how that happened because I usually have good
security. There was a shoot-out in the dance . . . (P)
. . . And it was planted from the other gang, so that the
minute the shoot-out went on, they would move in, through
the alleys and going through the basement. So that's where
I shot someone. In the alley . . . (P) . . .

E: And there was somebody there to turn you in?

S: . . . (P) . . . ah . . . (sighs) . . . I don't know what
happened, you know, it happened really fast--I shot the guy
and, I, ah, threw the pistol over the fence, and I grabbed
him and tried to bring him to the club. We always shoot
for the legs, and you know the guy's alive 'cause he starts
screaming . . . (P) . . . Well, oh, sometimes you run over
to see if he's conscious or something, if you have the
time. So I had blood all over me, and I ran for the club,
and then the cops moved in, and they picked me up. They
couldn't prove it, though. And I spent some time in the
state prison (an out-of-state prison).

E: I don't understand why out of state.

S: I don't know. They had a place there for junior, for young
kids, to do trial, or something, and so they shipped a lot
of us.

E: How old were you, Fred, at that time?

S: I must have been . . . (mumbles) . . . Really shook me
after that. I went into smack when I came out; I must have
been about 13, I suppose. A lot happened when I was 13.

E: Yeah. Were you there for six months, a year?

S: Seemed like a year, but I don't remember.

E: Seemed like a year. Did you try running away from there?

S: I tried. It was hard to get out. They really could catch
you . . .

E: What did you go through there?

S: Oh, it was hell. (Spoken in a soft, sad voice, but less
blocking than usual.) Actually, when I was there, there
was no one. I didn't care any more; I didn't care about
anything, really.

E: . . . (P) . . . I understand, that was heavy . . . (P) . . .
Do you have any memory of your father?

S: No, I've seen a picture of him, but I don't know anything.

E: Throughout the years, did your mother or your grandmother
talk at all?

S: Nobody talked about him. Even today I go home and try to
say to my mother sometimes, "Hey, Mom, who is this man,
what was he about?" and she won't talk.

E: So painful. Do you know why he left Puerto Rico?

S: I don't know.

E: Did he have a promise of a job here, possibly?

S: Yeah. I think he was an artist. And some of his friends
said, "Hey, there's an opportunity in a bigger country,"
and so he figured he'd go first and then send for my mother
later, but he never did send for my mother. And so my
grandmother had a little money and they had a little land

there and my aunt--they were all living together--so they all decided to come back here to look for him so he could support the kids he left behind. He got an apartment and I guess Rita and I were born, and then he left.

E: You don't know where he was working?

S: I think somebody mentioned he was doing dishwashing or something in some big restaurants.

E: But no painting?

S: Yeah, he was doing like oil painting. There was one around the house. It was beautiful, I still remember. I don't know why they threw it out. It was a picture of trees, this courtyard with a little fountain, birds, it was . . . (P) . . .

E: You said you saw your mother last Christmas. You say she's beautiful.

S: Yeah. Very simple. She's doing a lot better. She's still taking a lot of pills, sugar pills or whatever (chuckles), or maybe not. Maybe it's become a physical thing, probably has since she's had all those operations. She's had quite a few major operations. Heart of lungs, or something. Asthma. And some heart treatments. She's perfectly secure with her TV and pet dog.

E: She lives with your sister?

S: Well, they've all managed to have some arrangement where my sister's living with her, well she was. Maria was living across the street from where my mother was living. They're living up in Harlem now. Carmen is living in the same apartment with my mother. They have a lot of room in there. Carmen has two kids who are living there with my mother. Her husband left--he's in service now. Rita, the baby, lives in Harlem; she got married. Irma just got married; she's somewhere in Harlem.

E: Yeah. So everybody's married.

S: Except me.

E: Except you. Your mother is in better health? What's it like being with her now?

S: Well, it's nice, you know . . . (P) . . . she tries to . . . she's very much the same as she was, actually, when I was a kid. Trying very hard to cuddle me and give me love and affection, but afraid of doing so because she doesn't know me at all . . . I'm a total stranger to her. And when I embrace her and try to love her and hold her and kiss her and give affection, she starts to cry a lot . . . (P) . . .

E: When she tried to be mother when you were a kid? Why didn't it work?

S: It was something in both of us, actually. Her, probably. I don't know, I'm just trying to focus on her and what I see is that probably she felt for a long time a failure as a mother because she was not able to supply the full family, which is a mother and a father, and she realized that I was a man and she couldn't apply the same affection as she was applying to the girls to me. And I was rebelling against

that sweet motherly thing. I was probably upset because I
didn't have a man to fight with and wrestle and challenge
and live up to a man image. I couldn't identify with a
woman. I pulled away. And so that broke her up because
there was nothing she could do, I mean she tried to get
close, but I would push her away, but she didn't receive
very much. And she probably made attempts, and after a
while, as I grew older, I just resisted to a point where
I just ignored her and threw things at her.

E: I know you remember that you threw things at her. What was
the occasion?

S: Well, she would try to control me, like, "Where are you
going? Somebody told me you were out there fighting, and
you stay in the house today. You're not going outside,"
or "You're not going to eat here." And she tried to put
some form of discipline and restriction in my life and I
wasn't going to accept that.

E: Your experience with Zen masters in this country is not the
same as you had in the Orient, in the monastery where you
lived for a month?

S: You mean how I felt about that difference? It was kind of
hard, because in the Western world of looking at things,
everyone is an individual. And there is no such thing as
master, but self is master, you _are_ your own master, you _do_
run your life, and nobody tells you who you are but you,
and you have to find yourself--which is true. But in the
Orient it seems like there _is_ a master. There is a master
there who is above you, who's in control, who tells you
when you are not doing the practice right. And I used to
really get upset. I used to say, "What, me? Coming from
Harlem and such a big leader of a gang going to let this
little wrinkled man tell me that he's better than I am?"
You know, that became a very ego trip, eventually, where I
would look down at him and say he's on a very heavy ego
trip. But then I realized that when he came to America
that he was able to adapt to all the situations, which made
him a better man than I was, because I couldn't adapt to
his situation yet. So Zen is very much part of what I'm
doing right now. I don't know how long I will go on practicing this way--probably for life. I think it's become
very much a part of what I've been searching for, which is
self. Being able to understand and adapt and accept and
be myself and not be influenced by people and not be completely bewildered when I find that these people that I've
depended on, they've changed. And because I've changed and
I haven't been able to see the change happening and adapt
to the change, it's made me very lost and bewildered. And
I think having studied Zen and meditating and living with
people who are into Zen has made me more aware of myself
and of my environment and easier to accept what comes and
what goes from it.

E: Where are you now in terms of wanting to change things?

S: I'm not really in control of my environment, I'm not really
   in control of life and death. I don't know where I'm going
   to be tomorrow--it just happens. Right now I'm very satisfied with myself. I'm not completely lost. I'm not completely lonely. Alienated, shall we say. Or disabled. So,
   I think I'm . . . (P) . . . I have no desires. No real desires to fulfill. I have no fantasy dreams. Of happiness
   or of something good to do. That's what I mean by "when it
   comes, it comes." But it's not as if I were saying, "Well,
   what are you going to do, Fred? Sit on your ass all day
   in your room and wait for it to come?" Because I know people who would say that. They say, you know, you have no
   desire, you have no dreams, what are you going to do? What
   I've been doing is living. You know. It's what I'm doing.
   I don't have any money, I don't have any children or a wife
   or land or any possessions or . . . (P) . . . family I'm
   living with. I'm just traveling around, and I'm satisfied
   with what I'm doing.

E: When you come out of meditation, you start to speak to peo-
   ple--what was that like?

S: It was rebirth. Images and thoughts fascinated me. The
   fact of living in a house with people, the cooking my own
   meals, the going to the bathroom, the . . . (P) . . . sounds
   of words . . . (P) . . . The simple things that somehow we
   take for granted because we're so used to it because we do
   it so often that we're no longer aware of it, become so real.
   We may say that maybe this is just a thing that goes on for
   a little bit, and then after a while it wears off and then
   it's just like a drug trip, a head trip. But it really
   isn't. Because every experience, somehow, stays with you.
   And it becomes part of your life . . . after you come out
   of it you see things that were taken for granted.

E: You like that? There's something very good about it.

S: There's something very good about being able to see things
   as they are without already forming opinions about what they
   are or what they should be.

E: Is there anything scary about having things be so fresh and
   new . . . (P) . . .

S: On the contrary, everything is beautiful when it's fresh and
   new. A baby is always beautiful when it's first born. A
   flower.

E: How do you relate now to the drug scene around you, in the
   country? They claim to see things through drugs.

S: A lot of drugs are just escape and creating illusions, basically that's what they do. They create fantasies, and they
   live their fantasies through whatever it is they are taking
   to create the fantasies. I did some acid a long time ago,
   and did quite a lot of acid, and for a long time I thought
   I was such a holy man. I walked down the street with a
   sheet, a sheet I used to hold over my head, and I thought I
   was God. Jesus Christ himself, on this acid trip. After

the acid trip it was gone, and there was I, you know, with
all these people laughing. And I wondered whatever happened to that same person, where did it go? I would have
to run for the acid for to find that other person.

E: It was an acid self.

S: Yeah. And then I find that there are flashbacks through
acid. Acid is a door; it opens a door to yourself, to
true self. But it <u>closes</u>. And . . . and it's always hard
to get back to that open mind. I'm not saying Zen's better
for everyone; I'm saying it's better for myself because it
seems so much more natural and so much more real to just
sit quietly for a few minutes and empty my thoughts, silence my mind.

E: There was a time I recall when you saw the first interviewer that you were looking for a job but you couldn't find
one. You're not in that position of worrying now?

S: I don't have a job now.

E: And you're not worried.

S: No, I'm not worried about it. Some people I knew had some
candle wax, and I made some candles, and I made candles and
beads and little odds and things like that occasionally,
and trade with people for whatever they wish to exchange
for . . . (P) . . . But this is why I'm living, I guess,
in a commune situation where the value of a certain thing
does not become a mental struggle, such as money or food
or shelter. In the city life, you find a lot of people
worrying about materialistic things: homes and cars. And
if your car breaks down, or your job, and it creates a lot
of tension and anxiety, and . . . (P) . . . when people's
whole life depended on money they cannot go out into nature
and learn how to pick the right flowers or the right wild
lettuce that are growing around or peppermint plants that
are growing to make peppermint tea or make a little salad,
or go fishing . . . (P) . . .

E: How long did you stay on your visit to the family in Harlem?

S: Hmm, not very long, unfortunately. I would have liked to
spend more time with them. I guess for about two weeks.

E: Do you think when you left that they had the feeling that
however foreign you are to them, that you were OK?

S: Oh, yeah. After departuring from them . . . there were
tears in some of the eyes. And somehow . . . I said words
that I don't know where they came from, but somehow they
comforted them and the tears disappeared, and they realized
that I was not going anywhere; that I would always be with
them. Something of that effect . . . and . . . (P) . . .
even though I was a stranger, I was very much part of their
lives . . .

E: When you were a "discipline problem" your mother worried
and wanted to protect you.

S: I don't think she'll ever stop, I think she's still worrying right now. But now it's a lot different than before
. . . (P) . . . part of her worrying actually was part of

the fact that she was unable to do anything to discipline
me. And now she's realized . . . (P) . . . I'm 21 years
old and that I must have somewhere in this little tiny
head some sense of some capability of managing, because
somehow I have come back to see her, having gone to another
part of the world where she can never imagine, or California, even though the biggest movement of her life was from
Puerto Rico to New York--and that was such a dramatic
thing that it took years for her to, and even now she
hasn't adapted to the New York life. And she realizes
that I am capable of dealing with whatever has to be coped
with without running back and saying, "Mama, mama, mama,
help me, help me, help me," that kind of thing. When I
come home, I don't come home with problems, but I come
home with love and affection, and to share what I've discovered. And I think it gives her a lot of joy to see her
son not totally destroyed. But she'll always worry, she'll
always have the mother thing which all mothers have, which
is, you know, love and concern for a child.

E: Do you remember coming home and saying, "Mama, help me?"

S: Never, never. And I guess she expected me to. She always
wanted me to share my problems with her, always, yeah. I
remember one of the things she said, "Why don't you stop
going over there, why don't you just live here with the
family, get married? We love you, why do you run away from
us? What is there that we do wrong to you? How come you
don't like us?" You know, things like that which again expresses her need for wanting to share her motherly affection toward me, and her love.

E: Conversation was easier with your sisters?

S: Conversation was easier, yeah, because they had to say what
they had to say, and I had to say what I had to say (laughs).
We had spent more time together, in a way. Especially with
Maria. I guess when I was there I spent about a week with
Maria and a week with my mother. They lived right across
from each other, so I kind of got up in the morning and
went to visit Maria and had breakfast with Mother and supper, and slept in Mother's house, but . . . but I guess
the only one I could talk to was Maria, even though she
didn't understand my chain of thought through transcenden-
tal meditation, or mind expanding through a channel of endless life . . . she was not condemning, but yet, curious
and wanting to find more information and wanting to know
where I acquired the information and if there was any books
available that she could read. Whereas my other sisters
were just, "Yeah, is that what you're doing, wow, that's
great" (laughs).

E: You remember how you'd come home as a kid to find your mother sick in bed?

S: I remember times when I would come home and would become
moved by Mother's illness. And I would sit in a little
corner somewhere and pray and pray.

E: Pray to God?

S: Yeah. Fold my hands and kneel somewhere where nobody
would know I was doing this, somewhere in the closet or in
the bathroom, and would just repeat over and over, "I hope
to God that she gets well, I hope to God that she gets
well; I hope to God that she gets well." I guess occasionally Mother would say something like, "Oh, God, the problems," you know. God would always be in her mind, somehow
that word would always come out of her mouth when there
was some problem. And sometimes she would say things like,
like when things were bad, sometimes she'd say, "Thank God
we're alive." And, "It could be worse," and things like
that. Actually, she never did feel like giving up. When
they _insisted_ on taking us and putting us in some adoption
home, she said, "No, there's no reason to live," you know,
"without them it would kill me." That's what I heard from
my grandmother, and she just would not give up, you know,
she would not.

E: Did you have any specific fears that she might die?

S: Yeah. I thought of that, and when I thought about that I
would go out and steal and bring a lot of food home.

E: Did stealing first start with food?

S: Yeah. Well, we had very little food. We didn't have any
at all, I guess, at times. We were all hungry.

E: How old do you think you'd be when you first went out to
steal some food?

S: Oh, I don't remember, I was young.

E: Like before you ever went to school?

S: Yeah. I started out stealing candy from the candy stores,
and I would grab things from other kids . . . their toys,
and I would bring them home. Marbles and things like that.

E: Your mother probably didn't really notice?

S: Well, actually, after a while she did notice because I was
bringing home an awful lot. There were times where at
first she didn't notice so couldn't control it. There was
nothing she could do. And then I got to the point where I
stole an awful lot of things, and then she wondered, "What
are you doing, where are you going, where is all this stuff
coming from?" She was upset. She would say, "That's going
to make me sick, that's going to make me sick." And then
I would stop because I realized that if I made her sick and
then she'd die, and I didn't want her to die, so I just
stopped. I guess she was afraid of me being caught or shot
or arrested.

FOURTH INTERVIEW (APRIL 1972, THE NEXT DAY):
THE PRESENT SCENE: FEELINGS AND REMEMBRANCES

E: A year ago, it took you longer to get into yourself. Before yesterday, it would take you time to warm up or decide
what you wanted to say.

S: I think when I first started talking to Bill (the first E) was the time when I had just moved to the city and was looking . . . (P) . . . It just took a while to orient my-self and to feel a little bit at home. At home with the environment and at home with myself.

E: You had been in California only a couple months, I think.

S: And of course I was not suspicious of Bill, or not that I didn't trust him, but I was sort of bewildered by what this whole thing that we were doing was all about. Ex-changing money for my mind and my life, it didn't seem very comfortable, not that I don't trust you or that I don't trust the idea, it just puzzles me that someone would want to offer money for rap sessions. It all seems sort of un-real. And it still does.

E: Wonder how I can make it more real? You want to ask me anything?

S: Well, I haven't figured out why is it that it's unreal, why . . . (P) . . . I mean, why I'm sitting here rapping (chuckles) about something that's dead, probably that's why it's not real. And yet it's very much alive because it's molded me into what I am.

E: In that sense it's alive. Do you think we could understand where you are now if we didn't know the past?

S: Well, maybe, because, as I encounter people every day, I never deal with their past. We never talk about, you know, what your experiences were. It's just a picking up from where it's at. So that if I look at a person from the past point of view, I will be creating an image that no longer exists, even though that person has been molded by that past. So that any emotional hang-ups are based on the past in some sense. It seems more fresh or more real to me to look from where it is now. I don't know anything about your past, I don't know what your mother was like, or your father, or . . .

E: That's true, that you don't know me, in that same sense that I've come to know you.

S: I guess that the first tapes gave you an introduction to who I was, so that it gave you some foundation to what you were going to be dealing with.

E: I had some of the milestones of your experiences from Bill's tapes so that I wouldn't have to ask about those. When you were talking to a friend, you may not feel it necessary to go into the past, but as a psychologist trying to acquaint young people with lives that they haven't directly experi-enced, I feel it necessary to bring into the present the whole range of experiences that you've had. There are in-terests and potentials that started long ago that are still with you. What do you think of that?

S: Yeah, maybe some of the young readers who are feeling trap-ped by an environment can leave that environment. I'm sure that there are a lot of friends of mine living in Harlem that have gone beyond Harlem, that have gone to the Village

or have gone to other parts at one point or another. And
somehow returned back home because that's all they knew,
that's all they could relate to. But I never did figure
out why is it that I never felt insecure when I left, I
never felt like, "Well, I've got to go home," or, "That's
home where I came from," even when people speaking a different language and not being able to communicate or contribute and feeling somewhat isolated from other humans
. . . (P) . . .

E: That's a very good question. In your own family, you have
your mother saying, and maybe your sisters, "How come you
don't want to come back and live here?" Your sisters are
not very far from where they began.

S: I don't know; I really don't know. My sisters spent a lot
of time at home, and they had that sort of family grouping,
whereas I was always moving, and meeting different challenges and adventures, and not having any stable parents or
place. There wasn't one place where I knew I was home. I
don't know, it may also be . . . (P) . . . that if I had a
brother, it's possible that he would be in trouble, too.

E: You said that going to new places didn't make you feel so
insecure?

S: Well, there were times that I did, actually; there were
times when I felt very much alienated, depending on the
group, that is . . . (P) . . . There would be . . . (P)
. . . like, for instance, in the school where there were a
lot of middle-class white kids. Or in the Village where
the dialogues were so different from the ones I've heard
and the ways of doing things were so different, and the
clothing and the backgrounds. And there was nothing I
could say to feel in, or comfortable.

E: You felt out but you stayed?

S: Yeah, I stayed; I don't really understand why. I guess
probably because somehow I managed to overcome a lot of
inhibition of being in Harlem alienated from the rest of
the world.

E: When you were fighting so much, were you injured? Did you
get hurt some?

S: Oh, I have scars from knife fights. That was about 11 or
12. It wasn't a fist thing any more.

E: Were you ever injured so that you were out of commission
for a while?

S: No . . . (P) . . . no, not really. I was very lucky. I
had a slash on my arm that was infected for a while, and
I had a black eye so I couldn't see that day. Then I got
hit in my leg with a pike, and it swelled really bad--that
was the worst. I guess there were times where I just got
really beat up . . . (P) . . . but I recovered. They never
kept me away from the activity, for very long.

E: When your eye got hurt, how would you tend to it?

S: . . . (P) . . . I think it was at the school, yeah, I went
to the nurse. The teacher at school saw it, and it had an

infection and they just put peroxide on it. It was good
'cause they used to send me home a lot. So I stayed home.

E: What was your mother's reaction when you came in with it?

S: I never did show it to her. The truant officer would come
up once in a while and would tell her that I had been acting up in school, discipline problems. And she would cry;
there was nothing she could do except tell him she was
sorry, and say something religious.

E: God would not like to . . .

S: It was something about the devil is in me, or something
like that, or . . . (P) . . . I don't remember, but I know
it was something religious.

E: Yeah. You say you've been lucky. How has your health been?

S: Well, I had an ulcer once; that's about all. I've had very
bad teeth problems; I had cavities, that's about all. Considering my diet as a child, I would say that I am tremendously well.

E: When was your ulcer?

S: Oh, this was a while before I went to the Orient. It was
in between Peggy and the George trip. I was just breaking
up with that relationship and starting a new one. And it
was all basically psychosomatic. I don't know, I had great
tension, and I guess I needed a rest.

E: Did you go to the hospital?

S: Yeah, I spent about two weeks in the hospital. It was really bad when it first struck; it was just real strong, sharp
pain in my stomach, just paralyzed me and I just couldn't
move.

E: And that's about it as far as serious illness? No more ulcer symptoms?

S: Right.

E: You mentioned kids laughing at you a while back. What would
you consider one of your most embarrassing moments?

S: Embarrassing . . . (P) . . . Well, I don't know, when I was
embarrassed it made me very bitter and very angry during
the times when I had lost a battle, or when somebody destroyed my ego or when somebody would beat me up in front
of a lot of people, or in front of girls that I had been
trying to get to for a while . . . (LP) . . . that would
embarrass me, that I wouldn't live up to that image, to
what I was, and before . . . I was embarrassed not being
able to be accepted by the group . . . (P) . . . It was a
feeling of not belonging to anything, to anyone. It was a
feeling of not being able to, to fight my own battles . . .
(P) . . .

E: Now that you're not fighting battles, do you experience embarrassment?

S: Do I experience them now? How do I deal with them? . . .
(P) . . . I don't know. Now I just . . . (P) . . . I mainly sit back and watch them and look at them when I feel
like I made a fool of myself in some situation, or . . . (P)
. . . when I was flashing my ego too much and made a fool

of myself, I'd just sit back and I guess withdraw from the
situation rather than trying to master the situation by
dominating the situation, and try in some way to understand
this ego power trip that I'm on and accept the, the embarrassment.

E: You can't think of a for instance of where you've really
felt that you were on an ego power trip?

S: Hmm . . . (LP) . . . Actually, there were times when I
feared that I knowed something more than someone else.
Somehow I developed this . . . (P) . . . phony assurance
about something. And then I'd find out that I didn't know
that much about this certain thing. And I guess the way
I'd react to it is to say, "I don't know." and I'd withdraw
. . .

E: In terms of the range of feelings that people experience,
would you give me a for instance about joy?

S: (Chuckles) Well, moods. Right?

E: OK. Moods.

S: What gives me joy, did you say? . . . (P) . . . Well, actually, lately it doesn't take much to satisfy me. Just
walking on the street and seeing people with flowers out,
so it's joy to be able to identify with flowers and to let
someone else enjoy or share without notice. New things give
me joy. And it gives me so much joy to be able to sit back
and say, "Hey, I just learned something I didn't know."

E: Do you find yourself starting this "ego power trip" of
knowing everything with men more than women, women more
than men?

S: No, it used to be that way, but now it doesn't matter because I see . . . that we're all equal. I used to be the
dominant one, or the aggressive to a woman, and the woman
would always be the slave to me. It's part of the Spanish
culture. In some ways, the man is always the aggressor,
the worker. And the woman just stays home and has kids.
And this culture is so different.

E: This culture?

S: Um-hmm. I mean the Caucasian, or white establishment.

E: You find that it's not true, huh?

S: No, it's not true. 'Cause they're all happening today.
Women's Lib, and women are getting paid just as much as men.
And just discussing the situation and problems with women
in the world, that they're capable of doing just as much as
I am; certain ones are not. It depends on the individual,
actually. But in general, I would say that I don't draw
lines between women and myself or men and myself, and say
that I'm better than a man, or a woman . . . (P) . . .

E: Yeah. I'm going to ask you to do the same with "sad."
What makes you sad?

S: Well, for the longest time I have felt sad because of the
waste that I see in different countries and relating to my
past. When I first came to California I was invited to a
dinner party at some friends' house, a lot of people were

there. Everything on my plate was finished; everybody had
wasted some. And I remember when I was a kid when we did-
n't have a grain of rice or a bottle of milk for the baby.
And I would see the people, how they were wasting this and
people back home who are needing it now. It made me sad
because I felt that I knew all this and was unable to go
back and bring something back home . . . (P) . . . I felt
very selfish in many ways. And there are people back home
right now who don't have the time to enjoy because their
time is just filled about trying to find a meal every day,
overcoming fears . . . (P) . . . And I, I want so much to
be able to bring that world into this world, somehow, or
this world into that world . . . (P) . . . Or explain to
the people whom I'm eating these foods with, can I wrap up
some of this food and send it somewhere?

E: Do you remember being hungry yourself? You said a bottle
of milk for the baby?

S: I don't remember, but I recall the old lady coming and
talking about it, the lady who used to bring all the food,
she always used to talk about it was such a shame that the
little girl was always hungry. For the longest time I had
to struggle with that thought, how can I bring something
to people that they need that I see and hear? How can I
prevent myself from being selfish and indulgent?

E: You talk about giving yourself or parts of you, just like
giving food. Can that be done?

S: Well, I guess, yes, it can, actually, I have done it in the
past with the theatrical gang. My thoughts, my acting, and
I'm doing it right now, do it every day. I've learned to
become a reflection of other people, by being myself, by
not being what they want me to be, and not living to their
images or to their expectations but just by being myself,
so that when they look at me they see what self is. I think
that there's nothing you can do to help me. I can't see
through your eyes, I can't feel through your feelings, I
can't live your experiences. But I may know your reflection. Only what I see tells me to go on, to know that
there's hope, to know that there's hate, that there's whatever there is that you are projecting about yourself.

E: And that gives hope to someone else?

S: That gives whatever someone else has need for, what they're
looking for. At the time when I was younger I realized that
I was a dictator or a father or a gang leader, and this was
what they were looking for--my followers--so I gave them
that image. So I realized a way of--just being yourself.
But there were times when I guess at that point, I was being
myself, not that I wasn't, but I was being everything that
I could be. . . . But now I find that I cannot live that
image, I cannot live that past in this environment or at
this time, because I've seen different things. And what I
see, the only way I can help people through my daily life
is by being what I see, expressing it through my existence,

through my words, through my . . . (P) . . . my silence.

E: In the past, before you stopped judging good and bad, what
    would you have called bad for you, or unpleasant, maybe
    that even disgusted you?

S: . . . (P) . . . Wow. I can't . . . (P) . . . What's that
    word?

E: Disgust? A real negative reaction.

S: . . . (LP) . . . Well, taking the racial problem, I think
    that was one of the things I was disgusted very much with.
    Having to live a Puerto Rican image or a black image in a
    white society. And I would get very disgusted at times
    because I would find myself trying to be white. Trying to,
    to live up to the white culture, and to love the white art
    in order to be accepted in the white world . . . (LP) . . .
    to see the bitterness and anger in minority groups . . .
    that . . . (P) . . . made me sad, getting back to sad, or,
    made me disgusted. Sad. Because I couldn't live that
    dualistically. I couldn't live; I was being torn from
    white or black, from Puerto Rican to black, from Puerto
    Rican to myself . . . (P) . . . it was just impossible to
    live in a world without being anything, being able to say,
    when people say, "What are you?" to have to label yourself
    so that . . . so that there'd be some way of communicating
    . . . (P) . . .

FIFTH INTERVIEW (OCTOBER 1972):
THE PRESENT SCENE: WHAT NEXT?

E: So.

S: So then, let's see, what happened. Oh, from the country.
    I got tired of the psychedelic trip and just very, very
    lonely for a woman companion. It was an easy life and nice.
    But, somehow, I was restless, coming from the city. I want-
    ed to be around lots of people. I came back to visit Peggy
    and realized that that was all over. I decided I might as
    well live at a commune near the Zen Center. Actually, I've
    been thinking of living alone for a while and just getting
    my own place.

E: How about a girl? How does it feel with Peggy gone?

S: It's not easy for her, in a way, because I think somehow
    she resents me being around. I still believe she is very
    much emotionally attached to--to me. When I was with her
    I did show a great deal of affection, at least. . . . Med-
    itation brought us together. I did it partially to keep
    Peggy interested. At times I felt she was bored with me.
    She was a schoolteacher. An English teacher. Some of the
    people that are living in my commune are friends of hers.
    She comes over to visit them occasionally. But we sort of
    pass by each other, hardly noticing. Uh, I don't quite
    understand what she's doing. I guess she realizes she needs
    to change her life, and I'm in the way, in some way. And

that's perfectly understandable . . .

E: I was wondering about your schooling, when you learned
English. Was the first time you started to speak English
when you went to school?

S: I think I started speaking English when I was, well, let's
see, I think it was in day reform school. I guess you
call it a prison. It was a little old lady there who
taught English occasionally. She would come by and help
me with words. She would break the words down into what
she called syllables. That's when I started to read in
English. Miss Johnson was her name.

E: Did any of the teachers in your elementary school speak
Spanish?

S: The teachers spoke English, but I didn't speak any in
school--I mean I was always very withdrawn. Every time I
got a report card they'd say I didn't participate or "He's
very withdrawn" or "He fights a lot." I mean, I never
participated in anything other than occasionally I would
pick up a brush or do some fingerpainting or . . . When it
came down to spelling or reading or writing I would just
doodle away or sidle to the back and just stared at the
girls or ask to go to the bathroom. The teachers were annoyed, there was not much they could do because there were
no parents to get ahold of. Since I seem to have been
concentrating more on English since I met this old lady;
she really made an impression on me. And through George,
you know, people in the theater and listening and imitating
and going to plays and operas and musicals.

(Fred brought a tall, slender drum he had had made.)

S: My music sounds more Latin, to other people. I mean, I
can't really judge my own music. Because I'm just hitting
it without that much knowledge of the instrument. I control it with my hand with a little expression. Uh, from
what I've heard from other musicians, it sounds very Spanish, very Latin, bouncy. And that cha-cha feeling. It
seems like I've taken from three different cultures, Spanish, African, and American. Well, so far I've discovered
that the people that play this type of drum around here--
Puerto Rican people, black people, Filipinos, and Mexicans,
and there are a couple of others I know from Tahiti. It's
hard to get them together, sometimes, down where we play.
There may be twenty-five drummers. After a while some of
them just can't do it, and they walk away. It's so hard to
mix.

E: What music did you hear in New York?

S: Well, living on the Lower East Side for a while I heard
some jazz. I went to a few jazz nightclubs. It's hard to
take (laughs) after a while. Just sitting there my mind
keeps wandering; keep getting drunk and drunk. I guess I
could appreciate it now.

E: I just wondered how you could manage music and drums on your income?

S: Well, I pay very little rent, which is like 40 dollars.
Actually, I used to pay 40 dollars. Now I pay, because
I've moved into the closet, I pay 20 dollars a month. And
lately it's been very, very bad, my living situation. I
don't know where it goes.

E: Your ATD welfare is the same?

S: It's the same amount. It just disappeared . . . I had to
pay the army for a shrink to get out of the draft, and pay
for the drums.

E: You got a shrink in addition to the shrink that you got
along with welfare?

S: Oh, I only get to see one shrink--that's just ATD shrink.
They're supposed to assign me a clinical psychiatrist. At
one time they questioned me why I couldn't get a job. Obviously I'm so sick I just can't get out of the house (said
facetiously).

E: Can't go to work, so can't go to the shrink? So that part
of your ATD welfare bit was that you should be seeing a
shrink, huh?

S: Yeah, but I don't really want to go.

E: Do I recall that you saw a psychiatrist while you were living with George?

S: Yeah, I saw a psychiatrist, which I was with George, passing
time with him.

E: What did you get out of it?

S: Oh, nothing, actually, nothing at all. It just introduced
me to what psychology was. And a very bad introduction,
too. I felt very alienated from this man. Because what he
was doing, and how he was, which was he would sit way in
the corner of the room, and I would sit way in the corner
of this room and there was no other choice because his chair
was there and my chair was here, and I didn't know him and I
wasn't going to try to arrange his room. And we shook hands
when we first met, and he acted very businesslike. I wasn't
going to try to get close to him because his first vibrations
were very shallow; he built this wall against patient and
doctor. And I kept going to him, and all he did, he never
said a word. "How are you, it's a nice day, isn't it. Tell
me about your experiences today," were the only words I
would get from him every day. I saw him once a week. I
stopped going after a couple of months. I'm not saying it
was good or bad; it was bad for me at the time.

E: Whose idea was it?

S: Something I wanted to try. I guess there were people at
the time at the school talking about psychiatrists, and I
was taking a mental health course. George was paying for
most of it.

E: What did you want help with at that time?

S: I had separated myself from the school. I was lagging in
my work, smoking a lot of dope, not digging this big high
school scene. I felt alienated, that there was something
wrong.

E: I am interested in what you are planning to do now.

S: Yeah, I wish I had some money actually. This Christmas . . .

E: What would you do with it?

S: Visit my family. There are just times like Christmas when I think it would be nice to visit. I don't know what I'm going to do, actually. I signed up for a twenty-one-day meditation.

E: Last time I saw you, you were planning a long meditation.

S: That's right. And then I came back to the city, and I guess I never went back to the country. You hide from the city so much, you don't know your true state of mind. But while I was there I sort of looked for a musician to live with. I don't know if I would go another long meditation—getting into a lot of money. Last time I didn't have all the money. So I just sat there, and they couldn't call the cops or anything; they couldn't throw me out. They asked me for the money. I said I didn't have it. So what could they do?

E: Yeah (laughs).

S: They really have a racket; they are making a lot of money, they really do. But I don't care. That's their trip.

E: It doesn't make you mad?

S: Not really. They have to survive sooner or later; it's just the only way they can keep their game going. I'll probably get something from the State Welfare. I could sort of consider a job because I've been so lazy, sitting around the house. I've been hurting my arms and wrists. I've been trying to get in three or four hours a day of drumming.

E: What kind of job?

S: (Laughs) Who knows? Probably working jobs opening at Christmas, like at a department store, or collecting tickets at the museum.

E: Have you done any of that, in the last year?

S: No, I haven't . . . (P) . . . The only job I've done just for one day is babysitting. This has really been a bum week, in terms of not having money, and I've been sick with the flu.

E: You mentioned that you had enough of psychedelic drugs in the country. What are your trips like?

S: I felt like it happened—I wasn't in control.

E: Has acid ever put you in a bad place?

S: Well, there was a time, yeah, where I got very freaked out by it—where I started mumbling all kinds of things, without any control. And it all sounded very poetic, at least the girl I was with thought it was.

E: Why was it a bum trip though?

S: Well, it was a bummer coming down. Because it wasn't real . . . just jumping around and all of a sudden I just realized when I came down . . . I was totally destroyed, my image of who I was had disappeared.

E: And you weren't the poet?

S: And, yeah, I guess I couldn't accept not being a poet.
    It's just like playing a role and all of a sudden you're
    convincing yourself that that's your life. And, snap, you
    find yourself nowhere, without what you thought you were.
    And it was just weird, strange things came out of it. Not
    all that scary.

E: Generally you haven't had bum trips?

S: No. Not like I've seen in other people. Some people come
    to a profound understanding of themselves, that after they
    come down, they just, uh, retain that understanding.

E: Yeah. Has that ever happened that you come to a new under-
    standing of yourself?

S: Yeah, sure. Some of my acid trips have been like some of
    my meditation. Where I totally let go of my subconscious,
    and I saw some of the things, some of my subconscious,
    hidden fears. With acid, you might say . . . accepted a
    lot of things that I couldn't accept, so that when I came
    back, when I came down from the trip, I subconsciously
    learned something. That gradually in my life made a change;
    it's not necessarily a radical change. But very subtle,
    you know, very real.

E: Since I last saw you six months ago, how many acid trips
    would you say you've had?

S: Since last time we met?

E: Yeah.

S: There was, uh, let's see if I can recall--I went back to
    the country right after the spring (laughs). The minute I
    got there, somebody gave me some acid. Yeah, and then a
    week later, something like that, we went to a hot spring,
    and tripped out on mescaline . . . (P) . . . So it's been
    about two times since I last saw you.

E: Since you've been living near the Zen Center, they're not
    much into drugs?

S: No. So, therefore, I'm not in that environment any more.
    I'm not interested; however, I do have some LSD in my room.

E: So, it seems like drugs are no problem; you either decide
    to do it or you don't.

S: Yeah, yeah.

E: What's the difference between taking drugs now and taking
    drugs before, when you were really hooked on heroin? Do
    you worry about getting hooked again?

S: No. I guess the difference between then and drugs now in
    terms of my attitude--and my environment testing, well, I
    think it's just as simple a thing as experimenting. It was
    also the way of doing things way back. And I didn't have
    much of a choice. To be accepted, and I wanted to be part
    of what was happening.

E: Have you had any heroin since 16?

S: No.

E: I guess your experiment was really an experiment--you
    learned all you needed to know about it then.

S: Yeah. The drugs bring down. And I've got to find an ultimate high without an ultimate bring-down with it. I mean,
there's one already, life itself (laughs).

E: So you would like to change life a bit for yourself, but
it's certainly not drugs. What would be more in this life
for you now?

S: Well, I guess music is the only thing I'm really involved
in right now; and meditation, that's . . .

E: That's part of every day.

S: That's part of every day, yes, it's like sleeping and sort
of, uh, the music is the thing for right now. And I feel
very unsure, because I don't know that much of ways of con-
forming with other musicians . . . to create something that
yourself can understand. So that's about all I have on my
mind right now--that I really want to do, is music. There
are some times when I like to practice, and there's so many
things happening, draft and this and that, I can't even get
my mind still. I go over and meditate for a while, and I
just light up a joint and I just relax for a few minutes
or drink some wine . . . A lot of people say meditation
is a waste of time. I think it is too.

E: Oh, you do? Is that a new feeling about it?

S: No, not necessarily, no. It's just a feeling I had once.
Somebody said to me, "What are you doing?" I said, "I'm
wasting time."

E: So right now music doesn't feel like wasting time.

S: Yeah, it's another way! (Laughs)

E: (Laughs) Well, I see, you can really discount everything
you do.

S: I'm laughing now at how we're wasting time.

E: (Laughs) I gather it seemed like a long day to you.

S: It's been nice, though, very pleasant, very relaxed. Yeah,
I guess that's one of the feelings I get from Zen; I feel
very relaxed. More than I used to. I used to run around
trying to find things to do with my time, in very distorted
ways.

E: Would you tell me again your dream of this week that you
told when the tape was off, 'cause it may give me an idea
to understand you. I hope you can see that for me it's
not wasting time, but I can understand you're in a different place.

S: Well, I don't remember how it started out. Remember, I
said there's a guy next door that played the drums. He has
a friend in the same building. They're both on this super-
black trip. I can't explain what the black trip is, but
you know it's like using a whole lot of slang expression.

E: They're super-conscious of being black.

S: Yeah, and, you know, I don't feel like I want to contribute
to that conversation. I like to play music with the dude,
I'd like to learn something from him, but when he gets on
his rapping games about his shit, "I fucked this white whore

yesterday, and she wasn't really good. Those white women
are just a drag." I mean like that's cool, if you want to
carry on that conversation; I just said to hell with him.
I guess I'm too serious at times, 'cause I don't feel like
doing that. So I don't really know what it is with them.
I mean, they don't understand why I'm into Zen, and they
think I'm a weird dude, to be living in a closet. I guess
it's just very foreign to them, and if I tried to explain
to them it wouldn't make any sense. So, anyhow, they found
out that I used to go out with Peggy, somehow. And one of
the dudes saw Peggy passing by in the car and got in the
car and rapped at her a while, about me. I guess Peggy
told them that we had a bad time in the Orient and we had
a bad time here. Then I went to sleep and the next day I
guess when I was dreaming, I thought I heard them in a conversation, saying that Peggy had told the guy something
about, uh . . . that she had paid you to keep . . .

E: This is the dream now? Yeah.

S: Yeah. In the dream it was something about Peggy had told
this guy that she had been paying this lady called (the
present interviewer) to find out everything about me. And,
uh, the only way that she figured out that, uh, to get me
to come see you, was through money. So it seemed to me that
I was coming here because of a game that Peggy had set up
in her mind about what I was going to do in her life.

E: That might bring you back to her?

S: Yes. In a way I was all confused. I wanted to get away
from every single person I ever knew. I just wanted to find
a why,where I can be myself. Yet I do get interested in
other people.

E: Did they actually get into the car with Peggy one day?

S: I think that was in the dream, too.

E: I can see where many of us really are looking at you and
caring about you and are interested in you and you must
wonder, "What do they want of me?"

S: Really.

E: (Laughs) What do they want me to be?

S: (Laughs) Yeah, what do they want me to be? Can't they just
accept me for what I am like I'm accepting you? I'm not
asking for all this data or bullshit. You're a person; I'm
just, like, a human person, first impression, take it for
what it is. The next day there will be another different
expression, good, makes life interesting.

E: Don't try to put it together.

S: Really.

E: Yeah, I see.

S: That's like I figured it. I may be wrong. Maybe the world
isn't like that . . . maybe everybody has to manipulate in
order to live in this life. I can't explain what I'm trying
to say. At least that's the kind of person I am. And also
I find I'm very sensitive to people, and I'm very sensitive
to myself. And very impressionable, in many ways. So that

if you say something about me, I'll take it very seriously.
And I'll say, oh, really, maybe that's so. So people notice this, so it's very easy for them to say things, and
I'll freak out. So it's easy for me to be what they want
me to be. Because I'm so open to . . . but on the other
hand, it isn't so easy for me to listen to others. Well,
I'm wondering if I want to be influenced after saying I
didn't!

E: I can say I don't have the intention of having you change
in any way for me, but that doesn't mean that something
might not happen, for both of us, by being together. I
guess you must wonder, sometimes, that by telling so much
of yourself, you may change in the process? I mean, are
you making yourself the kind of person that you think that
I want you to be?

S: No. Uh, here's what I mean, you, in a way, are affecting
me. The way you conduct yourself, the way you are, the way
you speak, uh, the reactions that come out when you say
something. The way I react, so, in a way I am being influenced by you.

E: Do you think I'm asking you to change your values or the
way you think of yourself?

S: No, no, see, I learned a lot from you, just by rapping to
you and, uh, allowing myself to talk with you, so that when
I leave here I'll be a different person, and whatever I
find, uh . . . (LP) . . .

E: I noticed today your ideas really do flow. Today was very
nice.

S: If I was, ah, I can't quite explain it. But if your house
had a whole bunch of psychedelic lights and different posters
and, uh, you answered the door with a bikini and dropped
some acid in my mouth, you know, like when I walked in--that
would . . . (P) . . .

E: You're absolutely right. You know what I wear or what I do
is going to make some difference.

S: You choose the kind of situation that you want to be in and,
and, you know, you avoid the situation, you know, that you
don't want to be in. Obviously I've found out in my life
where drugs, where heroin, is at, and I found out where gang-
busting is at. I know if I went back to Harlem and that
situation, I would have to adapt to it. I would have to get
into something. I would have to either start as a youth
counselor again or the Rescuers, because I would realize
that there's a whole lot of suffering in front of me and
there's something I gotta do for it. And that's the reaction I'm going to get from it . . . (LP) . . . (laughs) . . .
I don't know; I'm trying to explain something but I can't
quite find the words.

E: You make me aware that you do act differently, in different
settings, with different people.

S: Yeah, I know. Sometimes I find myself going back to the
same stage and not understanding it's the situation that

you're in . . . I find myself becoming a musician but I
don't know very much about music (laughs). It's, it's incredible that I'm getting into music!

E: Like you feel different, getting into music?

S: No, but, that's not what I was trying to say. At my first
long meditation, I was just faking my way through the whole
thing. And it was true, I didn't know what the hell I was
doing. I was just, everybody was sitting on a cushion.
Now it's like . . . well, I was fucking around with other
musicians. They were playing, and I would somehow help
them out, with little pieces here and there.

E: What's faking about your getting into music?

S: Nothing (laughs). I'm not faking.

E: You really raised quite a puzzle there because as you copy,
and respond to what's there, then you can feel like it's
faking. You are sitting on a cushion and that makes you
feel like trying to do other people's thing, like meditate,
'cause it's different than what you've done before, so it
feels like faking. You're saying that your music trip is
still so new that it feels phony?

S: I don't know. I guess I don't feel like I'm into it yet.

QUESTIONS

1. Fred Gomez and Solomon Kompten were brought up in the
same city and in somewhat similar, though not identical, economic circumstances. By the age of 10 (before Solomon moved to
California) their behavior was strikingly different. What differences do you detect between the two environments, including
the family circles, that might help to explain such different
outcomes?

2. Is it correct to describe Fred as a rejected child? Did
he have any sources of affection and security in family members?
What evidence can be assembled from the record that bears on
these questions?

3. When a boy is repeatedly defeated in fights with another
boy, but constantly returns to the attack, this behavior is
sometimes interpreted as masochism (that is, taking pleasure
in humiliation) or as self-punishment as a means of reducing
guilt feelings. Do you think that Fred's history with respect
to Juan is best explained in these ways or in some other way?

4. Fred's life seems to divide itself into strikingly different chapters. Knowing only the withdrawn school child, you
probably would not have predicted the youthful gang leader;
knowing the gang leader, you probably would not have predicted
the peace-loving, meditating commune dweller of the interviews.
How do you explain the first change, which started about 8 or 9
and is attributed by Fred to overcoming earlier fears?

5. Fred's behavior as a gang leader would certainly be
described as aggressive. Do you think that it served Fred
mainly as an outlet for aggressive urges, or did it depend more
on yielding him other kinds of satisfaction?

6. Why do you think Fred responded so strongly to the first Peggy? What guesses can you make as to why Peggy behaved as she did?

7. Another of the big changes in Fred's life is described by him as wanting to give love instead of hating. This change was first manifested when he joined Roberto in what became in-formal theater groups designed to draw young people in Harlem away from violence and drugs. How do you understand this change as an expression of Fred's growth? Why did he himself give up violence and drugs? What satisfactions did he get from this new work? Do you see any continuity between his role as gang leader and his role as rescuer?

8. Why did the role as rescuer in Harlem eventually fail Fred?

9. Fred describes two situations where he remained for some time in a group even though he soon felt out of place there: the group in Greenwich Village to which he was introduced by the first Peggy and George's group of theater friends. Why do you think he stayed so long in spite of discomfort?

10. Fred's history includes strong relations with three white people considerably older than himself: the first Peggy, George, and the second Peggy. The basis of the attraction--on both sides--was somewhat different in each case, but not wholly so. What features do you see as being common to all three re-lations?

11. How do you think Fred's life has been affected by the conception of masculinity prevailing in his culture?

12. At several points Fred shows a sensitive awareness to the way the environment has governed his behavior. For example: "I guess I was that way because I was pushed that way, and I was in that sort of environment where I had to be that way." What evidence do you find that he was capable of taking initiative, making choices, and behaving in ways that were not simply dic-tated by environment?

13. Fred has been unable to achieve a stable sense of iden-tity as a gang leader, drug pusher, actor, group worker, or student, or by leading a simple country-dwelling life; he is still trying to find out about himself. Why do you think he has had so much trouble with identity?

14. Do you think that Fred will have further trouble with drugs? What evidence do you consider important in making this forecast?

4 Portia Slim

Contents

Introduction

At the time of this study, in the mid-1960s, Portia Slim was a senior at Radcliffe College, 21 years old. She was one of several subjects invited to take part in studies of personality. All the interviews were conducted by an experienced woman clinical psychologist. The material that follows is from the series of fourteen recorded interviews occurring between February and June. Through a variety of communications the story is then carried forward to bring Portia to the age of 30.

Portia was inclined to be voluble. You may also feel that she was somewhat rambling; the editors have tried to spare you by eliminating irrelevant and repetitive material and by dividing her continuous speech into topical paragraphs. Once you get used to her style, you will find that her ideas are clear and her reporting relatively vivid.

Portia's background is the most advantaged of the four subjects in this workbook. Comparison of her early life with that of Fred Gomez especially emphasizes the huge differences in the environments that surround the growth of personality. The material shows, however, that a favorable environment does not exempt a person from developmental tasks and problems.

FIRST INTERVIEW (FEBRUARY): SCHOOL HISTORY AND FRIENDSHIPS

E: Well, tell me about yourself.

S: Now let's see. I'm sort of curious as to why I got chosen
    . . . of course this is the dominant thing in my mind
    (laughs).

E: Well . . . on the original invitation to all of you, from
    what you said or wrote then, it looked as if you'd be in-
    terested in doing it and we'd be interested in having you
    do it.

S: I know I wrote . . . I wrote a very enthusiastic response
    because I had just spent the summer being introspective
    with a girl friend of mine. We were in California and we
    talked about ourselves, about our roommates, boyfriends,
    all sorts of problems of our lives, which was something new
    for me because for the previous two years my two roommates,
    ah . . . and I had not been especially close, that kind of
    thing . . . so it was really a good thing.

E: Fine.

S: Ah. Do you want sort of, ah . . . history?

E: Oh, just talk about yourself.

S: It's hard to know where to begin. My friends . . . I told
    them all about this great honor and they think it's wonder-
    ful. Ah . . . and there's a lot of kidding going around
    whether I'm going to be ah . . . a subject for normal psy-
    chology courses or for abnormal. And I think they're in
    pretty good agreement that it's going to be for the normal,
    because I am . . . a lot of people have told me how stable
    I am . . . um . . . matter of fact . . . and not very sen-
    sitive to slights received from other people, and I think
    that's probably true. And . . . I don't find it easy to get
    very close to people, but I find it easy to be friends with
    a good many people. And this year, much more than other
    years, a lot of . . . a few close friends which was . . .
    good too. And I have a very good family background. An-
    other interesting question that I'd love to solve . . . the
    answer to the question why my sister and I are so different
    (laughs). I think my mother wonders about it, too. Sort
    of a very striking difference. I guess I could define my-
    self by talking about me versus my sister, and you can see.

E: All right.

S: Ah . . . my sister's about 5 inches taller. Sort of
    surface difference. And she's a freshman at Syracuse,
    and she's interested in sorority life. And she always
    wanted to go to different schools from the ones I went to.
    For instance, I always went to a big public high school
    near my home, and she decided she didn't want to go there,
    and the ostensible reason was because she didn't think she
    could study in such a social atmosphere, but she also said
    that she didn't like the idea of competing with me. And I

think that's probably much more likely to be the strongest
reason why she went to a private girls' school . . . near
where we lived. And she had an extremely heavy social
life, so that I can't imagine it was just because of the
social aspect that she didn't want to go to my high school.
. . . I was always a reader. I would curl up with a book
in third and fourth grades. I remember going to the
library on Saturday, and I got to pick out seven books for
the week, and I could only read a book a day 'cause my
mother wanted me to play (laughs). So she would hide the
other six books on Saturday and I'd come back and whip
through the first book . . . and then I'd have to play
. . . (laughs). There weren't very many, ah . . . kids
in my neighborhood. There were two girls who were older
than I and a girl who's a year younger, and she was my
very best friend. Ah . . . and there just wasn't anybody
else at all. This was a neighborhood of older people . . .
about ten or fifteen years older than my parents. And
there were some boys, but they were very rough . . . and,
ah . . . I didn't want to associate with them. And ah
. . . and in fourth, fifth, and sixth grades of school I
had a lot of friends in school, but I didn't have very
many before because I was sick a lot. I practically
failed first grade because I failed attendance, and mother
was very indignant and she said, "We know Portia can do
the work. Well, she hasn't been here very much" (laughs).
I don't think I was, ah . . . there was anything physically wrong with me. I just . . . ah . . . I ah . . .
sensitive to ragweed pollen and so I would be sick, ah
. . . from hay fever the first month of school, and then I
got off to a bad start every year. And I had colds a lot.
(LP)

E: Your sister was older than you or . . .

S: Oh, she's younger, she's three years younger. And, ah
. . . this girl that was a year younger than I . . . that
was my good friend, I think I was accused rightfully of
bossing around a lot. And I think I bossed my sister
around to some extent too. And later on . . . she and my
sister became friends. It was nice for her because she
could boss my sister around. I think it was probably a
(laughs) good thing it worked out that way. It was nice,
ah . . . my sister had even fewer friends, I think, than I
did because there was nobody . . . nobody my sister's age.
This girl's younger brother . . . I suppose I should give
these people names. The girl's name is Sally, and my
sister's name is Sally too. This is going to confuse us
somewhat (laughs). Ah . . . let me see . . . And then we
moved to Panama Canal Zone when I was in the seventh,
eighth and ninth grades. And . . . that was a very lonely
period in which I spent a lot of time reading . . . I
didn't have the sense of liking to go outside and play

when my mother, ah . . . mother wouldn't make me go outside and play anymore because I was too old for that . . .
In grade school I'd sort of protest, but I really enjoyed
running around the yard and playing cowboys and Indians,
and so forth . . . and dolls. We used . . . we used to
play apothecary shop and make little things of berries
and grasses and things. We felt we were . . . we were
living the Williamsburg existence (laughs). I liked
especially to read about Colonial times and how you make,
ah . . . how they overcame hardships in the wilderness,
and so I used to like to overcome hardships in the wilderness. And there wasn't any wilderness around (laughs). I
did my best. But in Panama . . . ugh! . . . it was very
hard making the adjustment in school. I entered a month
late, and they were all very social. They'd been going to
dances since about fifth grade. I don't know quite why
this sort of society is . . . jumped up there, but that's
the way it was. They were all sitting around having
crushes on each other, And I got asked to a birthday party
right after I got there. Course the custom was to ask the
whole class. And I went expecting it to be a birthday
party like the old times, but no, it was a dance, and I
was just amazed. And so . . . I didn't know how to dance.
Ugh! Big problems! I adjusted to it pretty well, and by
the ninth grade I had a boyfriend of my own, which was very
pleasant. A big, tall handsome boyfriend . . . but I
wasn't very happy there. I didn't have any girl friends
who were very close to me. Ah . . . most of the girls
from American families as opposed to Panamanean--we called
them governmentals versus Panamaneans--lived in, ah . . .
exclusive suburbs quite a distance from the school. And
we had a small house in a sort of, ah . . . mixed
neighborhood, that is, a lot of Panamanean Spanish-speaking
families and a lot of governmental families, and the
governmental families were all, ah . . . they had young
children that I used to babysit for, 'cause there wasn't
anybody my age. And the Panamanean families sort of kept
to themselves . . . the two mixed in my school, but very
little elsewhere in the Zone, I think. I'm not sure how
true this is. And now I wish my parents had sent me to a
Spanish-speaking school, although, of course, I would have
jumped up and down and screamed if they had done that.
I'd have just hated it. But I would have learned Spanish.
There were some very good, ah . . . Roman-Catholic boarding
schools. But as it was, I was sent to this other school.
And the people there were nice but . . . . And governement
people were just down for a couple of years. And so it was
. . . a very fluctuating society.

E: How long were you there?
S: Three years. And there was a nice church which was . . .
    sort of an interdenominational Protestant church, and I

sang in the junior choir. We're Quakers, and the Friends
meeting in Philadelphia is very large and it's downtown,
so I didn't really know anybody in Sunday School. This
church in Panama was very active in many different ways
and my parents taught a Sunday School class for a while.
And I went to Sunday School, and I sang in the choir in
the service. That was good. And I started reading the
Bible, so I read three chapters of the Bible every night.
Started with the New Testament, then I read the Old
Testament. I don't quite know why, but I thought that
starting with the New Testament would be interesting, I
guess, or something (laughs). And I'm very glad that I've
done it. I--ah . . . it took me about a year and a half,
I think. I'd read however much it was . . . I think it was
three chapter or three pages, whichever was less (laughs).
It was really sort of . . . setting up this structure of
tasks to do, but I enjoyed it at the same time. And where
there was a lot of genealogical material I would skip that.
So and so was the father of so and so.

E: That must have been until you were about what . . . 12?

S: Ah, well . . . no, when I got there I was 11, and when I
left I was 14. It was seventh, eighth, and ninth grades.
Ah . . . I have this feeling that I didn't learn anything
in the school there. That . . . I think probably in junior
high school everywhere you sort of prepare yourself for
life more than actually learning academic material. There
was some problem when I got there because they were way ahead
in math from where I'd been. I failed a test and. oh . . .
oh, I was just so upset. I sort of . . . all the problems
of a new school, not knowing quite what to do, and now to
fail this test. But I overcame this problem. Um . . . I
was sort of different . . . and I felt that I was different,
in being probably a good deal more intelligent than most
people in the class and much more intelligent, and, ah . . .
there was another girl who was co-valedictorian with me
in the eighth grade, but she worked all the time. She was
a very . . . intense girl, and her mother made her work.
And I would get home from school and spend about a half hour
on my homework and that was it . . . and, ah . . . there
wasn't really very much for me to do.

E: I see.

S: My sister had more, a good many more, little friends in
Panama . . . I think she was in a Girl Scout troop and, ah
. . . there was a little girl in her class who was, ah . . .
smarter than she was, who Sally was a little jealous of
I think. And a number of other girls that she got to be
friendly with. And she was at . . . I guess a younger age
and not so sensitive and troubled with adolescence, and I
was all sensitive and troubled with adolescence.

E: Sensitive era.

S: And we'd go home every summer back to Delaware, ah . . .
stay with my grandparents. So there wasn't any continuity

in Panama, and when we were home for the summer it was just
me and my sister; cause we were out . . . about twenty
miles from Philadelphia, on this farm that my grandparents
owned. And I didn't see any other friends from home very
much at all. This sort of surprises me, now that I think
about it, that I didn't keep up the contacts with . . .
the girl who had been my best friend in the sixth grade
. . . her name was Sue . . . and who was also the girl I
spent last summer with. This friendship has lasted. And
then when I got back to Philadelphia and went to the high
school . . . ah . . . very big, very good high school . . .
somehow I wasn't, ah . . . able to establish my friendships with my old grammar school friends. And the first
year that I was there, ah . . . started out very badly. Redempt
Again I entered school a month late 'cause of the hay
fever problems, and, ah . . . it was sort of . . . it was
pretty difficult the first couple of weeks. And then a
girl whom I hadn't known very well in grammar school
approached me, and it seemed that there were sort of girl
sororities forming. These weren't really sororities . . .
they called them "pot lucks." And the idea was a pot luck
supper every Friday night. And she had not been asked to
join any of these groups, and I hadn't because I'd just
gotten back and . . . maybe for other reasons, I don't
know. And she said, "Look, why don't we form our own pot
luck?" . . . ah . . . I said, "OK, that's a good idea."
And so I looked around our classes for interesting-looking
girls who might not be members of such organizations. So
we got together a very, ah . . . heterogeneous group . . .
but it was fun . . . it was such a (laughs) weird group,
when I think about it. All kinds of different people.
Every once in a while we would add somebody. And ah . . .
we'd rotate from house to house and had these suppers and
then sit around and gossip. And we started out having
friends in common, and then we all got to be friends with
each other, and we for to know each others' circle of
friends, and it appeared that we'd all been in somewhat of
the same situation. Either we just moved to the area or
we'd been kind of out of the circle. And then the second
year, which was the eleventh grade, ah . . . I got put
into the rapid-learner classes . . . they called it . . .
a terrible name. The advanced placement classes, enriched,
I suppose you'd call them. And, ah . . . I hadn't been
placed in them the first year because I'd just come from
the Canal Zone and they didn't know what my talents were,
so I was just put in the regular program. Then I got put
in rapid-learners English, and suddenly a new circle of
friends emerged as the intellectuals of the school as
opposed to the others at school. And it was really funny.
There was a real clique of intellectuals at this high
school, which I hadn't realized my sophomore year there.

I became a member automatically by being in rapid-learner
English (laughs). Well, not quite automatically, there
were some people in our English who weren't . . . who were
more of the student government types. They've got, ah--
circles in the school. They've got athletic types, the
student government types, and the service club types, and
then the intellectuals. And we got . . . ah . . . we did
really funny things (laughs). Happiest years of my life,
I think, were eleventh and twelfth grades. The old pot
luck of tenth grade fell apart, and some of them graduated
to this new group. The people that I had liked best in
the pot luck I asked to the various parties being organized
by this new group and all. And the others . . . I really
don't know what happened to them, I'm sorry to say. They
probably continued to be excluded, I think. And that . . .
made me feel . . . slightly guilty, I guess. Although I
was very happy myself in this new, ah . . . circle of
friends. We had what we called YAAA, which was Young
Atheists and Agnostics of America . . . I was probably the
most religious of the group. I didn't want to admit how
religious I was (laughs). Ah . . . I got into a few
arguments about it, I think. We would meet, this time not
for supper but about once a week. We tried to get in
speakers, usually people's fathers 'cause there was a large
number of interesting fathers, so to speak. My father
spoke once about the political institutions in Latin
America, which is what his field is. And other people's
fathers were psychiatrists, mathematicians, and all kinds
of things. This was a co-educational group, which made it
much better (laughs). I started going out with . . . with
. . . first one boy and then his best friend. This was a
little touchy for them, but it was very pleasant for me
(laughs). And I dated him for most of the rest of high
school. He was very bright, an intense boy, and he was
. . . he was . . . fine thing to be going out with him
because he really . . . he really liked me, and he was
interested in . . . my thoughts and the kind of person I
was. And we'd have long talks about, ah . . . science and
all kinds of things. He was . . . I didn't really appreciate him at the time, I think. My parents liked him a
lot. And, ah . . . everybody in the group liked him. The
YAAA group (laughs) we were sort of, ah . . . ah . . .
known group at school. You know there goes one of those
YAAA people, and we'd agitate things. Like they were
building a stadium and we thought that money for the
stadium should be used for the library books (laughs). And
we ran most of the intellectual clubs like . . . I ran the
English Club. And there were others in the physics club
and math club, and so forth . . . and we didn't have anything to do with the . . . athletics or service clubs.

E: Yes. That carried you pretty well through your senior
     year.

S: Yeah. And I was studying pretty hard, too. It was the
    first challenging work I'd ever seen in school. There was
    the time in Panama when I had to catch up . . . was a
    challenging period . . . but, of course, I caught up . . .
    but . . . ah . . . junior and senior years in high school,
    these, ah . . . I was just in one rapid-learner class. I
    had the choice of being in math, but I decided that would
    be too much work, because I was taking one major subject
    more than a normal load. I think I probably could have
    handled another one, but I was just a little timid . . .
    I'm . . . ah . . . I wanted to be a teacher for a while,
    on and off. And I really got excited about being a teacher
    because of the English teacher I had sophomore and junior
    years. This is why I'm in English, really. He was a
    wonderful, wonderful man. He was . . . he was such an . . .
    ah . . . good example as well as a fine teacher. And,
    ah . . . he knew his literature. But he was . . . he
    trusted us so much. He would give tests and walk out of
    the room and give the same test to the first and fourth
    period classes . . . . By and large his trust in us was
    justified, I think.

E: They didn't cheat any?

S: There were a couple of people that I heard did . . . and
    people that I heard did, I've never been able to stomach
    (laughs). Ah . . . genial man . . . every once in a while
    he'd get angry at us, but not very often. A very fine
    person. And my senior year English teacher was another
    . . . really remarkable woman. She, ah . . . (pause) . . .
    every once in a while when there was some moral issue that
    she thought she ought to talk to us about she just would.
    She said she . . . she felt it necessary to give us a
    little pep talk on respect owed to teachers, dressing well
    in class, and things like that. But there were other . . .
    other things that . . . of that nature, and we'd all be
    sort of embarrassed while she was giving us these little
    talks. But I think we respected her a good deal for doing
    this, and her classes were so exciting. She'd get these
    good discussions going. We read good things and read a lot
    of papers. It was very, very good preparation for college.
    And very exciting.

E: English teachers can be. And meanwhile, your sister . . .
    when you were in this high school . . . was . . .

S: Was . . . well, she went to the junior high that I would
    have gone to if I'd stayed.

E: I see.

S: Instead I was in Panama, so there wasn't any competitive-
    ness there. And, ah . . . then when it came time to go to
    high school she decided that she hadn't been working as
    hard as she should in junior high and there was some, ah
    . . . she's part of the baby boom, and the high school that
    I went to was going to be very crowded. And I think that
    the real thing was this idea of competing with me, and that

she didn't like. Because all this time that I had been a
reader she had been definitely not a reader. And she once
told me that she used to get mad at me for not coming out
and playing instead of sitting and reading that silly book.
And, ah . . . it made a lot of difference in our school
careers, I think. I had sort of a backlog of information
and vocabulary, especially the ability to read fast, which
she didn't have at all. But, ah . . . I really enjoyed
school work, and I don't think she does. I can't figure
out whether she's, ah . . . less intelligent than I and
sensitive about that or not. It's my opinion that she's
not, but . . . I just don't know. She's not doing too
well at Syracuse. And I think it's because she doesn't
know how to study, more than anything else. Ah . . . she
isn't very well organized most of the time, I think.

E: I think intelligence comes in all kinds of shapes as well
as sizes.

S: Yeah, that's true, she's a very friendly, ah . . . self-
sacrificing sort of person. Ah . . . more apt to do favors
for people than I am. And . . . I don't know if it's true
that she's likely to have more friends than I. She
certainly dates a lot more than I do or would want to. Her
vacations are classics. Fourteen different dates during
the fourteen days of Christmas vacation. And I'm much more
interested in going out with one person at one time. And
I just . . . I've had some points in my life when I was
dating a number of different boys . . . and, ah . . . it
never seemed as satisfactory to me as liking one person and
góing out with him, getting to know him really well. And
she has just the opposite philosophy. I guess in the case
of Ken, I was the more . . . possessive. I recall that I
went away for a couple of weeks and he took out a couple
of girls. Oh, I was just furious. Long and bitter ex-
changes when we got back (laughs). I couldn't understand
. . . it was particularly bad because I couldn't understand
why in the world he'd want to take out the sorts of girls
. . . one girl is my . . . (laughs) enemy at school.
Terrible girl (laughs). And, ah . . . he said she was
interesting. Ugh! (laughs), and things weren't so good
after that. I decided that he really wasn't interested in
going steady as I was. And I became less interested in
going steady myself. So I broke up with him. Immediately
started going out with another boy (laughs) on a rather
firm basis also 'cause I . . . that's the way I operated
then.

E: What was the girl like that was your enemy?

S: She was a girl who was a year younger than we were, perhaps
two years. She was a grade behind us and I guess two years
younger. She came into my English class when I was a
junior and she was a sophomore. And . . . she had moved
from another school, and I, experiencing such difficulties

in moving from other schools myself . . . ah . . . decided
I ought to be especially friendly to her. And she, ah . . .
didn't settle into the group very well. She, ah . . .
she was younger than I and . . . she had a very sharp way
about her . . . sharp tongue. She'd say tactless things,
and she started coming to this . . . these YAAA groups and
acting as if she were running the group. Well, a lot of us
felt that we were doing her a favor by inviting her to
come. They were sort of mixtures of parties and discussion
groups. And, ah . . . she began inviting many of her
friends from her old school. And sort of awkward when this
girl you've asked to come to your pseudoparties, and they
were really parties, shows up at the next one with five
friends. And then just the crowning blow came . . . at the
end of my junior year; this was before Ken started taking
her out, before she was really my enemy. At the end of my
junior year my English teacher . . . got a fellowship. And I
decided to give him a surprise farewell party. I had
gotten dressed up . . . uh . . . sort of dressed up a
little bit. And she looked at me and said, "Portia, you
actually look nice. I can't believe it" (laughs).

E: Oh, dear.

S: Kind of girl that would say something like that . . . I
decided no (laughs). This was the summer part of which I
went away and I discovered Ken had gone out with Liz. And
I just, oh . . . she was an interesting girl. I think she
was intelligent, and more of a rebel than I was. He didn't
get along well with . . . his parents at all. I got along
very well with mine. And he was always defying them.
Whereas I would tend not to defy mine. We had . . . there
was a controversy over whether I would stick up for my
rights to come in later than they wanted me to come in . . .
it was 12:30 or something . . . it was a reasonable hour.
But Ken . . . wanted me to rebel just so that I could rebel.
I didn't see any point to that (laughs).

E: So . . . that girl was more or less the bone of contention
between you.

S: Yeah. And the issue of rebellion against my parents was
another one, I guess . . . (P) . . . other than that he was
a very easy person to get along with. He, at the beginning
he used to write these long poems. Oh, it was very sweet.
I have this manila folder full of writings from Ken of
various kinds. Unfortunately . . . he became very, ah . .
self-conscious. Not as friendly and outgoing as he had
been. And I've seen him very infrequently since. He was
usher at a friend of mine's wedding, and they said old Ken
was sort of insufferable now. Really too bad. He had a
little beard (laughs). I can hardly believe it (laughs).
He was a very short blonde boy. He looked very young.
The first time we went out (laughs) . . . let's see . . .
we were going to a dance at school, I guess. And we'd
just looked at each other, and it was so obvious that we

looked so young, both of us. I think we were crossing the
street . . . we just escaped being hit by a car, and we
were imagining the headlines, you know, "Two sixth-
graders (laughs) hit by speeding auto" (laughs). Really,
it was sort of . . . sort of the joke of the group about
how short we both were and . . . probably one of the
reasons he liked me (laughs). . . . There were other short
people around, so that wasn't the reason.

E: You could be babes together.

S: (Laughs) It was very good.

SECOND INTERVIEW (FEBRUARY): ENTERING COLLEGE AND MEETING JOHN

E: Tell us more about yourself.

S: Oh, dear (laughs). Of course, I've been thinking about
what I should add. And it strikes me that I didn't tell
you about how I'm extremely near-sighted and I was very
conscious, self-conscious, about this when I was young.
In fact until recently when I got contact lenses; that
helped quite a bit.

E: I hadn't noticed them.

S: Yeah, I've had them for about five years. They've, oh,
just made . . . just a complete difference in my personality. I got them right before my junior year of high
school. Junior and senior years were the great glorious
years, and a lot of it was 'cause I thought that I looked
so much better. My glasses are very thick and ugly. They
don't correct me all the way . . . even the lenses don't,
so that I still can't see things. And I get a little bit
defensive when I can't and people expect that I can. "You
can't see that?" and I have to say "No." I'm much better
about it than I was, but when I was in, ah . . . elementary school I used to have to sit in the very front of the
room, and new teachers or substitute teachers wouldn't
know this and . . . they'd put me in the back. I took it
as sort of a . . . personal attack (laughs). And I can
tell all these amusing anecdotes that weren't amusing at
all and they . . . I can . . . you know, break people up
with my tales (laughs) of these sad occasions. They don't
really seem very funny to me even now. And there'd be
other occasions when I'd get upset . . . . I was sort of
noted as the girl who cried and, ah . . . I think in the
first grade, somebody said, "Hey, Portia's crying again"
(laughs). I remember it very vividly. And I remember,
uh . . . sad things . . . (P) . . . from . . . that period
of time, more than happy things. I think I must have been
pretty unhappy in first and second grades ' cause I was
sick a lot from school. My earliest memory of all was a
very happy occasion, eating breakfast with my father. If
you want (laughs) that's significant . . . probably the

reason I was eating breakfast with my father was that my
mother was home from the hospital with my sister (laughs),
and I felt a little bit resentful of the fact that Mommy
hadn't been around and Mommy seemed to be busy with somebody else (laughs). I used to sing to Sally. She would
say, "Now you take care of Sally and go and sing to her,
and play with her," when she was lying in her crib, and
I was about 4 (laughs). So I guess they used that technique to help me adjust to the newcomer. Let's see . . .
um . . . I wasn't very good at sports, either, but I don't
think that bothered me very much, and I was all right at
jump rope. That was the big thing. Aw--everybody was very
good at jump rope. In fifth and sixth grades we started
playing things like baseball, Tsch! (deprecating noise).
I wasn't very good at them. I was afraid. I still am. I
don't like any sports where there's a ball involved 'cause
I'm afraid of things moving towards me. I don't know
whether it's because of my glasses or what. But I'm not
physically very brave about that kind of encounter. We
took a trip to Europe after the Panama stay, which was very
nice. Yeah, we went to Holland, we met my father there.
And then around up through Germany and down through Austria
to get to Italy and to France. We were fortunate to be
able to do it. . . . I'm near-sighted so I can read maps,
so I was sort of the family map reader.

E: Navigator.

S: Yeah. Right. My sister didn't go too much for that
(laughs) either. Mommy . . . and she are far-sighted and
they'd read the street signs (laughs). Daddy and I read
the maps. And I have a sort of business mentality. I'm
an organized, efficient person, I guess. And my mother
claims she isn't. Although it's always been my belief that
she could be better if she tried. So anything to do with
math she doesn't like, paying the bills or anything. My
father and I are very . . . I . . . much less than my father
. . . used to doing things like that. But I'm getting
better and better at it all the time. When I go shopping
I make a shopping list and then I get everything from the
list. And when she goes shopping she just wanders around
and sees things that she remembers that she needs and
(laughs) and forgets others that I've pointed out to her.
But she's just not going to force herself to be organized
enough. Um . . . after Ken I went out with another boy in
high school toward the end of the senior year. He didn't
really want to go out with me after the first date,
apparently, but, ah . . . it was a very strange situation.
And apparently . . . after the first few dates he really
decided that, ah . . . he wasn't so keen going out with me
and he <u>thought</u>, but he'd already asked me to go to the
senior prom and (laughs), and his best friend told him that
he just had to take me to the senior prom because if he

didn't take me nobody else was going to. And he realized
this. And he thought that he ought to sort of go along
with our dating relationship so that I wouldn't think it
was very strange that he stopped going out with me all of
a sudden and then took me to the senior prom . . . (laughs)
and, ah . . . so I didn't know this. I was . . . I was
fairly oblivious to subtleties of other people at that
time. And it's something that I worry about . . . in my-
self--today. Although I think I'm a lot better than I was.
But I tend not to notice that people are . . . under a
little strain or something. And, ah . . . to be somewhat
insensitive. I don't think I'm as bad now as I was. And
I'm a little bit self-centered, I guess. So I didn't
notice that anything was wrong. Ugh! (laughs), but it was
indeed. And after the senior prom suddenly the ax fell
(laughs).

E: Oh, dear.

S: Oh, gosh. I felt sort of bad about that for a while but
. . . ah . . . there wasn't any permanent scar. He, ah
. . . he was very different from me . . . he was very keen
on classical music, and he was trying to educate my ear.
And he didn't have very many friends . . . . He liked
classical music, and he knew a lot more about it than most
of us did. We all said we did because it was the intellectual thing to do. But he really knew just what he was
talking about. And he had been in love with this friend
of mine whom he'd sort of worshipped from afar about three
years and apparently . . . although he had thought he was
getting over it when he went out with me, he actually
hadn't been getting over it. This was a very . . . very
nice girl who I think was probably the most mature of us.
She was able to go . . . to be friends with a whole wide
group of people. Most of us had no contact with people
who were older. We didn't know people who were younger,
except for that infamous Liz (laughs). After we graduated
Liz became a ring leader in the school of rebellion and
trouble, apparently. I talked to my English teacher when
I came back, and she said, "Boy, that Liz . . ."--only she
said it more like an English teacher would say it. And,
ah . . . I said, "I've always disliked that Liz." And she
said, "Well, your instincts were right" (laughs). Ah--
she's just a troublemaker. She . . . you know, was very
sassy to the teachers.

E: Was she the one that gave moral lectures?

S: Yeah, yeah. Wonderful woman, but wouldn't condone any kind
of unusual behavior from somebody like Liz . . . (P) . . .
Well, then I went to college. And . . . my roommate was a
wonderful girl who is now married with a baby. And I'm
still very good friends with her, although I don't get too
much of a chance to see her. We got finally to be very,
very close friends by the end of the year. It was sort of

hard for both of us to adjust, and neither of us had ever
lived away from home for any significant period of time.
And . . . it worked out very well. We did much better than
most . . . and the college doesn't really know who to put
you in with.

E: Of course.

S: (Laughs) But she . . . I remember we exchanged letters, and
I said that I was a Quaker and Democrat, and I was interested in English. She wrote back and she said she was a Catholic and a Republican and interested in science (laughs).
And I thought, oh no! But we turned out to be more alike
than these things would indicate. At that point the relationship I'd had with Ken was still . . . and it's still
something I think back on with great affection. He did
things like try to get me interested in science. And, ah
. . . I didn't do much more than encourage him, I guess
(laughs). But ah . . . we'd go out and go to parties and
movies or something like that. And, ah . . . I would come
home very enthusiastic because sometimes he would be very
. . . very, very sweet and, "Oh, he's wonderful." But no
. . . we sort of severed relations at--toward the end of
freshman year, and I was very unhappy about that. And . . .
(P) . . . Then I got home for the summer, and I took French
in summer school that summer. And I went out with a boy
whom I'd known in high school . . . his name is Danny. His
best friend was going out with a good friend of mine, so the
four of us doubled all summer. The trouble was both Danny
and Barry were, um . . . I don't know . . . psychologically
upset. Each of them alone . . . Danny when he's not with
Barry is extremely fun to be with. You got the four of us
together and we were all kind of, ah . . . not too sure of
ourselves.

E: Edgy?

S: Yeah (sighs). One time we were sitting in the living room,
sort of all staring at the floor and not saying anything,
and my father came in and said, "What is this, a Quaker
meeting?" (laughs), and everybody went "Ugh" (laughs). Oh,
I don't know how sensitive . . . he is to the problems of
the young (laughs). But . . . ah . . . my parents had a
lot of trouble with my sister during the same period. Uh
. . . they were very worried about her because she was going
with a rather wild crowd that was older than she. And they
thought that they had had trouble with me and my slight
tendency, egged on by Ken, if you remember, to want to stay
out later than they said. But my sister . . . curfew had
no meaning for her. And, ah . . . oh, she started drinking . . . the people that she was going out with were a
drinking lot. Mother is very fearful that she had made too
much out of me and not enough of Sally. And that she'd
been sort of selling Sally down the river all her life because she wasn't quite as intellectual as I was. And she
was just so worried about this. I don't know how true it

is. I don't think it's . . . Sally . . . when questioned
says she never had that feeling at all. And, ah . . . I
don't think Mother's the kind of person that would do that
at all, but she . . . Mother got tremendously guilty. I
think she was undergoing menopause at the time and all
these things . . . she was sort of on edge that summer
. . . and she was very much more sympathetic to Sally than
Daddy was, so that these questions of discipline would be
this sort of . . . "Well, ah, it sounds all right to me,
but I'll have to ask your father." Of course, Daddy would
be against it completely, but Mother had already tentative-
ly agreed and all this stuff. It was very bad . . . Then
the second half of the summer I met this wonderful boy who
I thought was a good deal of my life for the next two years.
And whom I'm still . . . I don't want to be, but I am sort
of involved with. His name is John . . . very tall, virile-
looking person. I think about six feet tall. And oh . . .
I'd never gone out with anybody this good looking and dashing, with all this savoir faire . . . and, ah . . . great
stuff. I immediately ditched Danny in a rather callous
manner. Uh . . . Danny had been sort of depressing me. It
was getting depressing to be with him because he was troubled. I felt that I wanted somebody to help me (laughs)
more than I wanted to help Danny. But then . . . when John
appeared on the scene and he, ah . . . as I say, we were in
French class . . . and I offered . . . He asked me if I
would type a paper for him because he was a very slow typ-
ist, and I said sure, and then he took me out afterwards
and, ah, he was great . . . we . . . we went to, ah . . .
it was a folk singing place in Philadelphia. Sort of college place. There was a favorite song we wanted to hear,
and the singer didn't sing it until 1:30 or something
(laughs). Oh! . . . and then by the time we got out of
there it was much too late to, ah . . . I couldn't drive
at the time and neither could John. And so we walked home,
which was about four miles (laughs), and we were just talking and seemed to be so, ah . . . have so much in common.
It was just wonderful. Oh! Oh so golden, evening was very
warm, Philadelphia summer evening. And ah . . . ah . . .
just great, and he asked me, "Can I go out with you Saturday
night?" I was going out with Danny so I couldn't. I said
no. He said Sunday night. I said, "Oh, wonderful!" So I
went out with him Sunday night bowling. And . . . (P) . . .
and then I went out with him, let's see . . . for some reason there wasn't class one night and he took me to a play.
And . . . after the play we were sitting and talking about
why we had been attracted so to each other, and he said that
I seemed to be the kind of person that he would like to
marry. And I said, Oh! I was so surprised, amazing you
know. And I said, "My goodness me." And somehow or other

by the end of the evening we were going to get married
(laughs). That was . . . and it kept up for, ah . . .
well, as I say, for two years, off and on. There was this
eventual goal of marriage. Of course, I had thought about
it before. I guess girls do, sort of imagine what it would
be like to be married to X. And with John it seemed really
possible. It's very hard for me to talk about him. I'm
sort of . . . right now, resentful of him, so I'm not . . .
I don't know how good a picture I can give of him. He's
very, very intelligent. And he goes . . . he went to
Columbia. And very, very erratic and not disciplined, and
not very . . . not very self-disciplined, and totally
hostile to anybody else that is disciplined. And I think
that he feels guilty about not being disciplined and therefore any criticism of him is resented even more than it
would be ordinarily. I mean everybody resents criticism
but, ah . . . anyway, my criticism would be sort of
implicit rather than explicit, 'cause I'm, as I said, a
very disciplined, sort of organized person. And it's very
hard for me to change my mind. Uh . . . ah . . . for
instance, his friends were . . . ah . . . the boys he'd
gone to prep school with, and they drank a lot and they
were very different kinds of people than I was used to.
Unintellectual in the extreme. Very smart but just not
interested in sitting around discussing poetry all evening.
And, ah . . . and were very . . . (P) . . . We used to
have conflicts about them, ah . . . (P) . . . 'cause these
drinking parties were . . . I don't know, you just don't
get to know somebody if they . . . ... everybody stands
around just sort of pouring beer down as fast as they can.
I was very resentful of them. And they were also nice
people when I met them in other contexts. But you got them
all together at parties, as I once explained to John, and
they were all sort of interested in proving themselves.
And, of course, you get a bunch of intellectuals together
and they're all interested in proving how much they've
read, and so forth. But, ah . . . you get a bunch of beer
drinkers together and they're interested in proving themselves, and they do it by drinking a lot of beer. And
there's just nothing you can do. If it's an intellectual
conversation you can prove yourself too. But I'm not much
of a drinker, and as a matter of fact I tend to get very
relaxed and uninhibited, and I can do it even without
liquor at all. And there's many times people have thought
that I was a little tipsy and I hadn't had a drop to drink
. . . 'cause I was just feeling good and, ah . . . unrestrained. But the technique of these people was to drink
and not show it, just not show it in any way. You hand
wasn't supposed to shake, you weren't supposed to raise
your voice or get gay, just sort of glug (gestures--laughs),
and I like to drink and sort of relax and do a few silly

things, dance around a little bit to music, that kind of
thing. John would, you know . . . "Why do you have to get
so drunk?" And I'd say, "Well, I wasn't very drunk. I
was just feeling good," and he'd say, "Well, you know,
restrain yourself." I'd say, "Why?" It didn't embarrass
me, and it obviously did embarrass him. I just . . . I
wasn't, ah . . . sensitive to this because, uh . . . I like
. . . I just (P) . . . I guess I'm sort of an exhibition-
ist, and I . . . and I don't mind having everybody looking
at me and saying, "What a silly looking thing to be doing."
Uh . . . and I don't . . . when I drink I don't get unkind
to other people or . . . or rowdy in a way that would
disturb anybody. Except my date if he was embarrassed that
I'm . . . that I'm behaving this unusual fashion, but you
know . . . just seems . . . I was at a party recently where
I had this long dangling necklace on, so (laughs) we were
all . . . there was this cool music playing, and I sort of
. . . I took off my necklace and sort of twirling it around
the floor and jumping over it. And everybody was, ha, ha
(laughs), and I was going, ha-ha, and I stopped after a
while. And everybody thought this was a clever thing to
do. And . . . that was the kind of thing that was going
on, except nobody else was taking off their necklace and
jumping over it (laughs). Oh!

E: Just fun.

S: Try that at a party with John and his friends and you'd
feel like you're some kind of . . . . And John used to
like to prove himself by driving in an inebriated condition.
And, oh, my . . . parents had brought me up in such a way
that this . . . Oh! And the quarrels we used to have about
that. Oh! . . . And I . . . he's a very strong. Forceable
personality; I would usually give in to him. And he was in
perfectly good . . . control condition for any normal
driving. But, of course, if any . . . I don't know whether
he . . . I'm not an extremely good driver myself, so in
almost any circumstances he's a better driver than I am.
And he did drive cautiously because he knew he was drunk,
but, ah . . . there was always a rule that was in my mind
that if you're drunk you don't drive. And it's, as I say,
very hard for me to adjust to things that go against all
these rules. I suppose it's my superego or whatever that
I . . . that I've learned. The various things that I just
can't do, that I can't throw trash out of a car . . . it
seems to me . . . just . . . ah . . . sort of a moral crime.
People that throw beer cans out of cars I think are just
loathsome, I just can't stand them--the sort of people
that drop trash around the streets. Ah . . . this used to
upset John . . . (P) . . . because he didn't see why I felt
this way about some things and yet on an issue of civil
rights I'm in favor of civil disobedience. And his argument goes something like . . . you know, if you're . . .

if you're in favor of law as a thing to be obeyed because
it's a thing to be obeyed, then you ought to obey all laws
without question. And, ah . . . my defense was always that
I would obey the laws that seemed to me good laws. Like it
seems to me a good thing not to throw stuff out of cars.
And then if I really morally felt that a law was bad, there
wasn't anything wrong with breaking it. And, ah . . . it's
sort of a Quaker tradition, I think. And it's all, ah . . .
the situation in which you, ah . . . have faith in an
individual's power to reason about a thing like a law, and
to make their own decisions on a moral basis. And John was
brought up an Episcopalian, and I think he's sort of torn.
He doesn't think much of the Quaker kind of worship because
it's too much a personal thing. He thinks worship should
be more directed. For a while he was going to be an
Episcopalian minister, although you may (laughs) not have
thought so to listen to my description of him. But while
he was in high school he was really, ah . . . extremely
devout. And that kind of worship was very appealing to him,
whereas I like a sense of direct communication between God
and . . . and the individual . . . . Well, as I said, it's
hard to talk about John. His parents . . . are always at
each other's throats, and they mean well. But they're the
kind of people that are always quarreling. Tremendous out-
bursts of temper . . . just any time. Which is a way of
living that is foreign to me. My parents are controlled.
I think my mother perhaps is excessively controlled. She
. . . she gets . . . gets guilt feelings when she loses
her temper at all. And, ah . . . she'll usually try to go
some place else if she feels on edge and she's going to
explode at somebody. And I . . . I tend to lose my temper
and then get over it. I try not to be quite as controlled
as my mother, although somewhat controlled. But, ah . . .
my father is a very easygoing person. I don't think he has
to try very hard to control himself. It just seems to come
natural. That's the way it would be nice to be. I was not
used to any displays of temper. Especially condoning such
displays. Every once in a while some display of temper
would ensue and, ah . . . we'd get tramped on, and get
sent to our rooms as punishment (laughs). I would go to
my room and really brood about what an awful girl I was.
I remember very . . . ah . . . really feeling that I'd just
disgraced the whole family. I think once in a while mother
would say, after a party, when I had been bad and raucous
. . . she would say, "Now Portia, I was really ashamed of
you, you know. What will people think about the way I am
bringing you up?" This was her line, you know. What will
people think about me if you act that way. Which I understand from child psychologists isn't a good way for her to
act (laughs), for her to discipline me. But, ah . . . it
worked like a charm. I have this powerful superego . . .
(laughs) as a result. And, ah . . . I'd say . . . I'd just

feel like I was a worm and I'd go down all penitent and
I'd say, "Oh, Mother, I'm sorry I threw blocks at Sally"
(laughs). Sally, apparently, did not react to this form
of . . . she would go to her room and hum and sing (laughs).
She wasn't guilty at all (laughs). Well, ah . . . in
John's household . . . ah . . . people would storm out of
the room slamming the door. Every once in a while he'd
say, "I'm never coming back," and sort of tramp out of the
house, and, ah . . . you can very rarely eat a meal at
John's home that doesn't become involved in some great
debate over some rather inconsequential point. I recall
once they were arguing about how an accident had occurred.
And they were trying to describe this to John and they
practically came to blows (laughs). It was real . . . I'd
never been in such a situation of trying to pour oil on
the waters. I'd try to get everything in harmony. And
John would be in there fighting with the rest . . . And he
wanted me to be on his side at all times. Just sort of,
ah . . . moral issue . . . If you're committed to somebody the way I was committed to him, then I should defend
him. I could attack him when we were alone. But in the
company of others I was supposed to be a supporting member.
Well, I didn't see this, you know. . . . If I felt his
parents were right and he was wrong, well, I couldn't.
The way it would end up was that I kept quiet most of the
time . . . (P)

E: It's not satisfying.

S: (Laughs) Oh, dear. We had such . . . hmm . . . we went
out sophomore . . . I would go down to Columbia every other
weekend. And then . . . over the summer it was when I went
on this classical tour that he started going out with this
Holyoke girl, unbeknown to me. And he didn't write to me,
and I thought he just wasn't much of a letter writer. And
then he wrote me and said, "By the way I've been going out
with a Holyoke girl, but I've decided that you are the one,
and that she's all wrong." This letter arrived at the end
of this tour. Oh, I was so upset. Oh . . . Oh, dear.
And, ah . . . I went home and we had a long talk about it
and I just . . . ah, I was very upset . . . (P) . . . We
started going together again, and then we broke up in
about a month's time. And then after about two months of
school we started going together again. Let's see . . .
that's junior year? . . . Yeah, and then February of that
year he appeared in Cambridge. Just a black day . . .
blackest day of my life. He woke me up out of a sound
sleep at seven in the morning. I'd been up until two
studying for an hour exam. The hour exam was that day.
He announced that it was all over; he just couldn't go on.
I was just . . . oh, I was absolutely stunned. He then
left. I took (laughs) the hour exam and then went to the

dentist. It was an extremely painful (laughs) removal of a
nerve, of a dying nerve in a tooth. Ah . . . terrible
terrible day, just awful. And I immediately went into a
frenzy of dating. I went to mixers and I was . . . ah . . .
(P) . . . went on a lot of blind dates, none of which
were successful.

E: But . . . it was hard to get over John.

S: Oh, absolutely. And especially because I was used to
having a close relationship and arguing about . . . you
sort of . . . I . . . we would tell each other about everything. It probably wasn't too good an idea, either. But
we just felt that we had to. It was not that that's a
bad idea. But this . . . this feeling that everything had
to come out. You . . . you had to really dredge up this,
sort of, like, ah . . . finding bad things in yourself so
you could display them as proof of your honesty, you know.

E: Well, our time seems to be up.

S: OK, all about . . . ah . . . much more to tell about
John (laughs).

THIRD INTERVIEW (MARCH): IN COLLEGE: MAINLY ABOUT JOHN

S: I got up to John last time, as I recall. Beginning on that
saga. I told you what a glorious time it was. And we just
seemed so much alike, and we decided we were going to get
married after three days. Yes. I told you all about that
. . . and, ah . . . then the problem of sex came up because, ah . . . neither John nor I had had any experiences
beyond the sort of necking you do in high school. And John,
ah . . . had been more exposed to people that had been
sleeping with people, but he hadn't himself. Not for any
moral reasons , I don't think. At least he said it was
because . . . he . . . it just hadn't happened to happen
that way. And, ah . . . we both decided . . . well, he
was urging me to sleep with him and I was . . . resisting
. . . . I didn't think that was the right thing to do then.
And I had had a discussion with my mother in the early part
of the summer. She was very worried about my sister and
she said, "Oh, I'm just so worried. Sally won't know what
she's doing. And will, ah . . . just let her feelings
carry her away." My mother is very reticent. She won't
call a spade a spade . . . (laughs) in such discussions
(laughs). Ah . . . she gave us little talks when we were
9 because, ah . . . she . . . matured early and she thought
we would too. So she had to warn the two of us of the
comings and so she did. But she didn't like to do it very
much . . . at all. She gave us a little book (laughs) . . .
ah . . . and we had an idea of what . . . of what kinds of
people she wanted us to be. And, ah . . . so in this

discussion of mine, I felt that I should reassure Mother.
And I said, "You don't have to worry. I know you brought
us up right,and, ah . . . I certainly know myself that I
wouldn't . . . I wouldn't dream of sleeping with anybody
until I was married." I was just so sure, and Mother said,
"Oh, that's wonderful" (laughs). So we were riding downtown, and I remember it very clearly, it being in the summer, and, ah . . . having had this discussion . . . rather
recently with Mother, I was even more against the idea of
doing something behind her back. I guess I was feeling
very close to my parents; for the first time I was feeling
like they were treating me like an adult, and that was very
good. They were having such troubles with my sister, and I
think they were treating me like an adult . . . like an
adult sooner than they would have otherwise.

E: Yes, I see.

S: They were treating my sister so much like a little . . .
like a little girl (laughs). Ah . . . but John and I went
to the beach. And we walked up and down the beach one day,
and finally I decided it just didn't seem to make any
sense if I was going to marry him anyway, not to sleep with
him, so I said, "All right, I will." Ah . . . and we got
back to Philadelphia and I did. And then I felt . . . I
just thought it was . . . I wasn't at all guilt-ridden or
anything. I felt that it was just a good thing to do.
But I felt I ought to tell my mother, because I'd implied
so strongly that I wouldn't do such a thing . . . and so I
did . . . which . . . all my friends find incomprehensible.
None of them . . . one of them had after she got engaged,
been able to mention to her mother that she had, but my
roommate said her mother would just curl up and die. And,
ah . . . Mother was , , , ah . . . I think Mother was very
glad that I told her. So . . . she said, "Well, oh dear!"
(laughs). And I said, "Now, don't worry, Mother, I'm sure
it's all right." I was just so happy. I still thought
everything was great (laughs). And ah . . . we went back
to school. John was starting the second year at Columbia,
and I was a sophomore at Radcliffe. I was just so happy.
I . . . ah . . . this period, I look back to the first
semester of my sophomore year, just seemed like a golden
time when nothing was going wrong--although that wasn't
the case now that I suddenly remember. Ah . . . but I came
up to the school and I greeted everybody and I told them
that I met this boy that I'm going to marry. It's wonderful. And everybody was happy and I was happy. And then
my roommate, ah . . . this wasn't the girl that I'd had as a
roommate . . . freshman year because she had left school.
Ah . . . but this was a very nice girl. And a little young
. . . she was a year younger. and at the very beginning of
the year her brother had been killed in a very tragic auto
accident. . . .

E: Oh, dear.

S: And she had to go home, and her family was just distraught.
He was the middle child of the family and the oldest boy
and, ah . . . her parents had had great hope for him . . .
he had been sort of a golden boy, and he was just entering
high school. And . . . the family was just crushed. Polly
came back because her parents said, "You just have to go
back to school and continue as if nothing had happened."
But she just couldn't, and she had to take sleeping pills
every night. And I had to spend a lot of time talking to
her and trying to cheer her up, which wasn't easy. She
wasn't, ah . . . her family wasn't all that religious.
And she didn't have any . . . any solace, any place to turn
for comfort at all. That was sort of . . . hard on me. I
didn't . . . I didn't think of it as being especially hard
. . . And as a matter of fact, my hard time with Polly came
the next year when, ah . . . (P) . . . a reaction set in in
her against having confided so much to me . . . sophomore
year. She's a very, ah . . . withdrawn, sort of shy, girl,
and she had . . . she'd gotten hysterical a few times, and
she had really felt that I knew all the worst things about
her, I guess. And so . . . she . . . ah . . . so junior
year she and I didn't communicate much at all. Sophomore
year she had been needing all the help and I had been
giving all the help, and because I was very happy with
John and very happy in other ways, ah . . . it wasn't hard
for me to do this. But then junior year when things began
to go bad, especially with John, ah . . . (P) . . . I would
have liked to be able to talk to her, but I didn't feel
that I could. And she'd never . . . felt about anyone the
way I felt about John . . . I don't think.

E: It must have been hard to handle.

S: Yeah, sophomore year as I say . . . it was sort of like, ah
. . . a child that looks up to you and you don't need to
worry about what to do, you're just consoling, and if you
just have patience enough you can, and if she needs you so
much, 'cause she did then, you . . . then you can find the
patience. It's when she was . . . junior year when she
was recovering . . . ah . . . wasn't quite so unhappy and
was beginning to fell, ah . . . you know, "What did I do
last year. Ohhhhh, I must have told Portia all that."
Well, ah . . . so I was very glad to be able to go down to
New York every once in a while . . . sophomore year and get
away from (laughs) ah . . . Polly . . . Polly didn't like
that very much but, ah . . . (P) . . . she saw that I had
to go. Ah . . . I stayed with my aunt and uncle in New
York, and that was very pleasant. Things continued very
well . . . (P) . . . And I thought everything was just fine.
And it was for the first semester. And the second semester
. . . apparently John began to, ah . . . have a few doubts.
He'd just spent a year out of school working and deciding

what he was going to do with his life. And he decided to
change in various ways. My new theory is that he saw me
as . . . the embodiment of the kind of person he was going
to be. And, ah . . . of course, I was a very . . . a good
student and, ah . . . controlled myself and, ah . . . this
was what he wanted to do, and he'd really buckled down,
and, ah . . . toward the end of the year it began . . . it
negan to seem to him that he'd given up a lot . . . his
various drinking friends and the whole kind of rowdy
escapades he'd gotten into freshman year. But he had decided
even before I left for Europe that while I was gone he was
going to try to go out with somebody else. And . . . I
never have understood this because he was going to, ah . . .
establish a casual yet meaningful relationship. It was
going to last only as long as I was in Europe, and it
was going to be very definitely terminated when I got back.
But at the same time it was going to have some sort of
meaning and help him determine his life. I've never been
able to figure what the heck he thought he was doing. However, I went off to Europe . . . and my parents mentioned
in a couple of letters that he'd come over and played
croquet with the family, so I thought OK, fine. And then
about the last week I received this letter from him in
which he told me that he'd gone out with this girl, and
that he had now decided that she was not for him and he
was ready to welcome me back home. Well, of course, the
whole thing was horrible. This is the incident that I was
describing to my friend last night. We were trying to
decide, my friend and I, about the whole question of fidel-
ity, because he claims that he wouldn't mind if his wife
was unfaithful, and I say, "How in the world can you say
that? I would mind very much because it's an expression
of . . ." ah ". . . it's an insult. It's saying that . . .
that you're not satisfying me in some way, so I have to
go out and find somebody else . . . it isn't just sex, it's
the whole . . . the meaning of sex, and . . . and the fact
that you're having to find something in someone else that
your wife isn't giving you." I felt this about old John.
Because, ah . . . here he was . . . and he hadn't <u>told</u> me
. . . all this had been going on behind my back before
I'd left, even . . . and not a word had been said. Aw . . .
I was just . . . tremendously upset. And, ah . . . my
friends urged me to stay over a few weeks in Europe and
show <u>him</u> (laughs), boy! But, ah . . . well, I wasn't
having any of that . . . I zipped home immediately (laughs),
and he hitched up to New York to meet the plane, which was
a very noble thing to do. And, ah . . . I was very un-
comfortable with him. I didn't sleep at all on the flight
because I don't sleep on . . . such moving vehicles very
well. And so I was just exhausted when I got to New York,
and we got home to Philadelphia and, ah . . . then we sat

up all night talking, and I was . . . ugh . . . drooping,
but, ah . . . I didn't express myself very well. I had
very queer feelings about this whole thing, which I tried
to tell him, and he . . . and he agreed with me. He has
this habit of . . . of . . . of erring, and then he, he
recognizes quite clearly all the ways he was wrong, and he
just promises to do better and . . . you always believe
him (laughs). Ah . . . so . . . (P) . . . we got together
again for the rest of the summer. We broke up in the early
fall before going up to school. And he wrote me long
letters about how much he was sure, this is it. I guess
the break-up period lasted only the first couple of weeks
of school. So we began going out and, ah . . . it was . . .
uh . . . the . . . the whole thing was punctuated by
fierce quarrels, and there were lots of strains . . . that
. . . that were sort of continual . . . . Anytime X problem came up, it could cause a great reaction from both of
us, and probably more me than him. He can . . . he can
argue you into a hole (laughs) at any time. Oh, it would
be so maddening, we'd go over the same ground again and
again.

E: Very frustrating.
S: Yeah, oh it was. And at the same time we . . . I . . . oh,
I admired him in so many ways. And he admired me, and we
just felt it was so important that we keep on. I didn't
ever want to end it all, until more recently, but he . . .
would go through periods of just wanting to, and then he
would go through periods of optimism, and then he'd be sure
that we couldn't work out the problems. Well, one big . . .
the big split came, oh . . . February of last year. Ah
. . . it was . . . I don't know. Did I tell you about this
dreadful day? Oh, dreadful day. Well, he woke me up at
seven, called me, and I said, "John?" He said, "I'm in
Cambridge." "What are you doing here?" He said, "I have
to talk to you." I said, "I have an hour exam." He said,
"No, I have to talk to you." So we went out and had breakfast together. He said that he decided that we just had to
break up. I said, "What? Oh, no." And I . . . I was just
so . . . really stunned. And, ah . . . I don't remember
any of the rest of the conversation that we had. And finally he left and . . . I went and studied some more for
the hour exam, just sort of sublimated, and took the hour
exam and went to the dentist. Oh, terrible, terrible day.
And, ah . . . immediately that night I called up my old
friend who went to high school with me, Joe. And I think
that I went over for dinner to King House that very night,
I'm not sure. Anyway . . . I entered into a frenzy of activity. Ah . . . I'm not sure. Anyway . . . ah, I studied
very hard, and went out on a lot of blind dates . . . ah
. . . it was kind of a thing that I really don't like to
do . . . go out a lot with various people that you don't
care very much about. Ah . . . but that's what I was

doing. And, ah . . . in early May I went to a party and I
met this . . . this English, ah . . . major. He just
finished his thesis, and he was very happy and relaxed.
And, ah . . . the next thing I knew I was in the middle of
an affair with this person. I didn't believe what I was
doing but I seemed to be doing it. And, ah . . . this
lasted all through May, and it was very . . . it was very
. . . (P) . . . sex has always been very important to me,
and John had been the only one and I'd been . . . ah . . .
very unhappy that he was now sleeping with this other girl.
And that was one of the worst things about it . . . it made
me cringe every time I thought . . . about it. So this was
defiance, obviously. Very, ah . . . Well, I was going to
show him, boy! and (laughs) and, ah . . . it wasn't a very
smart thing to do at all (laughs), and, ah . . . it wasn't
very smart. Oh, dear. Ah . . . and then . . . (P) . . .
he was an awfully nice boy, this English major, but not at
all like me. And . . . he . . . had a lot of problems. I
seem to get involved with people who have a lot of problems.
He was 25 and a senior. I was sort of glad that the thing
was going to be ended by the ending of school . . . . Now
I was going to be . . . more level-headed, and I was,
really. I went to California with my friend Sue, and this
was a very carefully thought-out scheme to get away from
Philadelphia where John was going to be and his girl was
going to be. Sue and I went out to . . . ah, Berkeley . . .
went to summer school. And Sue is very interested in
psychology, and she had been seeing a psychiatric social
worker the year before. So . . . she became sort of
psychiatric social worker and I was . . . I talked to her,
and we would talk about all kinds of things . . . and, ah
. . . we'd analyze old John, and we got him all lined up
and what we thought of him. And, ah . . . let's see,
about the beginning of August I began getting these long
letters from John. And these letters played the old theme
of, ah . . . boy, he'd really been thinking this time . . .
he'd just changed in every way. And, ah . . . his parents
were very fond of me, and they wrote me a letter and said,
you know, "He really has changed. He's washing the dishes
and he doesn't quarrel any more." I couldn't believe all
this (laughs), but apparently it was the case. He took to
going over to my house and playing croquet with . . . with
my sister and, ah . . . (P) . . . ah . . . let's see . . .
and he called me and . . . so once again I gave in. I was
really very fond of him. And, ah . . . at the end of the
summer my parents came out and we flew home. And I saw
John and it went well for about two days (laughs), and
then . . . and it began to just collapse again. He was
worried that he felt that he couldn't communicate with me.
And this was . . . somehow my fault. I mean . . . I wasn't,
ah . . . (P) . . . I've never been able to figure out this

one either. Ah . . . I should have been able to make him
talk about himself by the kinds of perceptive questions
that I asked, but because I didn't ask these perceptive
questions, ah . . . it was obvious that I wasn't really
able to understand his problems and therefore he couldn't
. . . tell me about the problems. Well, this . . . this
didn't convince me very much. And I did my best . . . to
ask perceptive questions. And we'd have these terrible
. . . this was the beginning of the school year now, and,
ah . . . I would strive to ask a perceptive question, and
it would turn out that I just missed the point of the last
perceptive answer (laughs) completely. Ooooooh!

E: That was a miserable sort of thing.

S: And I went down to Columbia twice more . . . and just . . .
each time to . . . he got extremely drunk on Saturday
and . . . each time . . . it would be clear that I was
putting up with it rather than accepting it joyously as a
wonderful side of his personality. And, ah . . . so on
Sunday, the discussion would come . . . about how I wasn't
able to accept his drinking as part of him, and I would
say, "Well, gee, no, I would put up with it, but I just
can't welcome it, I can't do that." And, ah . . . the
second Saturday he was . . . ah, rowdy at the football
game. He insulted the man in front of him, and the man
turned out to be the judge at the court where he was later
tried because he was . . . he was arrested for disorderly
conduct. And hauled into the jail (sighs). For this little
effort he was kicked out of Columbia for a year. I saw him
again at Christmas time, and I had definitely made up my
mind that this . . . no point in going on . . . going
through these awful . . . conflicts and not getting anywhere, so I . . . I told him this. He can be . . . he can
be so charming, and, ah . . . (P) . . . when I got home
for Christmas vacation . . . I had made up my mind
completely, and then I really liked the first time I saw
him, and I thought, well, maybe I made a mistake, and the
second time . . . I really had . . . the second day I
really had a good time. The second day we went out to see
his friends' place in the country, where they were cutting
down Christmas trees; mostly it was sort of just sitting
around the fire and toasting your toes and drinking sort
of cider . . . (P) . . . it was cider and something else
. . . ah . . . And when I . . . and when I have anything
to drink if I'm feeling very good, and I was feeling
extremely good, I get . . . I do sort of antic things, and,
ah . . . so it turns out that my behavior on this Sunday
. . . so disgusted him with my . . . ah . . . he said, "Oh,
you got so drunk." And I wasn't at all. I know I wasn't.
All this was having a good time, as I pointed out to him;
I'd been acting this way before I'd had anything to drink
and didn't . . . it didn't change at all afterwards, but

. . . . This really disgusted him, and he didn't see me
again until Christmas Day. And Christmas Day we . . .
went to a play together, and I just really . . . hauled him
into it. And I . . . I said, I don't even . . . I'm so
disgusted about this whole thing . . . I just can't . . .
stand it . . . any more. And so . . . that's the last time
I saw old John (laughs).

E: Well, well have to stop there. I have to let you go to
class.

FOURTH INTERVIEW (MARCH): MENTAL QUALITIES
--JOHN'S AND HER OWN

E: Well, the last time we got up to about Christmas and
finally broke off with . . .

S: John (laughs). Oh, gosh. . . . I have been thinking about
him lately. Ah . . . a very forceful boy.

E: Yeah.

S: Ah, previously I've come with specific things that I want
to talk about, but I don't really have anything much today.
Ah . . . I thought that I may not have told you about how
. . . (P) . . . unsure of myself I felt at the time I was
in Panama. I mean, I let you know that it was an unhappy
time, but, ah . . . I guess . . . I was like every adoles-
cent, I was very sure that I was very unattractive. And
I just thought I was so ugly. My sister is very attractive.
And ah . . . she was at the age where she was reading my
diary . . . and getting into trouble generally. She would
say mean things, and I was just sure that I was so unattractive. I was wearing glasses at the time, and, ah . . .
my complexion was bad. But anyway, John . . . was one of
the first . . . probably the first person who thought that
I looked attractive, that I believed in. If you understand
what I mean.

E: Uh-huh.

S: My mother had always said, "Oh, of course, you look fine,
dear." But mothers are like that, I think (laughs). But
John had real ideas about me. He . . . he felt that, ah
. . . you know, sort of unusual good looks. He was all for
getting me to fix myself up, which I had been doing somewhat, in growing my hair . . . I had a sort of a Dutch-boy
cut until I came to college, and I started growing it then.
And, ah . . . oh, he was very insistent . . . that I buy
good-looking clothes. I'd been brought up not to . . . not
to care about my appearance so . . . all this caring that I
had done had been underneath the surface. And I'd keep
telling myself that it didn't really matter. But it always
did really matter to me. And then . . . and John came
along. It was supposed to matter now, and I . . . a lot of
conflicts developed over this question. He didn't think

that I had a whole lot of taste in clothes. Any time I
bought anything I'd be very insecure as to whether he'd
like it or not.

E: And he knew what you . . . what he wanted, obviously.
S: Yeah. I don't know, it may be connected with the fact
that he didn't know what he wanted for himself. Ah . . .
and so he was even more insistent about me. And, ah . . .
he has such a fine mind. He's so . . . penetrating in his
analysis of things, and it's very hard to argue with him.
And the more aware you are of how good . . . what he's
saying is . . . the less competent you feel to deal with
it . . . (P) . . . I can't decide whether the intellectual
stimulation was . . . was more good for me or not . . .
'cause it was definitely . . . intellectual stimulation,
but I usually would fight it at the time, and then . . .
and then . . . reassess my position afterwards and discover
that he'd been right or partially right. And . . . (P) . . .
since I've known him, ah . . . my ideas have changed an
awful lot. In everything I think I've gotten a lot more
perspective and . . . (P) . . . a lot more of an intellectual basis for what I . . . for what I think. (P) He
doesn't have the feelings that I have of obligation to
other people. I guess it's the most definite thing in the
back of my arguments with him. I have this . . . feeling
that I've been . . . born in a privileged position of
having a . . . good family and enough money to get through
college without any problems and, ah . . . a little bit of
money beyond that, which I have of my own from my grandparents, and, ah . . . I've sort of an obligation feeling,
of debt feeling, that . . . that I ought to make some
contribution to society. And John doesn't have this at
all. Things were very clear-cut in my mind between right
or wrong, black and white, and he was sort of a disrupting
influence. And he really made me think . . . about, ah
. . . what lay behind the things that I believe, which is
good. He didn't so much change them as show me that they
weren't black and white. Just more different shades of
grey, which is . . . we discussed this a lot in our letters
to each other last summer . . . he sees things in greys.
And . . . it means that he can't act because he sees good
and bad on both sides. And he admires me because . . . I
. . . still . . . as much insight as I've gotten . . . tend
to see things in black and white once I've made up my mind.
Ah . . . and I can throw myself into something . . . like
civil rights . . . which is what I'm going to. I'm going
to law school and then . . . and then work for the government or civil rights or something that has to do with some
cause that I believe in. And I don't think he can ever do
that because he just . . . he can't have that kind of belief in something. But they're just cases where there
aren't two sides to a question, there's just one in my

[handwritten marginal note: Debt to Society]

opinion. I've never met anybody that, ah . . . could
challenge me so effectively on these points, which . . .
really impresses me, as you can see, although it frightens
me, too, and was a very hard thing to undergo. But . . .
it's such a . . . such a thing to give up, I . . . I . . .
it really is hard for me . . . was hard for me . . . is
hard for me (laughs).

E: Probably both.

S: Uh-huh. And, oh . . . I spend I lot of time wondering what
I . . . what I meant to him. And I really don't know about
that either. For a long while I thought that . . . (LP)
. . . that I was . . . symbolic of the decisions that he'd
made in the year that he was out of Columbia. I had, and
still have, I guess, pretty . . . I don't know if it's
inflated or just justified opinion of my own intelligence
and . . . (P) . . . which I didn't used to have. It's sort
of gradually developed as I . . . as I kept conquering more
and more hurdles. In Panama the principal asked me to, ah
. . . if I were staying the whole time if I wouldn't like
to skip senior year because it was obvious that the school
couldn't offer me anything . . . comparable to what a year
of college could at that time. In other words I was going
to outgrow the school much too fast. And, ah . . . I was
very . . . amazed . . . this seemed to be a startling
proposition . . . (P) . . . I don't know whether it's just
that I have the kind of intelligence that does well in
tests and . . . in classroom situations . . . which may not
mean that I'm so smart in other ways, but means that I can
do that kind of thing . . . but every time I adopt some
attitude of humility . . . something happens . . . like
getting into Phi Beta Kappa, which (laughs) made me feel
pretty proud of myself!

E: I remember you said in Panama that you knew you were the
brightest one in class . . .

S: Yeah . . . but I . . . thought of it more in terms of the
fact that the rest of the people in the class weren't very
smart. You know, I kept thinking to myself, well, once I
get out back to Philly where there are a lot of other people
I'll be put in my place. And then . . . and then I wasn't.
And then I thought to myself, well, once I get to Radcliffe,
boy, everybody at Radcliffe and Harvard are brilliant, and
I'll be put in my place. And then I wasn't again and
(laughs) and . . . that's . . . I don't know . . . my
parents always react with such pride and happiness when I
do these little academic triumphs (laughs), and . . . ah
. . . (P) . . . And I know that what I want both for a close
friend and for somebody that I would marry would be somebody . . . (P) . . . as sharp as I am. Somebody like John
. . . and they're . . . it's just so rare. Sometimes
people . . . they're smart in a different kind of way . . .
they're not verbal . . . that kind of thing is very hard
for me to adjust to. Ah . . . (P) . . . I was going out

this summer with a boy at Berkeley. Man, actually . . .
he's 26 (laughs). Ah . . . he's getting his Ph.D. in
organic chemistry. Ah . . . (P) . . . awfully nice guy.
Very . . . very shy and quiet, ah . . . but he was really
anxious . . . he was really looking for somebody to get
married to, because after all he's 26 and he's going to
get a Ph.D. pretty soon and . . . then it's going to be
time, you know. And I was very definitely looking for
somebody to take the place of John, so that out of this
need we constructed this romance, which was, ah . . . (P)
. . . it was really a nice summer. Well, anyway, Bert just
wasn't literary. All his books were nonfiction. He liked
the things that weren't science, but they were all government and politics and so forth. Very politically active,
which was very nice change from John. And very . . . much
the same kind of warm, close religious family that I had
come from. More religious than my family. And, ah . . .
(LP) . . . but . . . just couldn't challenge my ideas in
the way that John had. He would just generally agree with
them. And this . . . was pleasing at first, but then it
got to be . . . terrible. He was too agreeable somehow
(laughs).

E: Wasn't as exciting?

S: Yeah, it just wasn't at all, ah . . . and then John started
writing me, calling me, and so I just gave in . . . which
was very, very hard on Bert. He'd been trying very hard
not to hurry into anything, but he knew that we just had
the summer to get acquainted . . . and he really was
anxious and very fond of me, and oh . . . feel bad about
that. Just . . . I was . . . so anxious to have somebody
to replace John . . . that, ah . . . (P) . . .

E: But it just didn't work.

S: Yeah. It just wasn't at all, ah . . . as you say, exciting.

E: Yeah. John had sort of made you feel like a . . . person.

S: Yeah (laughs). A thwarted person a lot of the time. Oh
. . . (laughs) so thwarted. Oh, gosh, we had these terrible
quarrels. I just would feel so bitter (laughs). Oh,
dear, we tried to make waffles once, and the waffle batter
stuck to the waffle iron, and he got furious and he threw
the waffle iron at the wall. And I just stalked out of
the room. Oh . . . I was so mad at him . . . he was so
mad at me and the waffle iron (laughs). Oh (laughs), the
kitchen was just in shambles . . . (LP) . . . Oh dear.
I'm dating somebody now . . . sort of like Bert in being
. . . I think I've finally grown up a little bit in
respect to this . . . I don't need to be dominated in the
way that John dominated me . . . . I would fight against
it, but at the same time I liked being sort of crushed, I
guess. There's something pleasing in having this very
strong person . . . opposing me . . . ah . . . and this
boy that I'm dating now is very strong, but he's not

hostile. You know . . . we don't get into . . . we got into
one tremendous quarrel . . . and he just . . . he just seemed
to me at the moment so obtuse . . . so un-understanding. Ah
. . . I never had that problem with John. He was always
. . . he always understood. He'd understand too well, though.
Aw . . . it was terrible . . . so deflating. Ah . . . "You
believe that because" . . . then I'd say, "No . . . no, it's
just not true at all . . . I believe." "Oh, wait a minute"
. . . (laughs), and oh gosh, really showing me what was
going on . . . (P) . . . We just felt that we understood
each other so well . . . so that it's very hard. I don't
know if it . . . it was just pure illusion so that it's never
going to be recaptured again . . . which would be very bad
because . . . it was a very fine feeling while . . . while
it lasted, and I still have the feeling . . . I bet he does
too . . . of there being a time when I really . . . when I
really understood him . . . (LP) . . .

E: Will you be at Columbia Law School next year?

S: Yeah.

E: That's certain that you have been accepted?

S: Yeah, yeah. That's . . . oh, that's another one of these
little challenges. They sent me the letter on January 1,
which is quite early.

E: Congratulations.

S: (Laughs) I . . . and I got into Harvard Law early too, and
. . . and, ah . . . Harvard Law was meeting on my application
before they said they'd meet. That is, the committee wasn't
supposed to meet until January 1. And I wrote in December
to add to my record that I'd been elected to Phi Beta Kappa
. . . and, ah . . . the woman said they were already considering my application. They had taken out a few to consider.
Obviously, they had taken out the few they were certain they
were going to accept. And, ah . . . (LP) I really feel that
. . . that . . . I can do anything which is, ah . . . John
is more like that . . . than I am. But (P) if I put . . .
if I focus my attention on . . . I can really do things . . .
I think I have real intellectual power, ah . . . John is sort
of automatically focused. And he used . . . to just say,
"Think . . . just forget about all this fuzzy thinking and
really put your mind to it and see all the aspects." And
. . . ah . . . and college work is like that, too. It's had
the same effect on me that John did, really. Taking a good
exam, that, ah . . . makes you get all your forces in there
and . . . build them all together. And writing a paper is
even better. Ah . . . in exams you've got to work in the
professors' own ideas, ah . . . and you know everybody
else is doing about the same thing. That's a little
dull. But, ah . . . writing a paper, you've some
little angle that you've thought of yourself, and you're
doing it yourself and you're organizing yourself.

. . . . I don't have a good writing style . . . but I've
always been praised for my good organization of papers,
and I can . . . really . . . explain things clearly. I
didn't use to think much of this until I read a few other
people's papers. I find it hard to believe that they
really do have a thought because they find it so difficult
to express it. You don't know what they're getting at,
and you think it's your fault . . . (LP) . . . And that's
what I really enjoy and really look forward to . . . the
kind of law school classes where . . . they're all taught
the Socratic method . . . if you get somebody that's good
at it, ah . . . real dialogue develops. It's . . . I . . . I
can think of nothing more exciting. There's not enough
discussions with teachers. It's really important to me
that I . . . continue with somebody that makes me think.
Ah . . . 'cause . . . I . . . I have this lazy streak, and
I . . . can see myself getting into a situation and not
. . . ah . . . and not using my mind very much. Just . . .
it is a fear in my mind that I'll just sort of sit back and
relax. Every once in a while I think about how nice it used
to be in high school and in Panama, just sort of sit around
and read and enjoy it and . . . it's, ah . . . it's a more
of an enjoyment to really work at it. So tiring some times.
I feel a lot of pressure on me to, ah . . . not pressure in
the sense of competing with people. It's pressure in the
sense of wanting to . . . to do everything just right. Ah
. . . (P) . . . and . . . I . . . I think I am competitive,
and it pleases me to do better than other people, but it
pleases me to do the best job that I can.

FIFTH INTERVIEW (MARCH): SUMMARY OF FAMILY BACKGROUND

    Portia's paternal grandfather was a mechanical engineer
who made a financial success in metal manufacturing. One son,
Portia's uncle, has continued the business. Portia's father
did not fit the industrial environment. He startled his parents
by deciding early to become a Quaker and a conscientious
objector, entered government work as an economist, and became
active in civil rights. The maternal grandparents are somewhat
more wealthy; the grandfather started as a wagon-maker but
turned early to the automotive industry. Portia reported
herself astonished to learn that her mother's family had had
"a cook and a maid . . . I just couldn't believe it; goodness,
it seemed like a story book." The maternal grandmother was
Irish; all the rest of the ancestors were from long-time
American families. The maternal grandparents were the important
ones in Portia's early life. They owned the farm in Delaware
to which the Slims returned from their winters in Panama. They
were sympathetic to Quaker beliefs, and Portia's mother had
already decided to be a Quaker before she met her husband.

Both of these grandparents were remembered for their courtesey
and thoughtfulness: Portia described incidents from their last
illnesses in which they still showed consideration for the
people around them. Grandmother was a "remarkable woman . . .
so energetic, such a way about her."

E: Did your grandparents do anything particular with you?
S: (P) . . . Um. Mother just recently wrote me about an
     article she read in the paper, increasing your child's IQ
     by making him responsive at an early age, and she said
     Grandma certainly did that for me and Sally (laughs). Ah
     . . . she used to . . . talk to us and make us talk to her,
     and Mother said it was so good, you could tell that you and
     Sally got such a kick out of communicating. Ah . . . and
     . . . Mother was, I guess, too busy or didn't have the
     patience or something. I must have been really surrounded
     by doting people in early childhood. Uh . . . from 1 to 3
     when my father was away I lived with my mother in this top
     floor of my grandparents's house in Philadelphia, and my
     aunts, I guess my two aunts were there too, and my grand-
     mother and grandfather . . . I just must have been . . .
     the darling of the household (laughs). They sent me to
     nursery school 'cause I didn't have anybody to play with,
     and I guess they thought that I ought to be with other
     children some. Ah, this was downtown Philadelphia, and I
     was 3, and there's this photograph that we have of it . . .
     there was this happy, happy Halloween party, big grinning
     pumpkin in the middle of the table and these little tiny
     kiddies all going "Huh La" (she shows big wide grin), and
     there's me and I'm just so mournful, oh! and there's this
     tragic look on my face, and they took me out after (laughs)
     only a few weeks. I think that was before I had my glasses.
     It must have been because I just couldn't see 'cause I
     really, I'm almost blind. (laughs)

     Shortly after, the Slim family moved into the suburban
home they have occupied ever since, The houses were set on
large lots with ample space for play. The parents were presently displeased to learn that the neighbors were highly
bigoted and that much of the land was held under deeds
containing discriminatory clauses. At one point they tried to
get the neighbors to sign pledge cards in favor of fair housing,
but none of them would do so. Their own lot was large enough
for subdivision, and father had a house built which he sold to
a family he knew at work, Latin Americans with somewhat dark
skin.The neighbors were wary of these strangers. Portia thinks
her parents ought to sell the house and leave the bigoted
neighborhood, as indeed they sometimes talk of doing, but they
love the house and still live in it. Portia describes in
detail her early childhood delight in the large well-equipped
yard where all manner of games could be played and imaginative

activities pursued. There were also indoor delights.

S: We had a lot of dolls, my sister and I. Christmas Eve
when the parents are busy doing all the Santa Clausing and
they want the kids out of the way . . . my mother thought
up this divine tactic of, ah . . . we had to get our dolls
ready to meet Santa Claus. This was very important. She
would clean them all up and make sure that they were all
just looking their best and take them all downstairs and
sit them in a chair. One chair for my sister's dolls and
one chair for my dolls so they would meet Santa Claus.
And I see now this was so my parents could engage in secret
activities (laughs). But at the time . . . this . . . this
is . . . this point didn't occur to me at all (laughs).
And I thought that every family fixed the dolls up.
E: That does sound like a good solution.
S: When we were sick . . . my mother used to get out her dolls
for us to play with as a special treat. She called them
the basket dolls because they lived in little baskets and
they had a lot of little clothes that she'd made . . . when
she was a girl . . . and they were small, they had china
heads. Oh, this was a very . . . important . . . occasion
when you're sick . . . I had a doll house which I just
loved. My grandfather had made it . . . I wonder if he'd
made it for me . . . because there was another . . . there
was another doll house out in the farm that had been made
for his daughters, I guess. My sister was never very
interested in it, and even when she got to be old enough
for . . . ah . . . dolls and houses and we put it out in
the hall . . . we could both play with it. She just wasn't
the eager doll house fan that I was. Oh, I just loved it.
Cleaned it up and arranged furniture, and then we would
walk the dolls around and have them do things. I still
like doll houses. I have this collection of . . . of
miniature furniture . . . you make it legitimate by calling
it a collection of miniatures (laughs). There's something
about these little tiny things . . . oh, it's really nice.
I certainly hope my daughters like doll houses (laughs).
For a good period . . . I used to spend my allowance on
things for my doll house. When I wasn't spending it on
comic books. I had a large collection of comic books.

Portia recalls that in the fourth grade she blossomed
forth in the school newspaper as a poet. The poem was about
Christmas and "it was terrible, just doggerel." "Three
stockings by the chimney hung/Even small Peter's who had sat
on the rung/ Of a chair." But the teacher was much taken by
this brave effort, and Portia became a sort of class poet. "I
guess Mother has the collected works somewhere" (laughs).

S: I kept it up, and I'm a little better at it now. I just

wrote a sonnet on the . . . on the sadness of not being
engaged, when all your best friends are engaged. I have a
a great mob of friends that are engaged (laughs). Ah . . .
and then it ended up with, ah . . . (P) . . . ah . . .
let's see . . . I rhymed . . . I rhymed . . . ah . . . identity
and entity. The idea being that I had to find my own identity.
I just . . . finished reading Erikson . . . I had to find my
own identity before I could consider being half an entity (laugh

SIXTH INTERVIEW (MARCH): DISCOURAGING THOUGHTS --MORE ON THE FAMILY

Asked about the progress of her senior honors thesis,
shortly due, Portia said, "I'll just finish in time." But she
described the progress as "very, very slow" and herself as
"very involved in it," so that she thinks of very little besides
her thesis and is having great trouble sleeping at night. In-
somnia proved to be an old complaint. As a child she had had
trouble and would wake up her parents who would soothe her,
rub her back, and perhaps give her aspirin. She recalled
failing a Latin exam in high school through misreading a
question; she should have taken time, with her poor eyesight,
to go up to the blackboard and make sure of the question.

S: Oh, I just got distraught! And my father got up and fed me
    warm milk and tried to calm me down. Of course, it didn't
    really matter at all, but it did at the time. It meant
    that I got a B for that semester.
E: Was that the only B you got during high school?
S: Yeah, except for a mark of C in gym.

At present S has a supply of sleeping pills--actually they
are tranquilizers--to which she resorts perhaps three times a
month, and especially during exams. Her doctor discourages
this and "seems to think it's a big crime."
Portia then mentions a series of frustrations this morning
when taking her roommate, Helen, to the health center for
treatment of a cold: parking difficulties, losing her scarf,
her umbrella blowing inside out. Soon she comes to another unhappy thought.

S: Helen is getting married in August. She has this damn
    bride's magazine (laughs) lying around. Very . . . oh,
    very annoying thing to read. You want to get married
    yourself and don't have any prospects in the future. And
    there's this bride's magazine telling you all about glorious
    honeymoons and trousseaus and choosing your silver and
    Woaah! (disgusted unhappy sound)
E: Oh, dear.
S: Just terrible. And, ah . . . (P) . . . Let's see what

else was I thinking of. I can't remember, my mind sort of
wanders . . . (P) . . . The real oppressive burden besides
my thesis at this moment is this Latin course which I have
to take, and it's just such a . . . oh . . . so oppressive.
Ah . . . starting with Horace and going on . . . Horace and
Tacitus and Livy are just great (excitedly). We should
close there, but no, we've got to go on with all this junk
. . . it was written in the late Empire. Just junk. And
write papers on it, worse yet. I can't bear it (laughs).
I just can't bear it. Seneca . . . Seneca's a fool! Oh!
(laughs).

E: But you're allowed to say it's junk?

S: Well . . . he . . . we can. But just . . . not even worth
the effort to go through and show how bad it is.

E: I hope you get through it all somehow.

S: Oh, well, I will. But I'm being very obstinate about this
summer. I've applied to one civil rights program with the
American Friends Service Committee. Ah . . . (P) . . .
but . . . I just haven't made any effort to do anything
else. And if I don't get into the program, I think I'm
going to sit around home and work for the Pennsylvania
Branch of the NAACP and just relax (laughs). I just feel
that I can't push myself into working this summer when I
just don't want to work at all. Going to law school . . .
it's very, ah . . . I'm so tired of working now, but I know
after the summer that I'll be . . . all fired up, and I
even am fired up thinking about it . . . stimulating
environment; Socratic method. And, ah . . . oh, gosh. So
exciting to . . . to . . . argue about things, I really
like it (laughs). I was getting very depressed a couple
of nights ago, and I said to Helen, "Helen, I just can't
ever get married, I like to argue too much, and furthermore,
I like to win." And Helen said, "Well, that's all right
you know." And she pointed out to me that . . . that, ah,
very often I don't like . . . to . . . to just vanquish
boys, and it's true. I don't like to just crush anybody
in an argument . . . anybody that I would marry would be
somebody that would be my own intellectual equal, so it
wouldn't matter (laughs). Wouldn't be capable of . . .
out-arguing him (laughs). And Helen said I was very easy
to live with, and Helen was very pleasant. This was
(laughs), oh . . . this was in contrast . . . to the discouraging thing that happened to me Saturday. Oh, dear.
Ah . . . I was . . . I got up early, and I was working,
and I came up to the room to have a little snack. And
Helen had just gotten up, and she was feeling very
depressed and she said, "Oh, I just can't work today." And
I said, "Oh, gee, Helen, I've gotten a lot done today. Ha-
Ha." And she looked at me and said, "You're the only person I know that would say that." And I said, "What do you
mean?" She said, "You're just insensitive." And I said,

"Oh, Helen . . . I am not!" Then I thought about it for a
while, and it was very obvious that I had not said the right
thing to her when I came up. I mean . . . she didn't want
me to say that . . . how good I was. She wanted sympathy.
And she said, ah . . . and I just got so depressed about it
all . . . and oh, no! I spent the whole day thinking about
it and worrying about it. I wrote a long letter to John,
which I never should have done, and mailed it to him, worse
yet. Helen said, "No, no, I didn't mean for you to do
that!" And I said, "No, Helen" (laughs), because that's
always what John said about me and about how insensitive I
was to other people's problems. And I just seemed all
wrapped up in myself, and oh, I just felt is was so true
Saturday. I don't feel so depressed about . . . . I don't
feel that it's so much the case anymore. Although since
Saturday I've been trying to work at . . . listening to
other people when they complain and . . . not complaining
so much myself. It's not that I complain so much, it's
just that I . . . that I tend not to think about other
people's points of view and, ah . . . (LP) . . . it's very
hard. It really is true, but on the other hand, it may be
true about everybody. I mean, it may not be something to
get depressed about. My mother is very good at . . . at
understanding the way you feel, and ah . . . (P) . . . I
don't know . . . even . . . what she does is not . . . she
just sort of sympathizes. But there's a difference between
sympathazing and really understanding . . . the way . . .
the way you feel, and she doesn't want, ah . . . a lot of
the time recently she keeps . . . eeeee! mothers, they
write you bull letters, and they . . . they show that
they're just completely unaware of what's going on. I guess
I'm like my father. My father is . . . has this . . .
tendency to be oblivious about other people . And what I
said to John in my letter was that maybe this was what was
making me so anxious to be in civil rights and work for
minority groups, because I was feeling guilty about not
feeling for them really. So that I felt that I had to
make up for it . . . (P) . . . And this is all happening
subconsciously, in my theory. Well, I don't know, but I
have this . . . feeling of . . . of justice . . . and . . .
everybody should have the same breaks. Now you see . . .
in the case of Saturday morning, Helen and I had the same
break . . . she could have gotten up at seven, too, and
studied just as hard as I did, and she didn't. And therefore . . . there is no reason for me to pity Helen because
it's . . . it's not . . . some injustice of the world that
caused her not to study, it was her own laziness, and
that's not sympathetic . . . but that's . . . you know,
that's sort of . . . looking at things from the . . .
fairness angle. Whereas it's unfair that talented Negro
people can't get to school at all because they don't have

any money. And they didn't have good education. And that's
unfair, and you have to wipe out unfairness, but you don't
have to waste your time on being sympathetic. That's the
way my father is, though, he really is, and that's the way
I am, I guess. I don't know why. And I don't like it in
my father. Very, very often it's annoying as anything
(laughs) when he doesn't . . . act sympathetic about me
(laughs). But . . . it's not very human . . . it's more
trying to set things down to computer exactness and give
everybody . . . you know . . . equal amounts of . . . of
. . . rations. In the beginning he would just say. "Well,
take care of yourself," and sort of wander off . . . (LP)
. . .   But he's . . . he's a little bit . . . (P) . . .
ah . . . (LP) . . . The question of my sister was handled
so different by my mother and my father. Because my . . .
my father has this very . . . rigid attitude about his two
daughters, you know, you give them the same amount of
allowance and, ah . . . Portia goes to Europe X number of
times, then Sally's going to Europe X number of times.
Portia gets her car at X age, Sally gets her cat at X age.
And, ah . . . Mother is very much prone to look at the
differences, extreme as they are, between Sally and me and
treat us as . . . as different individuals and, ah . . .
And I still have the streak in me of . . . of being the pro-
Daddy philosophy, you know. But . . . but Mother is really
right, It's impossible to imagine handling us the same way.
And I feel now as I wouldn't have felt a few years ago that
. . . that Sally ought to get a car pretty soon because she
. . . has more use for one than I did at her age, and there
isn't any reason why she should wait until her junior year
in college to get one. And . . . ah . . . she gets more
allowance than I did because she buys more clothes and
cosmetics and she smokes. And, of course, my parents don't
want to give her more allowance than I have, because they
hate her smoking (laughs), so that's all.

E: Do your mother and father get on with each other?

S: Oh, yeah.

E: The way that you and your sister do, ah . . . get on with
    each other, or how do they . . . interact, you father and
    mother?

S: Um . . . . The only time I am aware of any differences of
    opinion on them . . . between them, is on how to raise my
    sister (laughs); ah . . . they. . . it was . . . I didn't
    have any idea about differences in approach, whether it was
    because I was young or whether it was because there wasn't
    any difference of approach, I don't know . . . but since
    Sally has been in high school and now in college herself,
    ah . . . (sighs) . . . they've worried so much, and Mother
    felt in between in the sense that she agreed with Daddy's
    theories of how Sally should be treated, but she really
    felt sorry for Sally at the same time, so that Sally would

often be able to . . . win her to some concessions that
she knew that Daddy wouldn't want her to make. Mother
must have been under . . . a lot of tension for a while.
I felt under strain the one summer that I was home, the
summer after my freshman year. They did a lot of . . . of
wanting to know what I thought about X or Y. Put me in a
bad position . . . she's unhappy . . . and they want to
. . . . they want to fix things up for her, and they think
they know a better way for her to manage her life than she
does. They know they shouldn't force it on her, but at
the same time it's so very obvious . . . that . . . if she
were more controlled . . . and if she . . . if she had a
goal for herself . . . she doesn't seem to at all and that
distresses them, I think. Sally didn't see any reason, if
she wasn't doing anything the next day, why she should come
in early. My parents . . . had this . . . had this moral
attitude about getting to bed early anyway. And then they
had this more reasonable attitude that . . . that's more
dangerous, you know . . . a lot of drunk driving . . .
drunk drivers around after midnight, and so forth. And my
sister would just laugh in his face, when Daddy proposed
this theory and this reason for getting home early, and
she said, "No, don't be so silly . . . nothing's going to
happen." Nothing ever did happen but, ah . . . (P) . . .
she just didn't know how to . . . run her own life and yet
wouldn't . . . accept any guidance from anybody. Oh . . .
(laughs), it's really difficult for them.

SEVENTH AND EIGHTH INTERVIEWS (APRIL):
A NEW FRIEND--TED

In the evening of the day of the last interview Portia met
Ted, a Columbia law student on a brief visit to Cambridge, and
found him to be a "terribly, terribly nice boy." He and she
made a date for right after her thesis was handed in, and they
did not get in until four o'clock in the morning. Portia
describes Ted as "just wonderful," this in spite of the fact
that they think quite differently on public questions. He is
a Republican from Colorado, describes himself as a flaming
Republican, while she considers herself a flaming liberal.
After a few dates they began to talk about marriage; Ted considers this right because his father proposed to his mother on
their second date and the marriage worked out very well. Portia
spent her own spring vacation in New York.

E: How did the vacation go?
S: I saw Ted most of the time.
E: That's good.
S: Oh . . . (laughs), he got me to cut my hair. He wants me
    to keep on curling it, too. I don't know about that
    (laughs).

E: It looks nice that way.

S: Oh . . . (laughs), I really like it this way. It certainly
   is an improvement if you curl it, but such a bother
   (laughs).

E: So I take it things are going well between you and Ted.

S: Oh, very well (laughs). Very, ver well. Oh! We're just
   . . . oh, we're so happy (laughs). We spent all our time
   together. And he's going to be in Philadelphia this summer
   . . . he got a job. And, ah . . . oh, just, he's told his
   family about me, and they say I sound good except that I'm
   a Democrat and have to change that. My family (laughs)
   thinks he sounds good except he's a Republican and he'll
   have to change that (laughs). Oh, we were studying, we
   spent one night studying together in the Law Library and
   we were going to spend another night, but we never got
   there somehow. And he came up last weekend and I had him
   to dinner at the dorm. It was nice. So things . . .
   things seem to be going all right (laughs). In fact,
   really well.

E: Good.

S: My parents are off to Europe today. I didn't realize they
   were 'leaving so soon. I wrote them a letter, which is
   going to get to Philadelphia tomorrow (laughs). Mother
   called us and said, "You know we're leaving tomorrow?" and
   I said, "Oh, you are?" (laughs). I was sort of thinking
   about myself, and not remembering the date that she said.
   They should really enjoy that, though. That's wonderful.
   Mother just loves to travel. It's going to be a nice
   vacation for Daddy . . . 'cause he's been spending . . .
   he's been working awfully hard with . . . the job and, ah
   . . . civil rights activity that he's doing so much of.

E: Oh . . . what are they doing in Europe?

S: Ah . . . not business at all. They're just going to enjoy
   themselves. They're going to get a car, too. It's really
   neat, they're going to be able to . . . sort of decide
   what they want to do on the spur of the moment and do
   things, ah . . . 'cause my parents can be very young sometimes. I just think of them as being sort of fancy free
   and . . . driving around (laughs). It's really a . . .
   pleasant picture.

E: Yeah, I see. I take it they enjoy each other's company?

S: Uh?

E: I take it they enjoy each other's company--your parents.

S: They enjoy what?

E: They enjoy each other's company.

S: Oh, yeah. Oh, very much (laughs). We have, ah . . . Ted
   and I've . . . Ted and I've been talking about all sorts
   of things (laughs), deciding whether family vacations are
   a good idea and such. And I remember I was thinking about
   the family vacations that we had . . . 'cause we started
   taking them as soon as . . . as my sister was old enough

. . . (P) . . . to not object too much to a trip and new
environments. The first one I remember was when we . . .
went to North Carolina. And I guess I must have been 9
and Sally 6 or something like that. And every year after
that we took one. We would rent a cottage . . . various
places within a couple hundred miles radius of Philadelphia.
It was really sort of a family unity, and we'd do things
together, go off sightseeing and, ah . . . play and go to
the beach and . . . ah, it was really fun. Ted and I
decided that family vacations are a good thing (laughs).
And, ah . . . (P) . . . we all enjoy each other's company
pretty much . . . But I . . . (P) . . . it's just . . . I
think it's nice . . . and my parents are going off to be
alone without these responsibilities that have been
harrassing Daddy outside. He hasn't said that they've been
harrassing him, but . . . they would harrass me if I were
. . . the same sort of things with school work, which I
enjoy, but it just . . . sometimes it gets to be very
oppressive and sort of burdensome . . . and, ah . . . just
wish it would all stop for a while so that I would be able
to come back to it and enjoy it (laughs). Ah . . . that's
what vacations are for (laughs). So what I'm going to do
this summer . . . is sit around home and read and (laughs)
. . . work for the local civil rights organization. Probably try to get a few days a week . . . for different ones.
Unless I can get a really good thing going with one of
them . . . and, ah . . . and just try to take it easy.

E: And see Ted?

S: And see Ted. And, ah . . . (P) . . . Rest up for Columbia
Law (laughs).

E: How's Ted going to feel about having two lawyers in the
family?

S: Well . . . (laughs), it's so funny. He said, he said last
night, "Ah, gee, I'm going to break my long-standing rule
about . . . not dating female lawyer types" (laughs). And
. . . we're so . . . we're interested in the same things
. . . I mean . . . we might . . . we might even end up as
one of these sort of husband and wife working teams, which
he really hates the idea of, because the one that he knows
. . . I think a fairly good friend of his married a girl
who is going to law school next year. And this girl . . .
is just phenomenally brilliant. She was junior Phi Beta
Kappa . . . what a mind. The boy is not smart. He's a
very bright boy, but he's just nothing to her . . . and, ah
. . . Ted used to get so annoyed 'cause she would be around
all the time and they'd be sort of billing and cooing. And
he has this feeling of . . . smiling, cleverly plotting
females. The master mind of the whole show . . . and as
he puts it, she drives her Triumph to class every morning
and her husband rides his bicycle. Well, I know when you
have the sense that the person you're dating is not as
smart as you are, and you have this feeling of your

controlling him by means of . . . of sort of feminine
tricks . . . . It's really unpleasant for . . . (P) . . .
ah . . . Ted to contemplate. And he doesn't feel that
this . . . relationship like that, but he has this idea
that when . . . when a husband and wife work together it's
not so good, I think. (P) However, he doesn't have the
feeling that I shouldn't go to law school. I mean . . .
he . . . he wants me to be careful and think about it because I've expressed a lot of doubts to him which . . .
when it seems I can't go through more years of working the
way I'm working this year. But . . . I don't come up with
anything else . . . . I really need to have . . . the feeling that I'm accomplishing something and . . . being challenged . . . oppressive to be challenged when you just feel
you can't meet another challenge, but if there weren't any
challenges at all it wouldn't be good either. The only
kind of job I could get would be a nonchallenging job and
. . . I plan to work on my shorthand this summer. I suppose by the end of the summer I could get some kind of
fairly decent secretarial job. I think I'd really rather
go to law school. Ah . . . Ted wants to work in a . . .
in a New York firm for about five years. They . . . let
you try out different kinds of law, and then you decide
what you're the most happy with and what you can do. The,
ah . . . that's not so appealing to me, partly because
firms don't like women anyway . . . so . . . it'd just be
sort of an uphill fight to . . . ah . . . (P) . . . and
partly because I would want to work for a civil rights
agency or something of that sort. Ah . . . so in that way
Ted and I seem to diverge, but . . . we're both interested
in politics and government.

E: Yeah. How does he feel about civil rights?

S: Ah . . . I don't believe that he's ever been, ah . . .
active in civil rights . . . Now, I haven't been too active
in civil rights either. I've . . . I've told him a little
bit about what my father's doing, and he's very impressed.
It's very hard to fail to be impressed by what my father's
doing. There aren't too many Negroes in Colorado. And . .
your whole judgment must be colored by your upbringing and
. . . (P) . . . ah . . . the question of Negro rights isn't
very immediate, when . . . it's much more immediate to him
now . . . (P) . . . but it still isn't quite as immediate
to him as it is to me because . . . Philadelphia . . . so
I have a . . . I think I have more of this humanitarian
instinct than he does. On the other hand . . . ah . . .
he's one of the few boys that I've dated recently that has
. . . the same faith that the problems of the world can be
tackled and ought to be tackled, that your life is only
meaningful if you try to make some . . . progress take
place. I think his tactics would be the same as mine, that
is, working through government . . . . His aunt called up
. . . his aunt . . . his father's sister, ah . . . is

apparently a big influence on his life. He . . . he
respects her very much. She said, "Well, what's this I
hear? (laughs). Time to get a report on this girl," so
. . . Ted goes into his, ah . . . report (laughs), and
then she informed him that she, ah . . . had a diamond
that had belonged to her mother . . . that she never wore,
and he could look at it and . . . after he had talked to
her he decided that . . . we had been deciding not to decide . . . and he decided that we had better decide one
way but put off the wedding date . . . see what I mean?
So . . . (laughs), so yesterday he called me up and said,
"What do you think about a year from June?" (laughs). I
said, "Is this a proposal?" (laughs). He said, "What do
you think?" (laughs). I said, "You can't propose over the
phone." . . . He said, "Well, I was going to do it in a
letter (laughs), but" . . . and he really was . . . so
that . . . (laughs). But we've met since then, and he
asked me the same question. So it's all . . .

E: Yeah.

S: And so after this little confrontation had taken place
yesterday afternoon we had this little discussion over
religion . . . 'cause . . . we keep being afraid that . . .
we don't really know enough about each other, and so every
once in a while one of us thinks of a topic that has to be
covered (laughs). So I said, "What about religion?"
(laughs). And . . . he sort of briefly told me his philosophy. It's just amazing it was so much like mine . . . .
I hadn't . . . ah . . . (P) . . . it's mostly that we have
the same beliefs, and I have found an expression of them
in Quakerism . . . and he hasn't . . . he doesn't know anything about the Society of Friends, and he was brought up
a Methodist, so he sort of calls himself a Methodist. But,
ah . . . (P) . . . And he likes . . . ah . . . just like
me . . . he likes a good, ah . . . nice ceremony like, ah
. . . Catholic or Episcopal . . . ah . . . services are
sometimes _very_ spiritually . . . (P) . . . ah . . . fulfilling. But . . . there's just too much of the dogma . . .
that seems wrong to me so that, ah . . . (P) . . . I just
couldn't . . . join the Episcopal Church because I happen
to like their ceremonies . . . when in fact I don't believe
. . . hold any of their beliefs. On the other hand . . .
as far as I'm concerned, the Quaker meeting is the only
guarantee for me that I'm going to really feel, ah . . .
sort of spiritually awakened. (P) . . . I haven't been
very much at all this year. And I . . . I wish I could go
more. I try to when I'm home. My parents' going sort of
helps me to get on the ball and go myself. Everyone's very
. . . and you just _feel_ this intense . . . ah . . . medita-
tive atmosphere. It sort of just gets hold of you, and
it's very, very good . . . and I . . . I get an awful lot
out of it. It's . . . it's, ah . . . I don't know how much
I believe in God, but, ah . . . and I certainly don't have

any anthropomorphic version of God, but there is . . .
there is some feeling that I get when I . . . when I . . .
relax myself and . . . and kind of open myself up . . .
that . . . that would be a Quaker phrase, sort of opening
yourself up and becoming receptive to the Inner Light. And
. . . and the Quakers <u>very</u> definitely . . . are against
forcing anybody or . . . even saying that any one way is
right. Ted feels this too. He said he would describe his
philosophy as Christian existentialism. I don't understand
this too much, so he . . . he described it. It seems to be
that he doesn't feel that there's any one correct path but
that everybody has to make a choice for themselves, and you
can't label things good or bad.

E: Yeah.

S: And, ah . . . (P) . . . Oh, I tell you it's so nice. He's
the kind of person you really want to do things with. And
you can really imagine him doing things with . . . with
children and . . . and, ah . . . oh, it's so nice.

E: That's fine.

S: These family vacations stand out in my mind because they
were times when . . . very emphatically we were doing a lot
of things together. And it seems to me that the usual
pattern of our life was . . . my sister and I would do
things together . . . or my mother and I would do things
together. We didn't see too much of Daddy, though. Ah . .
although we saw him. We waited for supper until he came
home, and we had supper together. And, ah . . . and I can
remember doing things with him . . . particularly on
Saturday. He would work in the yard and we'd play. . . .
Oh , math homework. He did a lot of helping me with math.
. . I recall . . . and my sister, too. Daddy is very . . .
he's a little slow and deliberate. That is . . . he insists
on reading over the chapter. And sometimes you feel very
frustrated because you feel he could just look at the
problem and help you and then go away, and you wanted to
get it over with (laughs). But, ah . . . (P) . . .
actually he gave us more help in the long run . . . 'cause
he would sit down and work it out with you and make you
understand it better. (Getting up to leave, S struggles
with the zipper on her raincoat.) It's very annoying
that this won't zip all the way, and I can't figure what's
wrong with it. Maybe Ted can fix it. He's fixed a couple
of things on my car . . . ah, he's very clever. Oh . . .
see you Friday.

NINTH INTERVIEW (APRIL): VOCATIONAL CHOICE:
TEACHING VERSUS LAW

E: Well, how have things gone this week?

S: Fine. Fine. I've been writing to all . . . everywhere in
the world. I wrote to Harvard Law School and withdrew

myself . . . ah . . . and I wrote to John. I'd written him
a very depressed letter. I think I told you about that.

E: Yeah.

S: He wrote me back a long friendly letter in completely
illegible handwriting. I haven't deciphered it all yet.
I fear . . . it included a poem. There were two letters,
one written on the spur of the moment and one more medita-
tive. And, ah . . . this poem . . . apparently he's been
writing a lot of poetry. His mother said that he'd sent
her a poem, too. So, ah . . . and he said at the end of
the second letter that . . . that . . . that, ah . . . he'd
like to hear from me a sort of newsy letter and keep up
friendly correspondence. Well, I had big news, and I
decided I ought to tell him. Especially since I wanted to
tell his parents. Ah . . . and I didn't want them telling
him. It should come from me rather than them, if you see
what I mean? So . . . I wrote to him about Ted, and I wrote
to my friend Lucy. I got a lovely letter back from her
immediately and a bottle of perfume (laughs). Ah . . . I
asked her to be a bridesmaid, and she said she can hardly
wait. We can start picking up the dresses this summer,
which I think is a bit premature (laughs). She's lovely
. . . I met her at the end of my sophomore year in high
school, it was really nice 'cause I . . . when I had just
come back from Panama. And, ah . . . I was sort of looking
around for some close friends, and Lucy really filled the
bill . . . completely; we've been very good friends for
years. We don't write each other very much; we see each
other . . . a couple of times every year with little visits.
And her family is old friends with my family. Ah . . . I
wrote to my sister yesterday. I have to write my parents,
who are in Spain. Though I haven't gotten around the energy
to get an air letter, which is necessary for the (laughs)
venture. My aunt is coming up Sunday, and she's going to
meet Ted. Also, big machinations going on. He's finding
out from his family if I could come in June for their
family vacation. Oh, we just spent so much time on each
other. Really, it's detrimental to our work. We went . . .
we had the most fabulous date last Saturday. Sort of golden
evening. He said, "We can afford to eat like that once every
six months." But . . . (sighs) . . .

E: Have you decided when you're going to get married yet?

S: Well (laughs), ah, a year from June is the semi official,
official date, ah . . . but we keep . . . possibly it might
be earlier. As Helen points out, by September we will have
known each other six months and (laughs) fully enough time
. . . just . . . we solve all these problems . . . it's
wonderful. He's so . . . he's so, ah . . . sensible,
without being stuffy. It's just amazing. Ah . . . Tuesday,
I was very depressed in the morning. I was thinking about
law school, and how I didn't want to go but I did want to
go. I just couldn't figure it out. He took me out for

coffee and I told him about how . . . how I was depressed.
And I really wasn't sure if I wanted to be a lawyer wife.
And he just seemed to have slight prejudices against women
in the law . . . and it just . . . he's so easy to talk to
. . . and these things can be settled so rationally and
. . . and calmly and . . . I could never settle anything
with John. We'd just come to terrible clashes and each
. . . defend things as if . . . (P) . . . if we were
defeated . . . we'd be crushed. Sort of . . . a moral
victory, or as if you were defending your personality when
you were defending your position in Vietnam (laughs). Ted
is so . . . (P) . . . hmmmm. I have . . . I have this
feeling that . . . that he's considerate . . . that he's
respecting my point of view that I didn't have with John
. . . whether I was more paranoid . . . in those days
(laughs). But, ah . . . I just . . . I just don't worry
with Ted. I know . . . that when he disagrees with me it's
because, ah . . . he thought about it, and he disagrees
with me and not because he doesn't like me. See what I
mean?

E: I see. How did you decide to go to law? I don't think
that you ever told me . . . exactly.

S: Well . . . ah . . . last spring . . . after John broke up
with me, I was taking a number of English courses, and I
had always planned to, ah . . . teach English in high
school or possibly go on . . . get a Ph.D., and neither of
these was at all attractive. I was very tired of these
English courses, and I didn't feel I was taking anything
that I could talk to anybody about. And it all seemed so
divorced from reality. Just, ah . . . furthermore, I . . .
looking forward to graduate study in English, there didn't
seem to be any, ah . . . possibility of meeting any fine
young man if I went on! (laughs). Either a very depressing
thought of teaching English in high school or . . . (P) . . .
sort of grubby existence. I should think it . . . it
wouldn't be bad if you were married, but . . . I . . . I
. . . all these single women that taught me in high school
were pretty embittered (laughs). Ah . . . it certainly
isn't an atmosphere in which you meet a lot of men, at all.
And, ah . . . (P) . . . I started to get worried about how
it wouldn't be very intellectually challenging. Then going
to graduate school would be intellectually challenging, but
I really don't like the kinds of people that go into
English. They're very, ah . . . they think . . . they
think form and style are so important, and I think English
and form and style are interesting, but important I don't
think. And, ah . . . I wanted to do something important.
And I had, ah . . . I'd always been interested in politics
and, ah . . . been doing sort of social service things . . .
and I always planned on teaching as . . . as doing
something for other people. Ah . . . but with a group last

year that I was . . . I was teaching I wasn't doing a good
job of it at all. I just thought to myself, well, this is
so discouraging. This, ah . . . involved . . . fifth and
sixth grade girls. And the year got off to a bad start.
There wasn't any discipline maintained.   It was, ah . . .
reading . . . enrichment type of thing.   A couple of them
were in need of . . . remedial reading.   And there was
one who was fantastically bright and was in need of . . .
ah--enrichment, and of discussing a little more subtle
things than plot, and there was nothing you could do with
all of them at once. And just . . . just discouraging
experience, ah . . . (P) . . . So, I began to think of
what I could do that wasn't English. Ah . . . and on the
other hand, there was law school. Now law school anybody
could go, didn't matter what your background was. And you
were finished in three years. And you could then go out
and help the world. That's what I wanted to do. And . . .
so . . . my parents came up for junior parents' weekend,
and I went to see their friends, Professor and Mrs. Lott
and, ah . . . Professor Lott talked to me for a long time
about women and the law and various law schools. And he
was very enthusiastic. His wife is a lawyer, too (laughs).
And, ah . . . he was very pleasant. And he introduced me
to some girls who were at Harvard Law last year, and they
were very enthusiastic. And, ah . . . it seemed to get
better and better all the time. Wonderful idea. And so
. . . ah . . . all through the summer I talked to some
other people. And, ah . . . worked some in politics in
California when I was there last summer. I really liked
the idea of . . . of being out in the world in that way.
I started thinking about . . . maybe politics instead of a
government career . . . or civil rights career.

E: Were the reasons that you gave Ted what you just gave me
    now or . . .

S: Yeah, yeah. He just wanted to be sure that I had some . . .
    (P) . . . ah . . . specific idea of what I wanted to do.
    And he helped me . . . by . . . by mentioning the importance
    of the things you can do for city and local governments.
    Ah . . . and his point is that, ah . . . these girls who
    are interested in going into, ah . . . work with law firms
    have got . . . to be really, ah . . . go-getter types. And
    he thinks a lot of girls in law school become sort of un-
    feminine because they become very domineering, ah . . .
    thinking that this is the way that they have to be to win
    success in a law firm, 'cause you have to be just
    devastatingly chic, because you have to be better than the
    men that you're competing with.

E: Hmmm.

S: And he doesn't know if this is going to change in the
    future. And he thinks that it probably will change for
    the better . . . (P) . . . I don't. . . . And then I

explained that I didn't think that I was going to get
domineering, ah . . . I don't have any of what he calls
. . . what he calls the "killer" instinct. In fact, not
at all; I don't get any pleasure out of squelching people.
I've never seen that as a very attractive thing to do. Ah
. . . (P) . . . I don't think that I'll become any more
assertive than I am, 'cause I'm pretty assertive now. Ah
. . . and it seems to be a sort of facet of my character
that people have to put up with.

E: I was wondering if you could remember anything more now
    about what you were sick with when you were young . . .
    you had a lot of colds with asthma . . . when you were in
    the first four grades anyway, crying a good part of the
    time.
S: Well, not a part of the time but, ah . . . enough so that I
    remember it.
E: Yeah. You don't remember at all, do you, whether there was
    any stretch when you didn't want to go to school or got
    sick before you'd go to school?
S: Uh-uh. . . . Oh, I know there wasn't. My sister used to
    be that way. And, ah . . . the little boy down the street
    that was really a bad case of that sort of thing (laughs)
    . . . (LP) . . . Now, let me see . . . sometimes in grade
    school . . . (P) . . . Ah . . . in high school, too, I
    remember feeling, "Oh good, I'm sick and I don't have to
    go to school." But it . . . it may have been psychological,
    I don't know . . . maybe I made myself get sick, and then I
    was sick, and then I didn't go to school . . . it occurs to
    me . . . that I really liked staying home and reading. But
    after a couple of days , , , I . . . I got to want to go to
    school again. And I would always push myself to go to
    school in high school because there were things that had to
    be done, and I'd know I'd fall behind.
E: When did your sister start school? In kindergarten or
    first grade?
S: Kindergarten.
E: So you were in what . . . second grade, probably?
S: (LP) . . . Yeah . . . say she was in kindergarten, I think
    I'd be in third. Yeah, in third.
E: Third grade. She didn't go to school because she didn't
    want to go, or what? You said she was more that way than
    you were.
S: Ah . . . I have this sense that there were stretches of time
    when she didn't like school . . . and my parents . . . ah
    . . . had to sort of encourage her by telling her about how
    nice it was. I don't think she ever stayed home if she
    wasn't sick, and I don't believe that she had . . . the . . .
    sort of psychologically produced illnesses that kept her
    away from school . . . I think she was a healthier child
    than I was. Ah . . . but . . . (P) . . . I'm not sure . . .

. . . ah . . . (P) . . . I know . . . (P) . . . When I was
in kindergarten, first grade my sister was very jealous;
she wanted to go to school, too (laughs) . . . this is
really amusing (laughs) . . . and so she invented this
night school . . . it was her claim that every night when
everybody else was asleep the night school thoughts would
come, and she'd get up and go off to night school, and
there in night school they would do all the things that I
had done in school (laughs) that day (laughs), but better,
more exciting (laughs), more glamorous. Then she would
come home and go to sleep, and no one would know (laughs).
Well, I swallowed this hook, line, and sinker (laughs). I
didn't swallow it completely . . . I didn't believe it,
but at the same time I thought it might be true (laughs).
Oh, I was so mad. 'Cause every time I would say anything
about school, Sally would say, "Oh, we did that in night
school" (laughs). My parents were just . . . my mother
just laughs whenever she thinks about it, because it was
(laughs) such an obvious case of rivalry, and my sister
was so clever about it. My sister was . . . could be
diabolically clever (laughs), really. It was really a
sneaky thing to do. And . . . and . . . ah . . . (laughs)
I would resolve to stay awake and see if the night school
bus really came. Of course, I'd fall asleep (laughs). My
sister would say, "Oh, boy, it was even better than ever
last night" (laughs). I think, ah . . . her desire to go
to school diminished somewhat when she was actually in
school as a pleasant place pretty much . . . Do you want
to see a picture of Ted, by chance?

E: I'd love to see a picture of Ted. (S shows it.) Oh, he's
    nice looking.

S: Oh, his eyes are lovely, sort of blue, and they turn to
    green.

E: Yes, he's got naturally wavy hair. Does he have a dimple
    when he smiles?

S: Yeah, a little bit. He and his roommate were kidding about
    my dimples . . . ah, where did you get those dimples? And
    I said "What dimples?" (laughs).

E: Well, that's nice. He seems very presentable.

S: (Laughs) I hope he's presentable. Well, I don't even have
    to hope, 'cause . . . I know my aunt will love him.

TENTH INTERVIEW (APRIL): LOOKING TOWARD MARRIAGE

S: A girl in my dorm, Dora, has changed so since she was
    engaged. She seeing the world through Douglas' eyes rather
    than through an undergraduate's eyes, and she's really con-
    descending . . . Ah . . . Helen got this little cookbook
    called The I Hate To Cook book. And Helen told me after-
    wards that she had told Dora about the book, and Dora had

said, "Well, that's the kind of thing that Doug would never allow in the house" 'cause he expects her to be the gracious cook, you know, the gourmet cook, and the perfect hostess, and so forth. It's really terrible . . . you can see her mind saying, "What would Doug think of this," and then reacting in that way, and that's so bad. She used to be such a . . . sort of giddy girl . . . could enjoy herself and be foolish and young, sort of, and she's not foolish and young anymore . . . she's acting 29! (laughs). Dora and I were once very close, and ah . . . Helen and I are going to try and shock her out of it. The . . . the approach is going to be that I'm going to say, "You know, I'm worried that I might become a carbon copy of Ted. I seem to be doing . . . I seem (laughs), seem to be thinking what he's thinking and judging everything through his eyes. Do you understand this problem, Dora?" (laughs), and we're going to see if it works (laughs), 'cause it's really quite evident . . . and once Helen pointed it out and I noticed it . . . and Helen . . . saw what it was . . . it's, ah . . . oh, this whole thing about music . . . Dora and I used to have great hours together listening to rock and roll on the radio when she used to like rock and roll music. And Doug . . . "Oh, I can't stand it," and he likes violin, ah . . . (P) . . . string quartets, I guess. Yeah . . . well, Dora hates piano or violin but she . . . she remarked quite blithely, "Too bad that I don't like violin music, because I'm going to have to listen to it all the time," just . . . as if . . . whatever Doug liked was automatically going to be played, and whatever she liked was automatically not going to be heard at all. And . . . and you have to develop compromises on things like that.

E: What's going to happen to her relation to Doug, if she does change?

S: I don't know (laughs). Ah . . . and Helen points out that . . . that . . . that Doug likes her for what she was, not now. . . . He liked her when she was still different from him (laughs). And she's still gay, but she does it in this, ah . . . sort of young matron way. Strange (laughs). She does look like a matron, too. And Helen says, "She just always makes me feel gawky" (laughs). "And I'm not gawky" (laughs). Which she isn't; gosh, it's terrible.

E: Yeah, well, are you going to be a carbon copy of Ted?

S: Oh, no! (laughs). Certainly not. Oh, dear (laughs). Well . . . very definitely he's, ah . . . I could never be a Republican . . . absolutely not. He knows that (laughs) and, ah . . . he . . . knows a lot more about music than I do. And I really want him to . . . help me become acquainted with classical music. Ah . . . but ah . . . I would certainly never listen to it if I didn't want to listen to it. And violin concertos are going to have to be given to me in small doses . . . they're so squeaky (laughs).

And, ah . . . and I like rock and roll, and I don't think
he's too crazy about it, but it's the kind of thing I like
to listen to when I'm driving, and he does too; I suppose
that's not going to be a conflict. I'm trying to think of
some issue beside the Democrat/Republican one, which is a
real split.

E: Well, I had it in mind to ask you how you thought that
your marriage was going to . . . go, and what kind of a
marriage you wanted and . . .

S: Oh, OK. Ummm . . . he's just such a livable person. Livable, withable person. I've been . . . oh, I've still
been seeing a lot of him. We had our first little tiff.
Sort of a good sign. I'd been worried that we hadn't had
any little tiff (laughs); something unnatural going on.
Um . . . when was it . . . Wednesday night. Ah . . . because he has this . . . (P) . . . ah . . . he feels people
shouldn't hold hands in public. And intellectually I think
he's right. But I sometimes feel these tremendous urges
. . . for instance, in the library, ah . . . when he . . .
he was feeling very discouraged, and I reached over and
patted him on the shoulder. That kind of thing. And what
I want him to do is to say the minute somthing that I do
annoys him, you know, "Hey, stop!" And that's fine. But
what he did . . . he just . . . he just feels he can't re-
buff me in that way. And so he waited until we were back
in front of . . . of the dorm at the end of the evening,
and he said, "Now there's something I want to tell you.
It's about this holding hands in the library." He was
serious, this big build up. And it was really deflating
to me because . . . when I did it I knew that he didn't like
it, but at the same time I was doing it. I felt . . . I'd
been feeling a little bit guilty about doing it, and when he
said this, oh . . . just as if I'd done a terrible thing.
And I was so crushed; I said, "Oh, I'm so sorry, I'll never
do it again" (crying tone). And he got . . . (laughs) . . .
and he took exception to the fact that I was upset over such
a minor little criticism, and he said, "How can I criticize
you if you get so upset?" And I said, "But I'm upset because I know I was wrong," and I was sort of weeping. And
he said, "Oh, don't be upset (laughs). It upsets me when
you're upset." And then I got even more upset because he
was upset, that . . . so . . . (laughs). We settled that
one finally. And I told him that . . . sort of bring them
up as they come up and not wait for this big formal announcement, because it makes me feel as if I shot my grandmother
or something. And, ah . . . (laughs) . . . and also I'll
try not to get so (laughs) upset. Oh, dear. And, ah . . .
(P) . . . I think it will work out very well. I mean, I
wouldn't be undergoing it if I didn't think that it was
going to work out very well . . . (P) . . . We have . . .
we have the same kind of approach as to . . . things like
studying and, ah . . . (P) . . . well, this was a conflict

with John. He's the kind of person that cannot work for a
while then all of a sudden put in forty-eight hours of solid
work without any sleep, ah . . . writing a brilliant paper
and then collapsing into a heap, and I have this goal at
least of fairly . . . steady, ah . . . regular work. Things
get a little tense, like with the thesis, but they aren't
just uncontrollable. And, ah . . . Ted's the same way.
And . . . (LP) . . . he's such a neat person. I mean, you
know . . . keeps his room neat, that kind of thing. I have
to compare with John, 'cause that's what I have to do
(laughs).

E: That's inevitable.

S: (Laughs) And John's the sort of person that expected . . .
ah . . . (P) . . . well, I always felt that I wasn't going
to be able to be the kind of housewife that John wanted me
to be. That is . . . he wanted me to be a tremendous, ah
. . . (P) . . . inventive, exciting cook, and a fairly good
housekeeper, too, although not . . . not rigid, and he himself is something of a slob. And when I'm in the presence
of a slob I become something of a slob myself. I'm not . . .
I can go either way. And, ah . . . and I prefer to be neat.
And Ted is the kind of person that would . . . would hang
up his own clothes, which would be very helpful, and . . .
and would encourage me to pick up, and stuff like that. I
used to cook meals for John and . . . it wasn't that he
meant to be un . . . unkind, but he said . . . like he
didn't like a mixed salad so much as a plain green salad,
and would always end up very deflating. I prepared this
fine mixed salad. "Well, you know what I really like" . . .
(laughs), and, ah . . . and I said, "Oh, oh, OK," but it was
sort of a little crushing at the time. And Ted is the kind
of person who really doesn't care what kind of salad he has;
he just . . . he'll eat almost anything, as he has said on
many an occasion . . . (LP) . . . I think . . . I think he's
going to be sort of like my father . . . (P) . . . I don't
know whether maybe it's dangerous to be like my father, but
I don't know . . . I don't think it's bad to marry somebody
just like your father when you like your father. And, ah
. . . and my father is the kind of . . . exactly the kind
of person that doesn't care what is on the table and will
eat it and will compliment Mother on it, and there are a
couple of things that he doesn't like and we just don't eat.
And, ah . . . (P) . . . and he's also . . . he compliments
Mother a lot, which is nice. And Ted does that too . . .
(P) . . . He's a very thoughtful boy. The only problem is
. . . is the way he doesn't like to criticize me, and he
lets it kind of build up, and then it comes out in a solemn
pronouncement, which is . . . which kind of upsets me more
than anything else. But he's . . . he has said that this
is the kind of thing you want to find out. We want to sort
of establish ways of figuring out how to handle each other,

and how to tell each other's moods . . . when we're not
expressing them . . . I was in a very . . . punchy mood
Thursday . . . just sort of a bundle of gay, scintillating
repartee, and Ted was very . . . was very tired, and he
was very quiet. It was nice . . . he wasn't annoyed that
I was in this sort of mood.

E: How many kids do you think you're going to have?

S: I don't know. We decided . . . he doesn't want to have
kids until he's settled, and it'll give me a chance to
finish law school and, ah . . . get in a couple of years
of practice. And, ah . . . (P) . . . I've always thought
that four would be a good number. He says he doesn't . . .
he doesn't have any particular preference. There were two
of us, as you realize . . . I thought that was . . . that's
not enough. That's 'cause Mother couldn't have any more
children. But, ah . . . (P) . . . three or four, I would
think. Any more than that, and I wouldn't get a chance
. . . (P) . . . to go back to work until I was rather old.
And about two-year intervals I think is good.

E: Is he going to do the disciplining, or are you going to do
the disciplining? This is a big fantasy (laughs).

S: I think we both would. (Portia's tone is serious, not
responding to the half-invitation to treat it as a playful
fantasy.) That's . . . that's another thing, we have the
same . . . superego structure (laughs) about right and
wrong and sort of . . . adherence. He's a responsible person. So am I, I think . . . (P) . . . ah . . . and he did
. . . and he did say . . . it was a mistake to have children
when you were very young because . . . you had to have
enough age and authority to properly discipline a teenager.
That's what he said. Sort of . . . this never (laughs)
occurred to me. I . . . I . . . still seems to me that
even if you had children when you were 20, by the time they
were 15 you'd be 35, and that's old enough to give some
kind of discipline. Certainly you would seem prehistoric
to (laughs) them. But, ah . . . I can sort of see what he
means. It's sort of being around in the world long enough
to . . . to, ah . . . (P) . . . the right sort of balance
. . . perspective on things. And he's ah . . . and he
likes children, he says. And I think . . . and I think
we're the kinds of people that would be able to play with
them, and be on good terms with them, but certainly always
remembering that we were . . . we were parents.

E: Well, that's sort of the way it went in your family, wasn't
it?

S: Yeah, right.

E: People usually have either their own family or some other
family in the back of their mind as a model . . .

S: Or something to react against (laughs). (Portia's tone is
lighthearted again.) I've always felt my parents were too
inhibited. And I wouldn't . . . want to be that way.
There's a certain amount of inhibition that you have to

have, ah . . . just because you're an adult and a member of
society . . . (P) . . . It's not a good idea to rebel, in
silly ways . . . I can see sort of joining in games with my
children in a way that I don't think that my parents did,
although maybe they did . . . I don't remember . . . (P)
. . . and I don't really know quite what I mean. Once John
and I visited my freshman year roommate, and her baby was
just learning to crawl. And John got on the double bed
with the baby and sort of started crawling, and the baby
was crawling (laughs). And it was lots of fun, you know
(laughs). I can't imagine my father doing that. Maybe he
did, though (laughs); I can't be sure about these things.
I have a picture of me when I was, when I was 2, on the
beach with Daddy, in which we seemed to be digging a sand
castle together, so (laughs) now that I think about it.
Well . . .

E: I was wondering what you thought that your parents thought
about you.

S: (P) Well, I have a very high opinion of me. I think they
have too high an opinion of me. Mother's always . . . she
has this sort of awe-struck tone. She said, "Oh my goodness, we think this is just <u>wonderful</u>" (laughs). They don't
know what to do exactly. They don't want to praise me too
much because that will make me conceited. Ah . . . and so
in high school it was very much . . . de-emphasis, you know
. . . "Oh, you got all A's. Hmmm, pretty good." But, ah
. . . I sort of . . . I sort of felt unappreci . . . unap-
preciated. Of course, they were doing it because my sister
wasn't doing as well as I was, and they didn't . . . and
they didn't feel I needed any more incentive anyway. And I
mentioned this at one point, and things shifted gradually
after that (laughs). I got a little bit more, ah . . . sort
of pats on the back. And, ah . . . and Mother . . . and
when I expressed a complaint Mother said, "Well, you know,
we've always felt very proud of you. But we just didn't
want to . . . we didn't feel that we need to tell you that."
. . . (P) . . . Daddy sort of accepts me, and is proud,
proud of me in a sort of quiet way. Mother is really impressed by me . . . (P) . . . I remind her of her sister
. . . my aunt Allie, who was Radcliffe Phi Beta and is now
a noted authority in Graeco-Roman hearth objects. And I
remind her of her mother, who was also sort of an exceptional
woman. And, ah . . . (P) . . . she thinks of me as having
a lot of their qualities of . . . of intelligence and sort
of . . . an independent personality. Sort of different in
some ways. She herself was the middle child, and she was
very, ah . . . more of a meek person. Especially in their
family, where her elder sister was kind of a rebel against
my grandfather particularly. Mother decided that she was
going to . . . (P) . . . to, ah . . . conform very much
. . . she would always admire Aunt Allie, but she would
side with her parents more and, ah . . . try to do what they

wanted her to do. She has a very good quality for getting
people to talk about themselves and listening to them, and
she's really interested in people to an amazing extent.
I'm much more . . . I'm much more wrapped up in myself, and
I think Mother sees that, and she doesn't mind it. And she
. . . I think she thinks of me as . . . as, ah . . . sort
of, ah . . . (P) . . . ah . . . (LP) . . . Well, she doesn't
think that I'm too wrapped up in myself, because I have said
that I am, and she's said, "No, no, you're not." Ah . . .
but if I were . . .

E: Yeah.

S: Or if she did think I was a little bit . . . she would
    think this because I'm this different sort of person . . .
    Aunt Allie type of person rather than the . . . Mommy type
    of person. Ah . . . and I set myself good goals. My sis-
    ter, when she decides she's going to do something, does it,
    but it's usually something like, ah . . . well, she decided
    this summer she's going to work as a waitress and (laughs),
    and she has this same quality that I do but . . . but my
    parents don't approve of it quite so much (laughs) because
    the goals are at odds with their (laughs) goals. Ah . . .
    (LP) . . . sometimes she's a little puzzled by me, but
    since she remembers that her parents were puzzled by Aunt
    Allie . . . she really sees this analogy, I know she does.
    She . . . she feels very strong about this analogy . . .
    (P) . . . And, ah . . .

E: Did you hear a lot about it when you were young?

S: Oh, no . . . uh-uh. This has just come up . . . recently,
    and she must have felt it when I was young, but I certainly
    didn't hear about it. I wasn't treated as anything unusual.
    She . . . she was very careful not to . It's just . . .
    it's just recently, after I expressed the fact that I didn't
    feel (P) that I was appreciated for all I was doing. Ah
    . . . and she came up with more of these praises. And . . .
    and also just because I'm older and she can . . . and she
    can see things more clearly. But she always . . . she has
    in her mind a great store of anecdotes that show what a
    remarkable child I was, that she . . . she would pop out
    one every once in a while . . . and Mother . . . Mother
    feels . . . she sort of feels inferior herself . . . and
    she delights in telling anecdotes like the time my eighth
    grade English teacher in Panama, having been very impressed
    by me, in meeting her, said in astonishment, "How did par-
    ents like you produce a girl like Portia?" (laughs).
    Mother said she feels that way herself very often. Now I
    think that's crazy. My mother's a fine (laughs), very smart
    woman, and my father is certainly . . . (LP) . . . well . . .
    a dynamic man (laughs).

E: One can at least stand praise about one's children even if
    it does reflect on oneself (laughs). What do you think your
    sister thinks of you now?

S: I don't know. We've gotten to a good . . . phase in our
   relationship. That started . . . once I got to college . . .
   (P) . . . There was a lot of tension in the home before we
   went . . . left for school . . . because of difference in
   the way we operated. It's easy for her to appreciate what
   kind of a person I am because . . . it's sort of like appre-
   ciating my parents . . . . This . . . being a certain resem-
   blance in us and sort of like . . . and she's very fond of
   . . . of Mother and Daddy. There was a time when she wasn't
   fond of Daddy at all . . . but that's . . . that's passed,
   I believe.

E: What did she do?

S: Oh, mostly not adhering at all to the curfew set up and
   spending too much money. She's always in debt. She's terribly in debt right now. She claims she's going to earn
   enough money this summer to pay it all back. She went down
   to Syracuse and what did she do, she set up some charge
   accounts (laughs), which is something I just never thought
   of doing myself. There was a little trouble freshman year
   keeping up with the old allowance but . . . I would borrow
   ahead, and then I would go on a spartan regime for a couple
   of weeks . . . and it came out even in the end. But . . .
   Sally has a sense of borrowing and then . . . and borrowing
   some more and sort of never getting herself on an even keel
   again.

E: In Panama, she had been . . . I remember, getting into your
   things.

S: Oh! . . . Oh! . . . terrible (laughs). Oh hateful, hateful
   . . . child (laughs).

E: I don't know whether she was borrowing your things too?

S: No, no, no. She--it was more the technique that she wouldn't
   . . . deign to borrow my things (laughs); sort of . . . tremendous scorn . . . especially after . . . I was very insecure about myself when I was in Panama and, ah . . . Sally
   could play on it very adroitly.

E: Then she got into your diaries, if I remember . . .

S: Oh! Oh! I can't remember what else she did . . . along
   that line. The diary incident lived in my memory, but . . .
   (laughs) . . . it's very hard to imagine what it would be
   like to have an older sister 'cause I never had an older
   sister. Ah . . . (LP) . . . but I . . . I guess I can see
   that if my older sister . . . ah . . . seemed to surpass me
   in some way, I would try to get back at her by sneaking into
   her room and reading her diary. Oh, I don't know . . . it
   was such a sneaky thing to do (laughs), really!

E: I was wondering what your . . . most humiliating episode was
   (laughs) in your lifetime (laughs). I was wondering whether
   it was that.

S: Well . . . that's up there with them (laughs). See if I can
   think of humiliating incidents . . . (LP) . . . Hmm, there
   was the whole business of camp when I started my period and
   I didn't . . . and the question of Kotex was so humiliating

to me, and one of the . . . there's this big trash heap in
the center of our particular part of the camp. Ah . . .
and that's where we put all our trash . . . Kleenex and
stuff, and they were burned every once in a while. And, ah
. . . however, one could not put one's Kotexes there, which
I didn't know, because this wasn't a hot enough fire; they
had to be put into the incinerator down in the main part of
the camp. Oh, that was terribly humiliating. Goodness me
(laughs). So unfair (laughs). So I . . . and the counselor
had to tell me this. It must have been humiliating for the
old counselor, but it was terribly humiliating to me; of
course, that would have been just the moment to say, "Well,
look, I need some more Kotex by the way," (laughs) . . . but
no . . . I just couldn't. Oh! . . . I was forced to look
around . . . so embarrassed . . . Oh, dear! I used to remember it so well, all the other girls just had no idea, so
it was (laughs) terrible. I felt it was so unfair. Ah . . .
let's see. Humiliating incidents . . . (P) . . . Let's see
. . . (LP) . . . I can't remember any other outstandingly. . .

E: What was your most, oh . . . rewarding, nicest, happiest experience that you can remember?

S: (LP) . . . It doesn't pop into my mind too readily, as one
. . . a lot of nice things happened to me. I got into Radcliffe, that was very dramatic. I heard this girl had gotten into Wellesley, so I called home and, ah . . . the maid
that we have that comes in once a week was there, and nobody
else was there, so I asked her to open the letter and read
it, and she did, and I'd gotten in and . . . very . . . it
was very pleasant . . . (P) . . . And, ah . . . (LP) . . .
Hmmmmm . . . I used to remember sort of . . . eras in which
I was very happy. Ah . . . it was very nice when they made
a big fuss over the poem that I wrote in fifth grade. I
felt that I was, ah . . . somebody special, when that happened. And, ah . . . (LP) . . . I was co-valedictorian in
eighth grade . . . in Panama and that was nice. And I felt
. . . and there were times in Panama when I felt that the
class liked me, which was . . . which was a good feeling,
when they elected me president of the class. I guess that
was eighth grade, too. That made me feel nice. And, ah
. . . (LP) . . . well, I went to this dance . . . mixer type
dance last year and met a very cool boy. That was a good
experience . . . 'cause, ah . . . the question of my dancing
ability had been . . . had been a sore one and, ah . . . he
and I didn't have very much in common, but he was so appreciative of qualities in me that I didn't think I even had.
He told me, for instance, that I was light on my feet and an
excellent dancer, and he meant it, you know. And I . . .
and he was so obviously a fabulous dancer himself, that . . .
words had real weight coming from his mouth. I always felt
I was just a clumsy idiot on the dance floor. Oh . . . Oh
. . . the single happiest incident that comes to my . . .
just pops into my mind was the time when I got my contact

lenses, and the guy put them in for me the first time . . .
and, ah . . . showed me a mirror, and there I was without
those glasses covering up a third of my face. Oh . . . just
ecstatic. I just smiled, and I looked around, and my family
was there, and they all smiled at me, and they said they had
just never <u>seen</u> such a happy smile. And I said . . . (laughs)
Oh! those glasses were such a chore to me. I just realized
at that moment how much I hated them and how . . . what a
difference it made to my face. Oh . . .

E: That was maybe the first time you'd really seen your face?

S: Yeah, it <u>was</u> . . . it was . . . it was . . . yeah. It was
quite literally true, and, ah, I was . . . oh . . . I was
just delighted, and everybody in the room was beaming, and
I was beaming most of all. Oh . . . goodness . . . (laughs).
And now I don't mind wearing the glasses any more. And I
wear them without . . . without worrying about them. This
whole business with Ted has been very nice and pleasant.

E: Yes. That's actually, I was . . . I was assuming (laughs).

EXCERPTS FROM INTERVIEWS 11-14 (MAY, JUNE): A VARIETY OF LOOSE ENDS

Portia was asked to comment on her abilities. The following excerpts from her answers perhaps add something to what her conversation had already indicated.

On Business Ability
S: Helen and I were talking, and I was describing some traits
of Ted to her that I really admire. He keeps a very careful
budget, and he knows exactly what he spends on what. Helen
thinks that's terrible. And I think that that's admirable
. . . it shows control of your life, and I wish that I kept
a more careful budget, which I don't . . . I write my check
stubs and know what they're for. Helen just writes a check,
and she hopes she has enough money for it (laughs). I like
to be thought businesslike, and Helen thinks I'm extremely
businesslike. On the other hand, my family . . . well, my
family thinks that I'm extremely businesslike compared to
Sally, it's true. But I didn't used to be thought this . . .
I had to prove that when I was at college, and it gave me
satisfaction 'cause I could do it.

On Leadership
S: I don't know, I have a tendency to be a **little bossy**, a
little bossier than I should. Although I had a number of
positions of leadership, and last year I was **president of**
the dorm, and as you recall I was president of my class in
the Canal Zone, and I was president of a club when I was in
high school. Ah . . . (P) . . . it's very hard to **organize**
people, 'cause you can generally . . . you generally feel

that you can do things better than they can, and it's just
not worth the trouble of getting them to do it, but, ah
. . . (P) . . . and I'm not good at directing other people,
that is . . . if I put my mind to it I can . . . but somehow it just seems a lot of effort. I don't think I would
be good in an administrative position. Ah . . . it's sort
of why I didn't want to be a teacher, and when I think of
myself as a lawyer I think of myself as working in an office
. . . just be the person whom they consult for legal problems. I would be . . . running the legal part of the office,
but I wouldn't have any people under me, you know. I would
be . . . it would be pleasant . . . to be an adviser, and
talking to people . . . about something they didn't know
anything about. That would be a . . . sphere of getting my
ideas across . . . in which . . . and in which they wanted
to hear them, but in which I wasn't . . . yeah, I wasn't
directing their activities in some way.

On Entertaining Ability
S: I have these moods in which I like to be the center of gay,
happy groups in which we're all laughing and cheery, and I'm
telling funny stories and we're all saying funny things.
And I have this reputation, and, ah . . . you know, something like, "That Portia Slim, boy, is she a riot" and, ah
. . . it gives me a good feeling, and I like to do it.

On Social Ability
S: People think of me as being very blunt and outspoken and,
ah, very tactless. Oh, I don't mean to be, and it depresses
me when I think of it, but I am. Helen sort of accepts it
and doesn't mind it too much, but Polly . . . it bothers
her, I think. Ah . . . it's very hard for me to . . . be
. . . as social ability goes . . . to be close friends with
people . . . or at least it seems to be recently, although
although I had close friends in high school that I still
. . . am in contact with and I'm not having any trouble with
Helen. We have little tiffs, and then they come out all
right. And, ah . . . I have a number of close acquaintances
kinds of people. People that . . . if you said, "You know
Portia Slim," and they'd say, "Yeah, she's a neat girl. So
smart, so vivacious, so friendly," and, ah . . . but they
. . . don't any of them know me very well . . . and I don't
know them particularly well either.

On Thinking Ability
S: Yeah, I can, very definitely. . . . (P) . . . Trying to think
if I get too emotional and illogical. And, ah . . . theoretical questions are very interesting for me and things going
around in the world. I tended to see things too much . . .
ah . . . with emotions colored in, but John really took care
of that . . . in a good way. He's made me much more aware

of the need to be objective and, ah . . . thoughtful . . .
(P) . . . and question facts, too . . . Question what
you're told . . .

On Intuitive Ability

S: Intuitive ability is not good. If I make myself . . .
that's something that I'm trying to do. And I . . . I
really think that that's something that is necessary for
people to do, and I don't do it anywhere near enough. I'm
very, ah . . . (P) . . . and Ted and I are working on this,
too. . . . (P) . . . This is the kind of thing . . . he's
so sweet. He's, ah . . . oh such a nice boy (laughs), ah,
but we're sort of getting to know how to read each other's
moods and how to respond to them. That means a lot to me
to be able to do this with him, so that I'm . . . I'm working on it and sort of keeping my hand in with Helen (laughs).

Portia often spoke of her values, but the interviewer decided
to return to this topic in order to obtain a more explicit
statement.

E: One thing I was going to ask you about today was what you
thought of the state of the world today. . . . (P) . . .
Basically what you thought about the mess we're in, and how
much of a mess it is, and where we stand.

S: Hmmmm. When I was a freshman, I was very discouraged. I
thought the world was about to blow up. . . . (P) . . .
I suppose you go through a state at the beginning of your
life when you don't realize that there are many problems,
and you hear about the glorious pageant of American history,
and just sort of one happy thing after another, getting
better and better. And then when you find out . . . my
time of finding out was . . . (P) . . . I think it was just
in the last two years of high school there's corruption in
the government, and there's, ah . . . injustices at home
and injustices abroad, and the government doesn't seem to
know what it's doing in foreign policy. And, ah, the tremendous destructive power of atomic weapons was a frighten-
ing thing, given the incompetence, which I just discovered,
of governments . . . the least bit of incompetence really
disillusioned me.

Portia then recounted the numerous activities in which she took
part, aimed at influencing public opinion; this was prior to
the period of campus violence. In her junior year, becoming
involved with John who had no interest in political action, she
did less.

S: So I . . . my position today is of, ah . . . feeling that
things have continued this far, and they're going to continue with a lot of mistakes and a lot of foolishness going
on, but just not worth getting horribly upset about it because there's always been a lot of foolishness and mistakes.

Ah . . . I do feel fairly competent . . . confident that
atomic weapons aren't going to be used . . . although I
don't know if that's a justifiable . . . confidence . . .
If you think that the world is going to end immediately
in an atomic holocaust, there just isn't anything you can
do about it. That's a very deflating . . . feeling to
have. And you might as well just not have it, because you
can't live with it. Ah . . . so I don't have it (laughs).

E: Yeah.

S: There are more human questions about . . . uh . . . things
like race relations and the whole question of . . . of how
people relate to each other. People are so . . . (P) . . .
unfine, and they don't seem to be manifesting the good
qualities that as a Quaker I believe all people have . . .
of . . . of love for each other and, ah . . . willingness
to work together and . . . so many people don't have that.

E: Do you think that they really have it, or do you think
that the Quakers just assume they have it in order to get
on with the business of trying to make them have it?

S: Yeah, well, I think . . . the Quaker position is more that
they have power to have it. They don't have it, but
Quakers do believe that they could have had it if things
hadn't gone horribly wrong in their background. And that
they still can have it, which I'm less sure of.

E: Yeah.

S: Ah . . . if it's properly elicited, Quakers believe very
strongly . . . in direct confrontation as a . . . as a
pragmatically useful tool and this is stupid, frankly. I
. . . we did this in Berkeley last summer . . . . There
was a Friends meeting very near . . . . My friend Sue and
I attended a weekend study group on one of the first weekends we were there, dealing with the civil rights problems
in the Berkeley area. And one of the things that the study
group was all set on doing was going door to door and talking to people. Now this is all very well in neighborhoods
where people don't know what's going on, 'cause you can
inform them, but a neighborhood which was very politically
aware and very . . . very decided on their points, about
two thirds of them were decided against our position, and
you just couldn't talk them out of it. And Quakers believe
that if you approach them and lovingly . . . state your
position, you'll have some influence. I don't believe
this. Ah . . . what I do believe, however, is . . . that
there are reasons for these people's beliefs, and the reasons can't be changed by me, but they might possibly be
changed by great social changes or visits to the psychiatrist and just not by direct confrontation by some little
college student . . . or even by some mature adult. Ah
. . . (P) . . . people . . . all you can do is try to make,
ah . . . the set-up of things a little bit more sane. That
is try to . . . to . . . integrate . . . everything possibly sanely . . . ah . . . avoiding hysteria and just show

people that Negroes are very fine people and are just . . .
in fact, people.

E: Yeah. Have you ever had a real close friendship with a
Negro at all?

S: No, I haven't . . . that'a regret in my life, 'cause my
. . . I've always lived in, ah . . . quite good neighborhoods which are not integrated. We have a Negro maid that
comes in two days a week, and my grandparents had a number
of Negro servants. My grandfather had a Negro nurse and a
Negro cook and a gardener as well as this maid who worked
for my grandmother before she . . . before she worked for
us . . . this person . . . this Negro that I know the best
. . . very . . . very pleasant woman. I talked to her about
her children, and so forth. But it's a kind of bad thing,
'cause you're in the servant-master relationship. I would
really . . . really like to . . . there was a Negro in one
of my classes last year that I got on speaking terms with
but no real . . . well, wait a minute, now, now that's not
true. There are a number of light-skinned Negroes in Radcliffe that, ah, I'm such good friends with that I don't
think of them as Negroes any more (laughs). I don't remember about them (laughs). Ah . . . but they're . . . but
they're extremely light-skinned, which . . . which, ah . . .
makes you forget about it. There are . . . there are three
Negroes in my dorm, and two of them I know quite well. Ah
. . . and there's this little Negro girl that comes from
Washington, D.C., that was in a class with me freshman year,
and I know her quite well, too. I'm determined to have my
children go to an integrated kindergarten and first three
years of school, because that's when . . . (P) . . . ah
. . . you don't realize that there's any difference at that
age . . . it doesn't occur to you. And that's what it
should be.

E: Do you think you'll raise them Quaker and pacifist?

S: I don't think I'll raise them pacifist 'cause I'm not sure
how strongly I feel that war is never a solution. I do
feel that it isn't . . . but I don't feel it as . . . as
strongly and as dogmatically as, ah . . . a real pacifist
would . . . that is . . . had I been in a position to . . .
I think I would have fought in the Second World War. I
mean, I would fight against an aggressor and a real hundred
percent pacifist wouldn't. I'll try to raise them to, ah
. . . not be dogmatic in any way . . . ah . . . either about
the things that I believe in or the things that I don't believe in . . . (P) . . . to not . . . to not discriminate
. . . ah . . . on unfair . . . criteria. That's what my
parents taught me more than anything else. You know, don't
worry about how somebody looks or what somebody's skin color
is or what kind of background anybody has, but try to accept
them as they are. Oh . . . I think . . . the thing that
worries me much more than . . . than the imminence of war,

or even than the terrible poverty in the world, is this
. . . is this idea that . . . (P) . . . men can . . . just
never . . . ah . . . (P) . . . even under, ah . . . materi-
ally good conditions such as we have in the United States
. . . everybody . . . realize their potentials as really
good people . . . and that's the kind of . . . field in
which I'd like to work . . . ah . . . sort of trying to
promote justice and . . . and, ah . . . if I work with poor
people with legal problems . . . sort of trying to show them,
ah . . . (P) . . . justice exists. And, ah . . . help them
conquer their injustices. I may well . . . be often, ah
. . . on their side against the existing laws. I would
work . . . try to change the laws.

E: I was wondering what you thought your highest values were.
That is, the thing that you think really matters most.

S: Ah . . . human relations. Ah . . . what makes my life the
happiest or what is most important to me that other people
do? And what makes my own life the happiest is, ah . . .
the kinds of people that I'm with and the way that I feel
about them. And the feeling I have of . . . of, ah . . .
(P) . . . of affection toward people and of their affection
toward me. Ah . . . the kind of thing that I had at home
and that I feel in a different way at school. I mean, that
people like me. And that's very important to me. And it's
very important all these . . . all these . . . (P) . . .
men in my life (laughs).

E: (Laughs) Yeah.

S: And Ted is, ah . . . I've just been so much happier since
I met him, which, let me see . . . it must be seven weeks
now (laughs). I don't know, I'm about to lost count . . .
and . . . (P) . . . it means a lot to me to have somebody
to be very close to and, ah . . . and be concerned about
. . . I don't like just living for myself . . . . My goal
for myself . . . I mean, the thing that I would most like
myself to be is . . . is more . . . ah . . . concerned about
other people and have more of that intuition that . . .
that I said I lacked last week . . . (P) . . . be more of,
ah, a giving person more . . . and the kind of person that
I most admire is the sort of . . . sort of Quaker that can
love everybody. The really receptive warm people. My
mother is like that. And I admire my father in a lot of
ways but, ah . . . (P) . . . really, my mother is a little
bit more admirable because she's, she's so able to understand . . . to . . . to draw people out. She's really concerned with other people. My father is, but he's less able
to show it. And I think maybe he's just basically a little
bit less really concerned, and he is . . . ah . . . intellectually more sharper than my mother and, ah . . . very
efficient and admirable, as I said in a lot of ways, but,
ah . . . (P) . . . That kind of thing is very important
and hard to do, and I certainly am no good at it at all, but
I would like to be. It's . . . that's what I . . . yeah.

Thus far in the interviews Portia had not said very much about her sex history. The topic was therefore introduced.

E: Well, I was wondering, too, what you and Ted had decided about whether you were going to get together sexually before you got married or wait until after.

S: Well, we already have (laughs).

E: I sort of thought, probably.

S: Yeah. I'm a little bit, ah . . . I . . . I was going to tell you about this, but it's been embarrassing (laughs). (She repeats the story of her relation with John and her humiliation when he slept with another girl.) And this was the situation last spring, and I was going out with people and not getting involved with them sexually and then . . . (P) . . . I met this guy and sort of, ah . . . well, I was on a blind date, and this character was just loathsome, and I got very drunk 'cause I thought he was so loathsome . . . and, ah . . . (P) . . . we didn't . . . we didn't sleep together . . . we sort of . . . necked, and he asked me out for the next night, and I don't know why . . . some perverse instinct led me to accept, knowing full well what was going to happen. And it did happen the next night, and I just felt like the scum of the earth. It was right before the spring vacation. I went home and I just told myself, God, how could I do that, yatch! It was just horrible. The whole thing was just ghastly. Just ghastly. Ah . . . it wasn't enjoyable in the least. It was . . . it was zyugh! . . . And I thought to myself . . . well, yatch! thughg! And . . . it sort of warped my psychol . . . I don't know. And the people that I was going out with . . . there were two very nice boys . . . I . . . was seeing very different kinds of boys and, ah . . . (LP) . . . I wasn't interested in sleeping with either of them, and I didn't, but then I met this Bert, with whom I plunged into this deep affair because . . . if you see what I mean . . . I had . . . I had already demeaned myself just as much as I could, I felt, and after that it just really didn't matter. And I was . . . I was very interested in . . . in finding some affectionate person, and I guess, ah . . . I was interested in . . . in sort of purchasing their love in that way . . . I don't know if that's the case, but . . . that's the only reason I can think of for why I was . . . ah . . . And it was very satisfying to me physically 'cause I like it a lot (laughs), and I'm not at all inhibited, and I get a lot of pleasure out of except this one disgusting time when I didn't at all. And I met Bert . . . and, and he was such . . . a nice person . . . it seemed to me that this would be all right . . . (P) . . . At the end of that . . . I just sort of decided that if I met somebody that I'd like . . . and I wanted to sleep with him . . . I certainly would. And I carried on . . . in this way this past year. And, ah . . . (P) . . . it was getting me nowhere, if you know what

I mean . . . it was just . . . one more thing that I was
doing and, ah . . . it wasn't anywhere near as satisfying
in the long run as the whole relationship with John had
been . . . and I wanted that again, and I wasn't getting
it . . . (P) . . . so there were . . . let's see . . . (P)
. . . three boys at one time or another that I was sleeping
with this year, and then I met Ted. And, ah . . . before
too long we were sleeping together, but . . . before we
did, we were . . . we were in love with each other. And
he was . . . and he was just . . . I can tell . . . was
very fond of me, and it was going to be again the kind of
thing that I enjoyed with John, which was physical and in
a lot of other ways, which is . . . by far the most pleasing thing . . . and just . . . the real kind of thing that
I want. I think . . . my mother was too reticent in talking about sex to me, and I think possibly she's . . . (P)
. . . ah . . . she's just sexually not as unrestrained as
I am, anyway, and . . . (P) . . . probably the reason that
she's reticent is that she doesn't enjoy it too much herself. And . . . and I think I would . . . tell my daughters . . . ah . . . the importance of having a relationship
be more than sex and more than sort of good friends and
some sex but . . . have it be . . . where sex is just part
of, ah . . . very close relationship on a lot of levels in
a lot of ways. And that . . . (P) . . . if you don't feel
that you really . . . could marry him, then you just have
no business going around sleeping with him. But if you
feel that you really could, and you just are so close to
him in a lot of other ways, and it's very important to you
and to both of you, then you should rather than thwarting
yourself in a lot of ways . . . I think. And that's not my
mother's philosophy, certainly not my father's. My father
would die if he knew any of this! (laughs)

At the next to last interview, Portia made the following sur-
prise announcement.
S: Oh, I'm getting married in September.
E: Oh, you are!
S: Maybe (laughs).
E: I wondered about that. Oh . . . that's fine.
S: Ah . . . he . . . I hadn't said anything . . . like that at
    all, because I thought . . . it would just be an impossible
    dream to get married in September . . . everything would be
    so rushed anyway, and last Saturday night we were going out
    and, ah . . . he said, "You know, it would be awfully nice
    to be married in September . . . sometimes I think that,"
    said he . . . and I said, "You do! (laughs) Isn't that some-
    thing!" And, ah . . . (laughs). So we talked about it a
    while and then . . . we spent about three hours on the phone
    Sunday going through pros and cons and made a list . . .
    very, very . . . (laughs) mathematical . . . it was silly
    (laughs). I mean, I'm sure very few people in the world

would sit down and decide . . . about September versus other
times making little lists. Ted and I have now decided that
we're going to push for a small wedding and large reception,
and they can damn well introduce us to all their friends at
the reception, but we don't want a lot of strangers sitting
around (laughs), and it's a nice little church that's near
my house.

E: That's very nice.

S: Oh, it's very exciting.

In the closing interview, Portia asked the interviewer for an
opinion on whether or not she should seek psychiatric treatment.
This had been in her mind since the break-up with John, who had
told her that she had a great many problems and ought to find
psychiatric help. She herself thought that she did not need
such help, at least at the present time. She was much reas-
sured and pleased when the examiner announced having no in-
clination whatever to refer her to a psychiatrist.

QUESTIONS ON INTERVIEWS 1-14

1. Portia Slim and Solomon Kompten have in common that they
chose law as a profession and that they planned to devote their
best energies to civil rights. Considering the rest of their
experience and development, it seems that they must have arrived
at these decisions by different routes. For what reasons do you
think Portia was attracted by these goals? How do they differ
from Solomon's reasons? Do you think that Portia will stick to
them, as Solomon did not?

2. In the main, Portia seems to have been an accepted child
in her family. Do you think that this developed qualities in
her that made adaptation to her contemporaries difficult?

3. As the older sister who seemed to have the parents'
complete approval, Portia might be expected to regard Sally as
rather beneath contempt. In fact, she seems to have been puzzled by their relation and by the ways in which they differed.
Why was she puzzled? Did she feel inferior in certain respects?

4. How would you estimate the relative weights of father
and mother as models for Portia's behavior? Do you think these
weights changed as she grew older?

5. Portia describes herself as having difficulty in sympa-
thizing with others and being sensitive to their needs. Why do
you think she had these difficulties?

6. Portia's success with school work gave her a high opinion of her intelligence, but she became aware of intellectual
shortcomings through her conversations with John. How would
you summarize John's effect on her mental development?

7. Do you share the surprise of Portia's friends that she
told her mother about sleeping with John? Why did she tell her
mother?

8. The event that seems to have upset Portia most in her relation with John was his deliberate affair with another girl while she was abroad. Why do you think she reacted so strongly?

9. What sort of character sketch would you give of John, allowing that you know him only through Portia's reports? Why do you think he was attracted to Portia?

10. After breaking up with John, Portia went through a hectic period involving a certain amount of sexual promiscuity. She explained it as "defiance" and as "showing him." Do you think this is an adequate explanation of her motives?

11. Do you believe that Portia would have fallen in love with Ted if she had not had and then lost the relation with John?

12. Portia was contemptuous of her friend Dora, whom she described as making herself a carbon copy of her fiancé Doug and shaping all her plans according to what Doug would like. Do you see evidence that Portia was tending to make herself a carbon copy of Ted? Do you see evidence to the contrary?

SUBSEQUENT EVENTS

In April of the following year Portia visited Cambridge and consented to be interviewed. She and Ted had been married the preceding August and had an apartment in New York near Columbia Law School. Planning for the future was made difficult by the war in Vietnam and the prospect that Ted would be drafted.

S: If he goes into ROTC next year and then the next summer he goes to summer camp, then he can wait a year before he actually serves, then during that year I could finish law school. And then he would go into the army for two years, and it wouldn't be fighting, it would probably be working as a lawyer--maybe in the Pentagon or something like that, and we don't want to be tied down. Not that I don't want to have children, but it's nice to keep it two for a while, and we do all kinds of crazy things. We are sort of uninhibited, we sort of run around and scream, sort of stupid sometimes. We have a lot of fun doing it (laughs). It's really . . . and the other thing that is really amazing is, Ted said, "You know, you are not as exuberant as you used to be," and I said, "You know, you're much more than you used to be," and it sort of . . . I used to do really crazy things . . . and I'm rather more conservative, and Ted used to be very, very inhibited, and now he does such wild things. And he's so funny (both laugh). And we sort of dance around (both laugh). It just doesn't seem the kind of thing that parents should do.

E: How is his Republicanism coming?

S: He is a pretty liberal Republican (laughs). We have little arguments about Vietnam, otherwise we see pretty much eye-

to-eye. Oh, Vietnam is such a mess and it makes me so mad--
it just seems so awful and such a tragic mistake, a series
of mistakes, and Ted is more philosophical about it.

E: And how's your law school coming?

S: I enjoy it very much. I'm . . . even now . . . there's a
lot of pressure from exams, and that's not so pleasant, but
the work is very fascinating. I ran into some trouble in
January, which I have to tell you about, which is why I
didn't respond when you asked me how I was and I say OK.
I am actually great, but on the other hand I didn't want to
create a happy impression because I did have this problem
in January, which I will tell you about. I got very depressed all the time.

It turned out that there was a "practice exam," for which review
was necessary, and which was to teach students how to take a
law school exam.

S: And so I was trying to review, and I just couldn't seem to
get anything done. I had been working along pretty regu-
larly--do housework in the afternoon, sort of--and then I
would study at night, and everything got done, but I
couldn't find any time to do any reviewing. It just bothered me, so I would be so tired and I couldn't sleep at
night and I would cry, and Ted would get all upset and I
would say, "Oh, I'm all right, boo hoo," and finally I would
be all right and stumble on through another day, and then I
. . . oh, it just seemed as though . . . and I felt that I
had to do everything. Ted and I made an agreement that he
was going to do half the housework but I just couldn't
stand to remind him, try to nag him in any way, as I have
this image of a nagging person, and I just don't want to be
like that, so I would be . . . I just feared that my responsibilities were more than I could bear, and I didn't see
how this could go on. I went to see the doctor at the
Health Center and asked for sleeping pills, 'cause I had
been taking them at college, as occasionally I would have
trouble sleeping at night. I went in to see him, and he
turned out to be a doctor who didn't like to give sleeping
pills without examining things more carefully and he said,
"Now, you have some problem, don't you?" And I said, "Oh,
yes," and I broke down and told him everything, and he was
very sympathetic, and he said, "Now, I think you should
see a psychiatrist, and we have one here," and I said,
"Well, all right, but I'm all right, but if you think I
should see him I will." Well, he was a very nice guy. So
he said, "Now what seems to be the problem?" So I said,
"Well, I just can't seem to get everything done." So he
said, "Well, nobody can." And that was the essence of the
psychological advice, although it took a little more time
than that, and he said, "Now, you know, nobody at the law
school gets everything done. Everybody at the law school

is upset, you have a lot to do, it's understandable that
you get a little upset, and here are some nice tranquillizers, and take them for a while," and then hew saw me once
a week or every other week for three times, and then he is
now seeing me once a month. He sort of checks up to see
how I am doing. And the tranquillizers are very pleasant.
They just helped me get things going again. That's very
sensible, this remarkably simple advice--don't get upset if
you can't get everything done, 'cause nobody can. But I
guess I needed somebody to tell me, um . . . I calmed down
a little bit. Every once in a while I . . . (P) . . . I
feel sort of tense and kind of that I just can't do it, and
then I go to the little bottle of pills and take one. This
happens about once every three weeks. I was pushing myself
. . . I was making myself do the laundry every week, and
now if I don't get it done for a week and a half, I'm a
little better at that sort of thing.

E: Well, having to be a homemaker and a lawyer and help your
    husband be a lawyer, it's all . . .

S: But on the other hand, other people do it and, um . . .
    everybody says, "Oh, you are so wonderful to be doing all
    this," and I say, "Oh, it's wonderful to be doing it," but
    I can't do it. I was making it more than . . . I don't
    think . . . it's not that much. It takes some time, but
    you don't begrudge it, and if you studied all the time, and
    you couldn't study all the time, anyway . . . . I really
    enjoy cooking. I just love to cook.

E: And I take it Ted loves to have you cook.

S: As it turned out I can cook pretty well. I was surprised.
    My mother isn't too good a cook. Well, I guess it's my
    father. He has kind of prosaic tastes. Ted's very experi-
    mental. I sort of felt experimental, too . . . . And I
    spent the summer . . . I didn't like the way I spent the
    summer at all . . . just getting ready for the . . . well,
    I went out to visit Ted's family, and that was very nice
    . . . he has a fine family. I really like them . . . and
    I came back and started getting ready for the wedding, and
    I was going to, as soon as I got the wedding under control,
    then go and get some sort of volunteer job, but I never got
    to that stage. I was always doing things, addressing enve-
    lopes, having a fitting, or registering a pattern, or argu-
    ing with Ted over what crystal pattern, that kind of stuff.
    And I had all these hay fever shots, too, twice a week, and
    it did no good, which was very discouraging . . . um . . .
    so I was sneezing during our honeymoon, but I don't remember
    the sneezing but . . .

Shortly after the wedding they spent a busy time buying second-
hand furniture and getting their apartment ready for occupancy.
"We would just work and work, and it was very nice," said Portia.
Then they went for a real honeymoon at her Aunt Allie's cottage
in the country, where they took bicycle trips.

E: I seem to remember that Aunt Allie approved of Ted . . .
S: Well, everybody loves Ted . . . just wonderful, and every-
    body in Ted's family loves me. My family, even my relatives
    that I don't like too much, they are crazy about Ted. Every-
    body keeps saying, oh, it's so good she didn't marry that
    John. Ohhhhhh, that would have been terrible. Oh, we met
    John last summer. My parents insisted on having this party,
    this awful party, and what was awful about it was that my
    mother had said, "Now, would you and Ted like to have a
    party," and I interpreted this as a party of my friends,
    and I told her some of my high school friends to invite and
    some of my friends from college who were going to be in
    Philadelphia on vacation, and when I got down to Philadel-
    phia, I discovered that what she had in mind was a party to
    introduce us to all of her friends. Well, so we had kind
    of a mixture and it was awful--just one of the worst parties
    that I have ever been to, and, um . . . we were sort of wan-
    dering around and being charming to all of her friends and
    trying to keep our friends amused and trying to divide into
    two rooms, but anyway John came (both laugh), and after
    everybody had left, it developed into a card game. Um, John
    was also a great card player, and Ted and John and my sister
    and I don't know--two other people--playing hearts, I think,
    and . . . maybe it was hearts with two decks of cards--very
    wild game, and this went on and on until I swear about three
    or four in the morning, and I got very tired, and I was
    sleeping on one of the beds. This is the guest room that
    doubles as the card room--the room that my father built--
    all-purpose room. And John and Ted were just getting along
    famously, just amazing. I was very surprised, as they are
    different kinds of people, but they took to each other.
E: Well, now that you look back on it, do you think you were
    in love with John?
S: Oh, I was intimately . . . I was thinking about that the
    other night, too. A very different kind of feeling that I
    had 'cause I was unhappy so much of the time, there was a
    lot of strain in it, and I didn't really . . . especially
    after the time when I went over to Europe and he was going
    out with this other character . . . um, especially after
    that I didn't trust him and I worried a lot.
E: Well, I thought you were in love with him. The way you spoke
    about him and . . . but I know you are in love with Ted now.
S: Oh, it is the same feeling but there are other feelings too.
    I'm always confident with him . . . (LP) . . . John was very
    critical, and Ted isn't critical at all. I try to do what
    he likes. We have these funny dialogues where we are trying
    to find out what each other wants, and we are both trying to
    efface ourselves and do what the other person wants. And
    even when I am doing something that he doesn't like that up-
    sets him in some way . . . he just wishes I wouldn't, and
    he doesn't criticize me. He still loves me just as much,
    and I don't worry at all, but on the other hand, you're so

fond of him that you want to do what he wants to do, not
because he is going to criticize you, not because he's not
going to stop loving you, but because you want to do it and
do it right. It's just wonderful (laughs).

E: That's fine. When you were depressed, he tried to help you.

S: Oh yeah, I was never . . . the first doctor I saw was sure
there was something . . . tension between me and my husband, and said "How's your sex life?" And I would say, "No
problem with my husband, it's fine, it's just that I have
too much to do." I was placing too many burdens on myself.
He was sure that my husband was the one who was making me
do all the housework, and something like that, and there was
some feeling that he was. I didn't even have the feeling in
the back of my mind. I know I didn't . . . 'cause I knew
. . . that was part of what was depressing me . . . I knew
that Ted would gladly help me in every possible way, but I
didn't want him to. I wanted to do it myself, and I thought
I could, and I would get depressed when I coudln't, and that
was ridiculous.

Portia's psychiatrist declared that she was "in better shape
than the majority of law students," and this encouraged her
greatly.

S: I got a job for the summer that makes me feel very fine. I
will be interviewing for the Legal Aid people, the clients,
and giving advice, not too much at first, 'cause I don't
know too much about Missouri law--we're going to be in St.
Louis. Ted is going to work for a law firm there, and as
the summer goes on I'll know more and more about what to
say, and always with a practicing lawyer, because since I
haven't passed the bar exam I'm not supposed to practice
law, but I can give advice under the supervision of a lawyer. It will be approximately what I want to be doing when
I get out of law school.

E: I was wondering about how much of your relation with your
parents has continued the same, and how much of it has
changed now.

S: That's hard to say. It was sort of odd going home Christmas
vacation as I felt like a visitor, and I was sort of aware
of things that I hadn't been before. I was aware of how
much trouble it was to keep a house going so I was helping
a lot more and I wrote Mother a thank you note after vacation. I thought I ought to say something about how nice it
was to have her do these little various things that I had
always taken for granted.

Events for the next two years in Portia's and Ted's lives took
much the anticipated course. Both completed their law degrees
and passed their bar examinations; Ted was drafted and assigned
to do legal work at a post in Delaware. In a small nearby community Portia found a part-time job working in an old established

firm of lawyers. In a letter she characterized the job as "extremely interesting," involving "every kind of legal work imaginable." Although she was hired primarily to do research and
work up briefs for the senior lawyers, there was soon talk of
allowing her to argue some cases in court. She faced this
prospect eagerly, though "with some trepidation," but she knew
that "once I've made my first argument my 'stage fright' will
be greatly reduced, and so I'm anxious to get it over with."
She considered her employers "fine lawyers" from whom much could
be learned. "It isn't dealing with poor people as much," she
pointed out, but the firm sometimes took clients who were unable
to pay.

A great advantage of her position was that it did not require all her time. "So I am able to get my housework and cooking done without feeling so pressured and put upon, and without
having to make demands on Ted. I feel so happy with the set-up
that I doubt that I will ever work full time, at least not in
the foreseeable future." The freedom from pressure did much for
her "psychological well-being," and she doubted that her "Puri-
tan conscience" would be able to push her even into full-time
legal aid work.

Having children was being postponed until their life could
become more settled. Portia described herself as "terribly
drawn to all the nearby babies," but she could also see "how
tired down their mothers (and fathers) are." "Ted and I have
such good times together," she wrote; "we take trips, and we
plan to go to Europe when we are out of the army." But she ad-
mitted to a "wistful note"; "my intellect, fun with Ted, and
desire to do what he wants haven't quite suppressed my maternal
instincts."

Portia was once more available for an interview four years after
the original series. This was during the second year of Ted's
military service, the last of their expected residence in Delaware. The interviewer inquired about plans for having a family.
S: Uhm, we're planning a little trip to Europe after the army
    stint. If it weren't for that, the babies would fall natur-
    ally as soon as nature decreed, but because of the European
    trip, we're going to wait, because Ted has never been to
    Europe, and I have been fortunate enough to go to Europe
    three times! Ted has always had to work, so he feels very
    much that he wants to go there--do some traveling himself--
    he loves to travel, see things. So do I, we have a good
    time and go on trips together, so we're going to, so I try,
    I've started reading travel books, not particular guides but
    more, instead of reading baby books (laughs), get my mind
    in gear and figure out where we're going to go. It's very
    exciting. We want to go to some places that I haven't been,
    but, of course, many of the places I've been, there are
    things Ted wants very much to see, so we're going to go
    there too. Of course, they're worth seeing again, so there's
    no complaining from me. We're going to work on our languages,

too. Ted is going to do German and I'm going to try to do
some French, so I think we should have a good time, and
that will be just about a two- or three-month trip--just go
as soon as the army lets go of us, and then move out to
Seattle after that. Although he's thinking now about Washington, D.C., because the Republicans are now in power.

E: He's still a Republican?

S: Uh-hum.

E: And you're still a Democrat?

S: No, well, I registered Republican. With me it doesn't
really matter what label I call myself. My ideas don't
change, and as long as he's interested in politics, he
doesn't want a wife going around calling herself a Democrat,
so I'm going around thinking the same thoughts that I always
did and calling myself a Republican. He worked one summer
for a Seattle law firm, but the job he had was quite a different sort of thing--consulting work, and he enjoyed it,
but he doesn't think he wants to do that either. He's going
to go out to Seattle next fall and talk to friends of ours
working in law firms, interview with law firms, and see what
the picture seems to be.

E: And then you can start your babies (laughs).

S: As soon as we get back from Europe.

E: Yeah, that's a firm decision (laughs).

S: My cousin, the story of my cousin is depressing me, because
she and her husband got married shortly before we did, and
spent a few years not having babies and then decided they
were going to have babies, and discovered that they couldn't.
Well, they adopted a baby, just adopted it. It arrived
from the adoption agency in January, and she's pregnant now
in April (laughs). And my mother is very anxious to have a
grandchild to talk about, cuddle.

E: How are your parents?

S: They're fine, they're fine. Mother--they sort of, uh, enjoy
themselves now that they don't have me and my sister around.
Mother just loves to have us up there, but I think she likes
the fact that we're not there all the time.

E: And where's your sister?

S: Oh, Sally is having terrible problems. She left college
and went to California. Decided to go to secretarial school.
Mortified my parents by moving in with three guys--completely
platonic relationship, uh, but it didn't look right to my
parents, uh. That didn't work out too well. She was doing
all the housework--little frictions like that. Well, so
then she moved in with some girls, finished the secretarial
course, got a wonderful job. And she was secretary, recep-
tionist, tour guide, helpful person . . . she's been working
there ever since, about a year now, and she got salary in-
creases . . . but then her boss got sick . . . so she's
quitting the job as of June and going back to school. But
. . . this would all make my parents extremely happy, the
fact that she had been so successful with a job, and so

forth. If it were not for the other problem, which is that
she met the owner of a restaurant who is a 35-year-old married man with two children, and a very pleasant person.
Ted and I have met him a couple of times, and he's just a
delightful person, and his wife apparently has a lot of psychological problems and has been getting, I think, more and
more difficult to live with in several different ways, and
so they had separated before my sister had started dating
him and . . . I guess they're planning to get married eventually, but that's in the far distant future. Right now
she's living with him. My parent's dont like that at all,
so I've tried to be the, uh, bridge between the generation
gap here, and I spend some long times talking to my sister
on the phone trying to explain to her why it is my parents
are upset. She thought they'd be pleased that she was going back to school. Of course, they didn't focus on that
at all, they focused on her new living arrangements.

The conversation shifted to Ted's relations with Portia's parents.
S: Daddy's hard to get to know, um, he's . . . I don't know if
    he's shy, but he's reserved. He doesn't sit down and talk
    to you right off the way my mother does. Ted and my mother
    got along from the very beginning. Um, Ted didn't <u>dislike</u>
    Daddy, he just didn't feel like he knew him very well. This
    past summer when I was studying for the bar exam and Ted had
    already gotten to Delaware and was in the army and he was
    very lonely and he would go up to Philadelphia to stay with
    my parents as often as he could, practically every weekend.
    And so he got to see a lot of them and just sort of sit
    around and drink beer. He had never thought of my father
    as the kind of person to sit around and drink beer, and the
    fact that he probably did in the summer time sort of sur-
    prised him and pleased him, and Ted and my father really
    have a lot in common, so that it's not surprising that once
    they got to know each other better they should get along.

E asked about the problem of reconciling marriage and housekeep-
ing.
S: Well, um . . . it was not marriage and housework so much as
    marriage and law school and housework, and, um . . . I don't
    know why I have problems which other career women don't seem
    to have or seem to handle better than I do, but I seem to,
    and so I've just accepted them and I think I can live with
    them much better than that first period of time. Now I have
    no trouble in getting everything done, and I don't ask Ted
    any more, because I . . . I just don't know what it is, but
    I just don't want to have him doing housework! I just can't
    explain it . . . it just doesn't seem sensible . . . it
    seems like I'm a modern woman and I should be perfectly
    willing to accept him to do half and me do half, but I just
    can't do it, I . . . I can't stand it. I had originally

thought that when the children were in school I would be
able to go back and work full time, but now I'm not so sure,
and it doesn't disturb me any more. So, I'm just not going
to force myself. And I could also, um, I suppose there are
other ways out of the dilemma. For instance, hiring somebody to help me, which I've done. I now have a cleaning
lady who comes in, and I'm sure I'll continue with having
somebody help me out, but I like to cook and I don't want
to hire anybody to cook, and I want to take care of my own
children, I don't want to have a housekeeper to bring them
up. Another of my friends from law school has a full-time
housekeeper and spends most of her legal salary for the
housekeeper, and, to me, she's missing all the excitement
of having a child.

The next news of Portia came a year and a half later, several
months after the end of military service and the trip to Europe.
She and Ted were now settled in Seatlle, "both working for law
firms with a corporate and business practice," and they were in
the process of buying a house. Some of the lawyers in the firm
for which Portia worked had interested themselves in a suit
brought against a large private housing development which was
discriminating against prospective black tenants. Portia as-
sisted this group and became much involved in the case.
     After this letter more than two years went by, bringing
Portia to the age of 30. Then came a printed card announcing
the birth of a daughter. This event was more than commonly
welcome, a sort of personal victory; according to an accompany-
ing written message, Portia had had two miscarriages, and the
possibility of having children had been for a time in doubt.
The baby, she wrote, "is delightful and full of smiles and
chortles." Portia hopes to go back to part-time work in a few
months, though as yet she has no job offer. Tacked into a post-
script was another recent victory in her life: the suit against
the housing development had been won before the Supreme Court.

                         FURTHER QUESTIONS

     1. What explanation do you give of the troubles that led
Portia to consult a doctor during her first year at law school?
Why do you think she tried to do too much?
     2. In view of Portia's experience the following year, do
you think the psychologist who conducted the senior-year interviews was wrong in not advising her to seek psychiatric help?
     3. Continuing the topic of Question 12 in the previous set,
to what extent do you now think Portia has succeeded in retain-
ing her individuality and not becoming a carbon copy of Ted?
     4. Would you characterize Portia's and Ted's marriage as
successful? What evidence do you bring to bear in making this
judgment?

5. As the "good" child in the family, Portia might be expected to take her parents' side in disagreements with the "bad" child, Sally. Why do you think she did not do this, but instead became a kind of mediator?

6. Which of the four subjects in this workbook do you like best? Which do you like least? (Don't let anyone grade you on this, but the questions deserve searching answers, with a serious attempt to unearth your reasons; in this way you may discover some of the preferences and preconceptions which you have brought to the study. It would be instructive to join with other students in a frank discussion of these questions. Their preferences might prove to be very different.)